Richard Henry Lee
of Virginia

D1451773

Richard Henry Lee
of Virginia

A Portrait of an
American Revolutionary

J. Kent McGaughy

ROWMAN & LITTLEFIELD PUBLISHERS, INC.
Lanham • Boulder • New York • Toronto • Oxford

ROWMAN & LITTLEFIELD PUBLISHERS, INC.

Published in the United States of America
by Rowman & Littlefield Publishers, Inc.
A wholly owned subsidiary of The Rowman & Littlefield Publishing Group, Inc.
4501 Forbes Boulevard, Suite 200, Lanham, Maryland 20706
www.rowmanlittlefield.com

PO Box 317
Oxford
OX2 9RU, UK

British Library Cataloguing in Publication Information Available

Library of Congress Cataloging-in-Publication Data

McGaughy, J. Kent, 1964–
    Richard Henry Lee of Virginia: A Portrait of an American Revolutionary /
J. Kent McGaughy.
        p. cm.
    Includes bibliographical references and index.

        ISBN: 978-0-7425-3385-1

    1. Lee, Richard Henry, 1732–1794. 2. Revolutionaries—United States—Biography.
3. Politicians—United States—Biography. 4. United States—History—Revolution,
1775–1783—Biography. 5. United States. Declaration of Independence—Signers—
Biography. 6. Politicians—Virginia—Biography. 7. Plantation Owners—Virginia—
Biography. 8. Merchants—Virginia—Biography. 9. Virginia—Biography. I. Title.
E302.6.L4M43 2003
973.3'092—dc22   2003015081

Printed in the United States of America

Contents

Figures

Acknowledgments

$\mathcal{I}$ have devoted much of the last fifteen years to the study of the life and times of Richard Henry Lee of Virginia. What began as an inquiry into Lee's authorship of the *Letters from the Federal Farmer to the Republican* under the guidance and direction of Philip L. White at the University of Texas at Austin has mushroomed into a full-length biography of the man and the role he played during America's Revolutionary era. Along the way, I have received a tremendous amount of support and encouragement from numerous individuals and mere words cannot adequately convey the gratitude I have for all the assistance they have offered over the years.

While conducting research at the Virginia Historical Society in Richmond, I received valuable assistance from several archivists, librarians, and scholars, among them Nelson Lankford, Francis Pollard, Joseph Robertson, Lee Shepard, and Ed Reid. I would also like to express my sincere appreciation to the Virginia Historical Society for awarding me a Mellon Research Fellowship that allowed me to take full advantage of the archives in Richmond.

One of the primary objectives of my biography was to introduce the reader to the private side of the public man. To that end, I benefited from the assistance of Jeanne Calhoun who then served as the associate executive director of Education and Research at the Jessie Ball Du Pont Memorial Library on Stratford Hall Plantation as well as the Du Pont Library's archivist, Judith S. Hynson. Additionally, I would like to thank Ms. Hynson for her assistance in securing a copy of the portrait of Richard Henry Lee that appears on the cover. I would also like to thank Quinn O'Brien, who currently owns the property where Lee's home, Chantilly, once stood for allowing me access to the property and to Russell G. Brown for conducting a guided tour of the site and its environs. I also owe a posthumous debt to Virginia Sherman. Her commitment and dedication to the history of Westmoreland County prompted her to sponsor an archaeological excavation of the Chantilly site. The result has been the preservation of numerous artifacts from Richard Henry Lee's home, which can be viewed at the Westmoreland County Historical Museum in Montross, Virginia.

Several faculty members of the departments of English, History, and Political Science at the University of Houston provided a tremendous amount of advice and encouragement. I would like to acknowledge Joseph Glatthaar, Karl Ittmann, Robert Palmer, and Bailey Stone. I would also like to thank the Department of History at the University of Houston for providing financial assistance by awarding me the Murray Miller Research Scholarship in 1995. I would also like to thank those faculty members who read portions of my biography at various stages of completion: Dorothy Baker, Lawrence Curry, Ross Lence, Cathy Patterson, and Eric Walther. Most of all, I would like to thank James Kirby Martin. Without his constant and unwavering support, this project would never have been completed. I owe him a debt I can never repay. I would also like to thank all of my friends and colleagues at Houston Community College, Northwest for their support while I worked to complete my biography, especially Gisela Ables, Michael Botson, Patience Evans, Irene Guenther, James Thomas, and Mark Tiller. Jordan Carswell and Lori Grieg of Houston Community College, Northwest provided invaluable technical support and assistance with the illustrations that are included in this biography.

I would also like to thank all of the editors and staff members at Rowman & Littlefield for their contributions toward making this book possible, including Mary Carpenter, Scott Jerard, Erin McKindley, Lori Pierelli, and Laura Roberts.

Lastly, I would like to thank my wife, Kimberly, for her assistance, her patience, her support, and her unfailing confidence in me; it is to her that I lovingly dedicate this work.

Note on Sources

$\mathcal{T}$he following sources are cited in multiple chapters. They are cited in full upon first reference, then shortened thereafter.

PRIMARY SOURCES

American Colonial Documents. Edited by Merrill Jensen. New York: Oxford University Press, 1955.

American Husbandry. Edited by Harry J. Carmen. New York: Columbia University Press, 1939.

The Documentary History of the First Federal Elections, 1788–1790. 3 vols. Edited by Gordon DenBoer, Lucy Trumbell Brown, and Charles D. Hagerman. Madison: University of Wisconsin Press, 1984.

The Documentary History of the Ratification of the Constitution. 18 vols. Edited by Merrill Jensen et al. Madison: State Historical Society of Wisconsin, 1976–.

Fauquier, Francis. *The Official Papers of Francis Fauquier, Lieutenant Governor of Virginia, 1758–1768.* 3 vols. Edited by George Reese. Charlottesville: The University Press of Virginia, 1980.

George Mercer Papers Relating to the Ohio Company of Virginia. Edited by Lois Mulkearn. Pittsburgh, PA: University of Pittsburgh Press, 1954.

Journals of the Continental Congress, 1774–1789. 34 vols. Edited by Worthington Chauncy Ford. Washington, D.C.: Library of Congress, 1905.

Lee, Richard Henry. *The Letters of Richard Henry Lee, 1762–1794.* 2 vols. Edited by James Curtis Ballagh. New York: Macmillan, 1911–1914.

———. *Revolutionary Virginia: The Road to Independence, a Documentary Record.* 7 vols. Edited by William J. Van Schreeven and Robert L. Scribner. Charlottesville: University Press of Virginia, 1975–1983.

Letters of Delegates to Congress, 1774–1789. 18 vols. (to date). Edited by Paul H. Smith. Washington, D.C.: Library of Congress, 1976–.

Madison, James. *The Papers of James Madison.* Edited by Robert A. Rutland et al. Chicago: University of Chicago Press, 1973.

Mason, George. *Papers of George Mason, 1725–1792.* 3 vols. Edited by Robert A. Rutland. Chapel Hill: The University of North Carolina Press, 1970.

The Revolutionary Diplomatic Correspondence of the United States. 6 vols. Edited by Francis Wharton. Washington, D.C.: Government Printing Office, 1889.

Revolutionary Virginia: The Road to Independence. 7 vols. Compiled and edited by William J. Van Schreeven and Robert L. Scribner. Charlottesville, VA, 1975–1983.

Washington, George. *The Writings of George Washington.* 39 vols. Edited by John C. Fitzpatrick. Washington, D.C.: Government Printing Office, 1931–1944.

———. *The Papers of George Washington: Colonial Series.* 7 vols. Edited by W. W. Abbot, Dorothy Twohig, et al. Charlottesville: The University Press of Virginia, 1990.

SECONDARY SOURCES

Anderson, Fred. *The Crucible of War: The Seven Years' War and the Fate of Empire in British North America, 1754–1766.* New York: Alfred A. Knopf, 2000.

Armes, Ethel. *Stratford Hall: The Great House of the Lees.* Richmond, VA: Garrett and Massie, 1936.

Chitwood, Oliver Perry. *Richard Henry Lee: Statesman of the American Revolution.* Morgantown, WV: West Virginia University Library, 1967.

Egnal, Marc. *A Mighty Empire: The Origins of the American Revolution.* Ithaca, NY: Cornell University Press, 1988.

Friedenberg, Daniel M. *Life, Liberty, and the Pursuit of Land: The Plunder of Early America.* Buffalo, NY: Prometheus Books, 1992.

Hendrick, Burton J. *The Lees of Virginia: A Biography of a Family.* Boston: Little, Brown, 1935.

Holton, Woody. *Forced Founders: Indians, Debtors, Slaves and the Making of the American Revolution in Virginia.* Chapel Hill: University of North Carolina Press, 1999.

Lee, Edmund Jennings. *Lee of Virginia, 1642–1892: Biographical and Genealogical Sketches of the Descendants of Colonel Richard Lee.* Philadelphia: 1895.

Lee, Richard Henry, II. *Memoir of the Life of Richard Henry Lee and His Correspondence.* 2 vols. Philadelphia: William Brown, Printer, 1825.

Maier, Pauline. *The Old Revolutionaries: Political Lives in the Age of Samuel Adams.* Revised edition. New York: W. W. Norton, 1990.

Marks, Frederick W., III. *Independence on Trial: Foreign Affairs and the Making of the Constitution.* Baton Rouge: Louisiana State University Press, 1973.

Montague, Ludwell Lee. "Richard Lee the Emigrant, 1618–1664." *The Virginia Magazine of History and Biography* 62 (January 1954): 3–49.

Nagel, Paul C. *The Lees of Virginia: Seven Generations of an American Family.* New York: Oxford University Press, 1990.

Potts, Louis W. *Arthur Lee: Virtuous Revolutionary.* Baton Rouge: Louisiana State University Press, 1981.

Price, Jacob M. *France and the Chesapeake: A History of the French Tobacco Monopoly, 1674–1791, and of Its Relationship to the British and American Tobacco Trades.* 2 vols. Ann Arbor: The University of Michigan Press, 1973.

Royster, Charles. *The Fabulous History of the Dismal Swamp Company: A Story of George Washington's Times.* New York: Alfred A. Knopf, 1999.

Selby, John E. *The Revolution in Virginia, 1775–1783.* Williamsburg, VA: The Colonial Williamsburg Foundation, 1988.

Thorndale, William. "The Parents of Colonel Richard Lee." *National Genealogical Society Quarterly* 76 (December 1988): 253–67.

Prologue: "We Cannot Do without You"

*W*hile heading south on Virginia State Highway 202 in Westmoreland County, I finally saw the sign that read "Richard Henry Lee's Grave." I followed the posted directions to the burial site, and after driving just over a mile along an isolated country road, I saw a brick enclosure in the middle of a well-kept field. Inside, I found graves for Richard Henry's parents and grandparents, and his cousin, George Lee. The sixth grave belonged to Richard Henry Lee. Members of his family had the following inscription carved on his tombstone:

Here was buried

Richard Henry Lee
of Virginia
1732–1794

Author of the
Westmoreland Resolves
of 1766

Mover of the Resolution
for Independence

Signer of the
Declaration of Independence

President of the
Continental Congress

*United States Senator
from Virginia*

"We Cannot Do Without You"

Clearly, as the marker indicates, Richard Henry Lee played a pivotal role as an American political leader during the Revolutionary era. His career in public service began in 1757 at the age of twenty-five and continued, with only brief interruptions, until 1792 when Lee was sixty years old. During this period, Lee participated in almost every political controversy, from the Stamp Act crisis until his death in 1794 at the age of sixty-two. Yet the plaintive statement "we cannot do without you" strongly suggests that, to friends and family, he was far more than a prominent figure on America's political landscape. While standing by his graveside, I resolved to search out the man largely forgotten by history—Richard Henry Lee, the planter and merchant, the husband and father.

Throughout his career in public service, Lee remained a controversial figure. His contemporaries accused him, at various times, of promoting his private interests at the expense of the public good. Although such accusations were unjust, they have unfortunately been incorporated into the modern scholarship regarding Lee and his role in the American Revolution. The confusion is largely the result of historians' devoting too much attention to Lee's political career at the expense of his private life.[1] Consequently, the modern portrayals of Lee are little more than caricatures of the man; historians have avoided his complexities by simply characterizing him as "paradoxical."[2]

One of the more persistent and problematic interpretations of Richard Henry Lee is the characterization that he had "no profession beyond public service" and that he found "little joy in family life."[3] First and foremost, Lee was a tobacco planter and father. He managed affairs on his own plantation while also assisting his older brother to run an even larger plantation, Stratford Hall. Consequently, Lee's role as an eighteenth-century gentry man cannot be understood in isolation from his family. He was but one person within a large, extensive family. All members of the family played a role that supported the larger family interests, and maintaining an active role in government was simply one aspect of that overall effort. In this context, Lee was not different than several of his brothers or his contemporaries living in tidewater Virginia; thus, it is misleading to overlook his many other pursuits and describe him simply as a "professional politician."[4]

Additionally, basic factual errors about Richard Henry Lee that persist to the present day hamper the ability to acquire a complete understanding of Lee's role during the Revolutionary era. The most notable examples, of course, are suggestions that Lee led the effort to remove George Washington as commander in chief of the Continental army in the years 1777–1778, events characterized as the "Conway Cabal."[5] Another factor that has confused Lee's legacy has been the incorrect identification of Richard Henry Lee as the author of the *Letters from the Federal Farmer to the Republican* and the *Additional Letters from the Federal Farmer to the Republican.*[6] Writers and historians since the 1780s have presented their portraits of Lee through filters based on these two factually incorrect identifications. The first made Lee an object of vilification, the second a person to celebrate, and both represent the foundation of the ambiguous legacy of Richard Henry Lee. A fundamental concept that many scholars over the past two centuries have failed to fully grasp is that consistency of thought over the course of a lifetime, unfortunately, does not lend itself well to isolated examinations or limited topical surveys. As a result, the totality of Richard Henry Lee remained obscured, hidden in the dim shadows of the distant past.

The problem with the extant secondary works on Richard Henry Lee is that scholars tend to focus only on specific aspects of his life to justify a particular point they wish to make, at the expense of understanding the man in his entirety and the world in which he lived. My goal is to bridge the gap between Lee's private interests and public career because, in actuality, one cannot be understood without the other. Lee was, first and foremost, a merchant and planter; as far as he was concerned, political office was not an end in and of itself but rather a means to some other end. However, he served in public office out of a sense of duty and obligation, and he would willingly make personal sacrifices to further the public good. The financial successes experienced by Lee as a planter–merchant in the private sphere, however, directly affected his popularity and political influence in the public sphere. These factors, consequently, made Lee a frequent target of his business and political rivals, men who often resorted to rumor and innuendo as weapons in their efforts to lessen the influence of the Lees of Virginia.

II

From the moment the first member of the Lee clan arrived in Virginia, they began building a transatlantic commercial empire that depended upon carefully placed family members straddling the Atlantic Ocean. Each successive generation of the Lee family contributed to the expansion of the Lee enterprises. Yet, while they were pursuing their family interests, they were also contributing to England's national efforts to achieve economic self-sufficiency from her rivals on the continent. The English crown relied on enterprising merchants like the Lees of Worcester, England, to achieve the king's desire for a commercially integrated global empire.

In pursuit of these imperial objectives, Parliament and the crown readily extended exclusive privileges and helped create new opportunities for those Englishmen willing to settle in North America. The Lees proved to be only one of many English families that left England. By the middle of the seventeenth century, the Lees had established a thriving business in the fur and tobacco trade. Their close association with the provincial government afforded them greater opportunities, as well as access to royal patronage. The relationship between the Crown and these provincial businessmen proved to be mutually beneficial as the Crown provided patronage to the colonial leaders; they in turn provided a loyal foundation for the Crown's imperial ambitions.

The Lees of Virginia proved to be a remarkably resourceful and successful clan. Through an elaborate framework consisting of various members of their extended family, the Lees of Virginia accomplished what modern business historians call "the vertical integration of the transatlantic trade"—a process that allowed them to exert influence over every aspect of commercial activity, from receiving and distributing patronage to the sale and distribution of a variety of American- and English-made goods. The Lees, through their extended kinship network, proved more resourceful than other planter–merchants, which explained their successes in the seventeenth and eighteenth centuries.

By the middle of the eighteenth century, however, the situation started to change. As the Crown achieved its commercially integrated empire, it began shifting its priorities and focus. Instead of conferring exclusive benefits to the Americans, Parliament opted to promote the interests of a growing number of politically influential British merchants. They formed different business groups, also based on family ties, and they engaged in the practice modern business historians call "backward integration"—a process in which they worked from their positions as factors and agents and seized control over the transoceanic trade.[7] To accomplish their goals, the British merchants formed commercial alliances with lesser planter–merchants in the Chesapeake colonies and with businessmen primarily centered in Philadelphia. Together, they organized a formidable group that challenged the established planter–merchant families like the Lees of Virginia. The resulting conflict between the British merchants and the great planter–merchants in Virginia peaked in the 1750s and 1760s and soon defined one's allegiance to the Crown, setting the stage for the American Revolution.

As the Continental Congress debated the question of American independence, Richard Henry Lee told his colleague Patrick Henry that the colonies must separate for the preservation of society. By 1776, British imperial policies presented a serious threat to the world that Lee's family helped create, and that is what he sought to protect by supporting the decision for independence. Consequently, Lee represents the epitome of the conservative revolutionary through his efforts to usher in dramatic change to preserve what already existed. In the process, Richard Henry alienated many other prominent individuals with competing political and economic interests in other colonies—a situation that caused conflicts in Congress and came perilously close to threatening the success of the War for American Independence and the viability of the new nation. In the end, the resultant controversies damaged Lee's reputation and established an ambiguous legacy in relation to his contributions toward establishing the American republic.

III

The era of the American Revolution is still enshrouded in popular myth. Much of the existing scholarship fails to adequately address the competing economic interests within the context of the first British Empire. Instead, some scholars have preferred to portray them as virtuous, disinterested revolutionaries, while others have gone to the opposite extreme by presenting them as leaders of a grasping, self-serving elite. Both interpretations are equally distorted. What has been lost is the forgotten middle ground. From the moment the first English colonies were established in North America, a careful balance was maintained between private commercial interests and English imperial objectives. Personal profit and patriotic service became thoroughly enmeshed.

Families like the Lees made their fortunes by establishing commercial networks based on transatlantic kinship ties. In the process, the Lees of Virginia helped create a transatlantic commercial and cultural community that advanced England's (and later Great Britain's) interests as much as their own. As Richard Henry Lee emerged as a leading revolutionary, he did not embark on this path because of some narrowly defined set of private interests. Lee participated as a leader of an effort that contributed to the dissolution of the Atlantic community and that marked the establishment of the United States as an independent nation. He sought to preserve a way of life and a pattern for opportunity that brought success to his family as well as several other planter–merchants in Virginia. The world in which Lee lived depended on tobacco, transatlantic commerce, and unfettered access to western lands. If any of these particular interests were adversely affected, then Lee, and others who were in the same position, would aggressively protect their interests—and the same held true for all of Lee's contemporaries. Modern scholars may read this and decry the absence of ideology, but such criticism ignores the reality that ideology is merely a reflection, or an extension, of a person's private interests. Ideology and interest go hand in hand and cannot be separated and treated as two separate entities.[8]

To fully grasp the meaning of these events, scholars must first abandon attempts to understand prominent individuals like Richard Henry Lee exclusively in the public sphere. In the end, the prevailing "whiggish" view of the virtuous revolutionary must be modified to accommodate the simple reality that, no matter how well intentioned, private interest does affect public action. As historian Carl Becker once noted in a letter to Arthur Schlesinger, Sr.: "we all have a wonderful talent for identifying our interests with the cosmic purpose, but we do it honestly enough for the most part."[9] By acknowledging these points, perhaps we can uncover the forgotten human dimension of Richard Henry Lee and other participants in the American Revolution. In the process, I hope to bring those of us living at the start of the twenty-first century closer to a person largely lost to history, and I hope to rediscover the man his family could not do without.

NOTES

1. Although Richard Henry Lee has been the subject of numerous articles and dissertations, there are only two published full-length biographies of Lee. Lee's grandson and namesake, Richard H. Lee, published the first, titled the *Memoir of the Life of Richard Henry Lee and his Correspondence*, 2 vols. (Philadelphia: William Brown, Printer, 1825); in addition to this, there is Oliver Perry Chitwood, *Richard Henry Lee: Statesman of the Revolution* (Morgantown, WV: University Library of West Virginia, 1967). Both of these works present sympathetic portraits of Lee.

2. Pauline Maier, *The Old Revolutionaries: Political Lives in the Age of Samuel Adams*, rev. ed. (New York: W. W. Norton, 1990), 164. With regard to the limitations found within Maier's interpretation of Richard Henry Lee, it is important to note that her study was not meant to be a full-length biography of the man but rather an essay designed to place Lee in context within a larger group of individuals and set of ideas. That being said, it is important to note certain depictions of Lee found in Maier's essay because the view is still held that it represents the "best interpretive sketch of [Lee's] political career." See Jack N. Rakove, *Original Meanings: Politics and Ideas in the Making of the Constitution* (New York: Alfred A. Knopf, 1996), 386 n. 35.

3. Maier, *The Old Revolutionaries*, 176 and 192.

4. Maier, *The Old Revolutionaries*, 176.

5. The majority of scholars has now shifted to another extreme and has consigned the "Conway Cabal" to the realm of myth. Unfortunately, such an interpretation of the events of 1777 to 1778 leave more questions unanswered. As a result, the Cabal and the major personalities involved warrant closer study.

6. See J. Kent McGaughy, "The Authorship of the *Letters from the Federal Farmer*, Revisited," *New York History* 70 (April 1989): 153–70.

7. For more on the British merchant community and "backward integration" in the eighteenth century, see David Hancock's excellent study *Citizens of the World: London Merchants and the Integration of the British Atlantic Community, 1735–1785* (New York: Cambridge University Press, 1995).

8. Maier, *The Old Revolutionaries*, ix–xi.

9. Carl L. Becker to Arthur M. Schlesinger, late 1918. *"What Is the Good of History?": Selected Letters of Carl L. Becker, 1900–1945*, ed. Michael Kammen (Ithaca, NY: Cornell University Press, 1973), 59.

A Virginia Dynasty

I

$\mathcal{I}$t was February 1748, a very busy time for large tobacco plantations like Stratford Hall. Richard Henry Lee sat on the docks of Lee's Landing with his older brother, Thomas Ludwell Lee. He had just turned sixteen years old, and he was about to embark on an adventure that few Virginians had an opportunity to experience. He sat there anxiously waiting for the tobacco ship that would take him across the Atlantic Ocean to England, where he would complete his education.

Lee's Landing was one of several ports of call selected by the British Crown to serve colonial Virginia. Richard Henry's father, Thomas Lee, built a modest dock system that could accommodate the ocean-going vessels that were so vital to Virginia's economy. As Richard Henry sat on the docks, he could look to the northwest and see the majestic white cliffs that first attracted his father to the area; to the east, he saw the wide Potomac River that seemed to have no end as it flowed into Chesapeake Bay.

The Landing provided a convenient place for the Lees to store their annual tobacco crop as they waited for the ships to transport it to England. In addition to the wharves and piers jutting out into the Potomac River, Thomas Lee had a number of warehouses built, in accordance with government contracts, to hold tobacco and other dry goods. As a result, Lee's Landing served as an important link between the tidewater planters of the Northern Neck and British markets.

As Richard Henry waited, he witnessed a tremendous amount of activity. He could see slaves and indentured servants bringing massive barrels of tobacco, called hogsheads, down the "rolling roads" from the tobacco fields. Still more slaves lined the barrels along the sides of the piers so that they could easily be loaded onto the ships. Additional laborers, both slave and free, emptied the warehouses of dry goods, making room for more products as they arrived from England.

On this winter's morning, Richard Henry could readily appreciate that his family was one of the wealthiest and most influential families in the colony, but that had not always been the case. Just over 100 years earlier, his great-grandfather Richard Lee "the Emigrant" had arrived in Jamestown in 1639 with very little to his name other than the patronage of some influential men. By the time Richard Lee died in 1664, he presided over a vast transatlantic commercial empire that went beyond any of his contemporaries could imagine.

Now, Richard Henry Lee prepared to embark on a journey that would allow him the opportunity to contribute to his family's transoceanic interests. Getting an English education allowed young Lee to establish contacts with British merchants and other businessmen connected to the Lees of Virginia. In many respects, the Lees had come full circle. In 1639, Richard Lee left his home in Worcester, England, to make his contribution to his family's fortunes. One hundred and nine years later, Richard Henry made preparations to leave Stratford Hall for the same reasons.[1]

II

At the beginning of the sixteenth century, Worcester was a prosperous community in western England located along the banks of the Severn River.[2] More than half of the town's population, including John and Jane Lee, engaged in the production of manufactured cloth. As one traveler noted, Worcester was a city "full of people . . . generally esteem'd very rich, being full of business, occasion'd chiefly by the cloathing trade, of which the city and the county carries on a great share."[3] The Lees of Worcester were among many small clothiers that acquired wool from the surrounding rural districts brought in by boats traveling up and down the Severn between Shrewsbury to the north and Bristol to the south. Once the Lees had a finished product, John Lee, like the majority of small manufacturers, sold their cache to a great clothier, who then transported large quantities of cloth to London, where it could be sold on the international market.

John and Jane Lee's mill first opened for business in 1615. As clothiers in Worcester, the Lees had a slight advantage over some of the other manufacturers in the vicinity. Jane's father, Edward Hancock, already owned more substantial textile factories in Worcester and in nearby Twyllings. The marriage of John Lee and Jane Hancock, in part at least, represented a business merger of

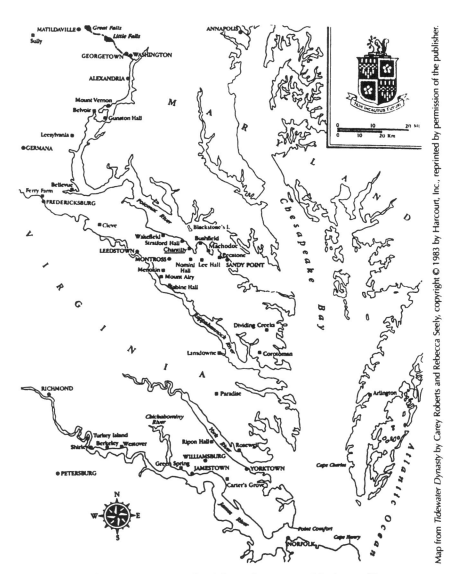

Figure 1.1. Tidewater, Virginia, in the eighteenth century, with places of importance to the Lee family marked.

sorts. Kinship networks along these lines allowed for the economic growth of families living throughout the English countryside, and the Lee–Hancock connection proved very successful. The partnership between the Lee and Hancock families serves as an illustration of the dynamics contributing to Worcester's growth as a major economic center in the fifteenth and sixteenth centuries.

After John Lee married Jane, his mill became a subsidiary of Hancock's larger factory. Their combined interests afforded them greater opportunities to purchase the cloth made by other small textile mills. Afterward, Hancock would arrange to transport the cloth to London, where it would be traded for various products around the world, including luxury cloths from Europe; velvets, silks, and satins from the Mediterranean; wines from France and Spain; and spices from Asia. Once Hancock arranged shipment of these products from London (with the exception of the wines brought in from Bristol), they would sell them at the markets to townspeople and to families from the surrounding rural districts.

As John Lee's business grew, so did his family. At the time of John Lee's death in 1629, he had three surviving sons: John Jr. (b. 1616), Richard (b. 1618), and Thomas (b. 1622). In 1639, ten years after the elder John's death, Jane Lee passed away and left her small estate to her three boys. In her will, Jane Lee stipulated that her brother, Thomas Hancock, would retain control of each son's inheritance until his twenty-fourth birthday. This mandate made the Lee boys wards of Thomas Hancock, and this arrangement soon proved beneficial for all parties concerned.[4]

Thomas Hancock now controlled a thriving family enterprise. Although manufacturing cloth remained central to the business, Hancock was much more than a clothier. A more appropriate characterization would be that of a mercer, a merchant who traded in cloth but also supplied a wide variety of miscellaneous goods for which no other specialized supplier existed. Hancock's success as a mercer depended heavily on his ability to maintain constant and direct access to the London markets and fairs. To this end, Thomas Hancock arranged for two of his wards, John and Thomas Lee, to go to London and open a merchant house. John and Thomas would receive cloth from their uncle and trade it for various imports that would then be shipped overland to Worcester. As John and Thomas Lee set up shop in London, Thomas Hancock made preparations for Richard to leave England and settle in Jamestown, thereby providing a direct connection between Hancock's growing enterprises and the newly developing American market.

Thomas Hancock's success as a mercer depended heavily on his ability to secure the patronage of prominent members of the community around him. For Hancock, this meant that he had to foster favorable ties with the leading families in the region that included the Throckmortons, the Packingtons, the

Gowers, and, of course, the Bishop of Worcester.[5] The patronage of these prominent personages among the local gentry not only afforded economic advantages for merchants like Thomas Hancock, but they also helped lay the foundation for access to Parliament and the Crown as well, which was crucial to the merchant seeking to engage in the American trade.

Hancock's connections served him and his nephew well. As Richard Lee made preparations to leave England, Sir Francis Wyatt, the recently appointed royal governor of Virginia, hired Lee as his personal secretary, and the two men traveled side by side across the Atlantic Ocean to Jamestown. Lee developed a close association with Wyatt, and his close association with the new governor only enhanced his prospects in Virginia. After his arrival in Jamestown, Richard Lee spent the first three years employed as Wyatt's personal secretary. In 1642, Wyatt relinquished his post as royal governor once his replacement, Sir William Berkeley, arrived in the colony. Wyatt gave Lee an impressive recommendation; therefore, Berkeley conferred upon Lee the position of secretary of state, thus allowing him to retain a salaried position as a colonial official. At this juncture, Lee entered a small circle of colonial gentlemen who worked together toward managing the Virginia colony in the name of Charles I. Patronage extended downward from the king to Berkeley; from there, the royal governor selected those who would share the responsibilities of colonial government and administration, while King Charles I could more effectively control the taxes and other monies the crown received from colonial trade.

Richard Lee's relationship with Governor Berkeley continued to grow, and over time, it became increasingly profitable. In 1643, Lee finally found an opportunity to begin pursuing his interests in the fur trade. The governor gave Lee a 1,000-acre land grant just north of the York River. Once Lee secured the grant, he and his wife, Anne Constable Lee, left Jamestown and built a home along the shores of the York River, where he then established a trading post along Virginia's frontier. There, he would trade a variety of English-made goods for animal furs and skins. Periodically, he would load the furs onto a shallop, bring them to Jamestown, and make arrangements to ship them back to London. He would share his profits with Governor Berkeley and other patrons, both in Virginia and in England.

Lee's new home on the York River, which he called Indian Spring, was located near a small Native American village known as Capahosic Wicomico. As long as Lee lived near Indian villages, he could maintain a steady trade with the native inhabitants of the colony. Similarly, as long as he provided access to furs to all interested parties in Jamestown, his position and his patronage from the governor remained intact. Consequently, as Lee fulfilled the duties of his office, he also began the process of steadily building up his commercial interests and his transatlantic ties with his uncle, Thomas Hancock.

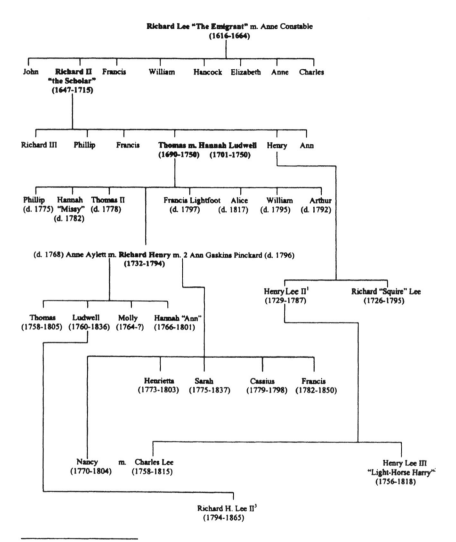

Richard Lee "The Emigrant" m. Anne Constable
(1616-1664)

| John | Richard II "the Scholar" (1647-1715) | Francis | William | Hancock | Elizabeth | Anne | Charles |

| Richard III | Phillip | Francis | Thomas m. Hannah Ludwell (1690-1750) (1701-1750) | Henry | Ann |

| Phillip (d. 1775) | Hannah "Missy" (d. 1778) | Thomas II (d. 1782) | Francis Lightfoot (d. 1797) | Alice (d. 1817) | William (d. 1795) | Arthur (d. 1792) |

(d. 1768) Anne Aylett m. Richard Henry m. 2 Ann Gaskins Pinckard (d. 1796)
(1732-1794)

Henry Lee II[1]
(1729-1787)

Richard "Squire" Lee
(1726-1795)

| Thomas (1758-1805) | Ludwell (1760-1836) | Molly (1764-?) | Hannah "Ann" (1766-1801) |

| Henrietta (1773-1803) | Sarah (1775-1837) | Cassius (1779-1798) | Francis (1782-1850) |

| Nancy (1770-1804) | m. Charles Lee (1758-1815) |

Henry Lee III
"Light-Horse Harry"
(1756-1818)

Richard H. Lee II[3]
(1794-1865)

---

[1] Richard Henry Lee's cousin who was appointed guardian of Thomas Lee's children in 1754.
[2] Robert E. Lee's (1810-1870) father.
[3] Richard Henry Lee's grandson and author of *Memoir of the Life of Richard Henry Lee* (1825).

Figure 1.2. The Lees of Virginia, a partial genealogy.

Richard Lee had amassed an impressive fortune for himself and his family in Virginia. Not only had Lee acquired over 10,000 acres of land, either through direct purchase or the head right system,[6] but he also managed a warehouse in Gloucester County known to local residents as "Lee's Store." In this facility, Lee stored his tobacco and furs; he also placed a wide variety of English-made goods that he traded with other planters for their tobacco. Lee's fortunes increased still further in the mid-1650s, when he became a partial owner of a transoceanic ship and when he owned and managed three separate tobacco plantations: Paradise in Gloucester County; Dividing Creek in Northumberland County; and Machodoc in Westmoreland County. By 1660, Richard Lee had clearly become one of the largest landholders and ranked among the wealthiest men in Virginia.

While Lee worked to expand his holdings in America, civil war erupted in England. As the conflict drew to a close, Parliament tried and executed King Charles I, and the Stuart dynasty came to an abrupt, albeit temporary, end. Then came the advent of Oliver Cromwell, and Lee, Berkeley, and other Stuart sympathizers had to leave their political posts in favor of new appointees loyal to the new government in England. Consequently, Lee retired from Jamestown; afterward, he moved his family out of their Indian Spring home, settled on new lands they had acquired in Gloucester County, and built a new home they called Paradise. Lee's success shows that the English civil war only slightly disrupted Lee's activities in America. As Lee consolidated his holdings in Virginia, he continued to make preparations to promote his interests on the other side of the Atlantic Ocean as well.

As Cromwell's government took control in London, Parliament took its first deliberate steps to manage the nation's growing economic interests in America. Seeking to regulate colonial trade, Parliament passed the first of a series of navigation acts in 1651. This initial act prohibited the use of non-English ships for the transportation of colonial goods. The adopted measure had the support of London-based merchants who wanted to prevent Dutch interlopers from profiting off of the American trade. Virginia planters like Richard Lee denounced the measure as an infringement on their tradition of free trade, and Lee's name appeared on a short list of candidates to travel to London to lobby for the repeal of the 1651 Navigation Act.[7]

Lee's efforts in London to abrogate the trade restrictions were of no avail. Parliament left the navigation act intact, but members agreed to make one concession to Chesapeake colonies. Parliament agreed to ban the production of tobacco in England, which threatened to undercut the price of tobacco grown in Virginia and Maryland. There is little reason to doubt that this sort of limited victory regarding the regulation of colonial trade prompted Lee to expand his ventures to include an oceangoing ship and a warehouse to store tobacco and English made goods. These actions represent distinct efforts on Lee's part to adapt to Parliament's regulatory measures. Once Lee became a co-owner of an English ship, he could readily comply with the navigation act without reducing his profit margin in the tobacco trade.

As Lee prospered in Virginia, there is reason to believe that his uncle, Thomas Hancock, did not fare so well in the aftermath of the civil war. In the decade following the execution of Charles I, Hancock's active participation in the transoceanic trade ended, but Richard Lee remained a respected and well-liked individual among the citizens of Worcester in spite of his long absence from that community. On two separate instances, Lee or his sons were recipients of money from the estates of Worcester clothiers in the 1650s and 1660s.[8] Consequently, with the restoration of Charles II, Lee made preparations to leave his Paradise plantation and return to England. Upon his arrival, Lee decided to establish a merchant house of his own in London, which would allow his growing transatlantic commercial empire to continue to grow and prosper.

Richard Lee's business interests forced him to make numerous trips to England during the Cromwellian interregnum. At one point, he had to demonstrate that he was "faithful" to Cromwell's regime and prove that he was "useful to [the] Commonwealth"; but these were terms Lee readily agreed to so that he could maintain his growing business enterprises. After the Stuart restoration, Lee decided to establish a permanent residence in London. He left the management of his three plantations in the trusted hands of his business associates in Virginia and made preparations to take his family with him back to England.

Upon their arrival in England, the Lees settled near London. Lee bought an estate on the outskirts of town called Stratford-Langton. From this location, he consolidated his holdings on both sides of the Atlantic and achieved what would be called in modern parlance "the vertical integration of the tobacco trade." On the London end of his business, Lee arranged for the shipment of English-made goods to his warehouses in Virginia. He would then trade these products for tobacco, furs, and animal skins, which would be transported back to London. All of these transfers, of course, would be done on English ships that he partially owned, which allowed him to reduce overall costs and remain in compliance with the navigation acts.

As Lee established his London merchant house, he also looked after the education of his two oldest boys, John and Richard II (ages seventeen and fourteen, respectively). He introduced John to a number of London-based merchants, grooming the young man for the day when he would assume control of the Lee family enterprises in England and America. While Anne and the younger Lee children remained at Stratford-Langton, Richard and John periodically traveled to Virginia to oversee matters on the American side of affairs.

During this period, Lee became actively involved in the slave trade, arranging for the transportation of eighty African slaves, which netted him another 4,000 acres of land through the head right system in Virginia. In addition to this transaction, Lee purchased land in Maryland.

By 1664, Richard Lee had established an impressive commercial empire in the twenty-five years since his arrival in Jamestown. He launched his enterprise after securing the patronage of other, more prominent men. Lee now was one of the most influential men in the colony and thus in a position to dispense patronage to others. Smaller planter–merchants in Virginia often looked to Lee for credit, for land they would either purchase or rent, for convenient access to English-made goods, as well as jobs for their sons. By the time of his death in 1664, at the age of forty-five, Lee had gone to great lengths to ensure that his sons would continue the family business. John Lee returned to Virginia and made the Machodoc plantation along the banks of the Potomac in the Northern Neck his primary residence. After Richard II returned to America, he took up the management of Paradise and "Lee's Store" in Gloucester County. A third son, Francis Lee, remained in London in accordance with his father's wishes so that he could take his place as the family's London commercial agent. As each of Richard Lee's oldest sons took their place either in Virginia or London, a second generation of Lees assumed control of their father's burgeoning transatlantic commercial empire.

In the mid-seventeenth century, the Lees shifted their Virginia interests away from the fur trade in favor of tobacco.[9] Several factors made this decision crucial. First, by the 1670s, English clothiers were relying more heavily on manufactured cloth and less on materials made of animal skins and furs. In addition, the number of creatures with luxurious furs sought after by some manufacturers had steadily declined in the Chesapeake Bay area to the degree that few could sustain profits in the fur trade. Consequently, as this shift occurred, large planter–merchants like the Lees struggled to maintain a competitive edge in the fur trade, despite their political connections, while smaller planter–merchants began to grumble about the monopolistic control of the trade that was still in the hands of Virginia's provincial government. The shift toward tobacco illustrated the Lees' remarkable ability to adapt to challenges against, as well as changes within, Virginia's provincial government and economy. It occurred as the colony had to confront a series of upheavals during the latter half of the seventeenth century.

As Richard Lee II assumed his place as the patriarch of his family's interests, the smaller, disgruntled planter–merchants soon found a spokesman in the guise of Nathaniel Bacon, who had recently arrived in Virginia fully intending to make his fortune engaging in the fur trade (only to be sadly disappointed). By June 1676, Bacon had gained enough support in the House of Burgesses to secure the passage of a measure prohibiting all trade with the Indians, only to modify it later to allow for biannual commercial fairs at which all interested parties could attend and engage in trade. Richard Lee II voiced his objections; he denounced the actions of the June Assembly and declared that Bacon led a "zealous multitude" that was jealous of the more successful planter–merchants in the colony. He made it abundantly clear that he had no intention of obeying the statute passed by Bacon's supporters in the House. Lee's public stance, however, soon landed him in jail, where he remained imprisoned for two months. He secured his release only after Bacon had suddenly died of the "bloody flux," or dysentery, in October 1676.[10]

Bacon's Rebellion and its aftermath taught Lee a valuable lesson, that political upheaval potentially had disastrous consequences for his family's economic interests. The rebellion resulted in some modifications of the provincial system; many of the changes gave the king more control over colonial affairs in order to prevent future rebellions from occurring. Those planter–merchants who were staunch supporters of Governor Berkeley took umbrage at this new situation. As a new royal governor, Thomas, Lord Culpepper, arrived in Virginia, where a factional split existed within the planter elite. Those who were designated as the "Berkeleyites" resisted Culpepper's administration at every opportunity; in opposition, moderate planters formed a second faction, known as the "Trimmers." The moderates quickly found a leader in Richard Lee, as he urged compromise because he feared that the hard line adopted by the "Berkeleyites" would only invite more intrusive policies from the Crown. Eventually, cooler heads prevailed, and the new governor rewarded the "Trimmers" for their support.[11]

For his part in the affair, Lord Culpepper rewarded Lee with a lucrative political appointment as the revenue collector for the Southern District of the Potomac. In 1680, the House of Burgesses revived an old tobacco duty of two shillings per hogshead of tobacco shipped to England. As revenue collector for the Southern District of the Potomac, Lee received a fee for every ship that entered the Potomac River, as well as a 10 percent commission on all of the revenue collected from the tobacco duty in the southern portion of the great river. In the 1680s, especially after Culpepper's appointment, Lee directed as much traffic as possible into the Potomac and the Northern Neck, while at the same time he expanded the Machodoc estate. As Culpepper left Virginia and was replaced by Francis, Lord Howard of Effingham, Lee continued to cultivate strong ties with the provincial regime. These proved to be very good times for the Lee family in Virginia. Richard II remained an active and loyal supporter of the royal government, and he further strengthened his transatlantic interests by working with his brother Francis Lee in London.

The situation, however, suddenly changed as Lee received word that Parliament had deposed King James II. Once again, England divided into Parliamentarian and Royalist camps, but this time, both sides sought to avoid bloodshed. James II, sensing that the end of his reign had arrived, fled to France, where he chose to live in exile rather than risk the same fate his father had suffered in 1649. Once King James II had departed, Parliament extended an invitation to William, Duke of Orange, and his wife, Mary (James's daughter), to cross the English Channel and assume the roles as king and queen of England.

As these events transpired, Richard Lee was somewhat uncertain what his next step would be. He found it exceedingly difficult to break his long-standing ties to the Stuarts because he was convinced that his family's success depended entirely on the patronage that had flowed from Charles I, then from Charles II, and lastly, from James II. The geopolitical aspects of James's flight to France were also of concern to Lee. At this time, France had emerged as the single largest market for Chesapeake tobacco. Lee would ship his annual crop and other tobacco he acquired to his brother in London, who would then sell a significant percentage of the shipment to the French purchaser. The accession of the Duke of Orange to the throne of England posed a direct challenge to these arrangements.

As a resident in the Northern Neck, Lee soon realized that the majority of his neighbors had chosen to recognize the new monarchs. Families such as the Fairfaxes and Culpeppers reaped tremendous benefits and acquired vast estates in the Northern Neck with the blessing of the Crown. By 1690, Lee had come to the realization that he would have to find some honorable way to win back the favor of the Crown and the provincial government. Lee's accomplishment of his goal came in the wake of the Crown's massive land grants to the Fairfaxes and Culpeppers. In addition to the acreage, William and Mary also allowed these to families the right to collect quitrents—annual payments for land that normally filled the coffers of the English Crown—in recognition of their support. They could keep this revenue for their own personal use rather than give it over to the monarchy.

Several small planters resented this sort of preferment bestowed on these two families and simply refused to pay the amounts owed. Tensions rose, and another rebellion, reminiscent of the one led by Nathaniel Bacon, seemed eminent. At this juncture, Richard Lee stepped forward and announced his intention to pay the rents he owed to the Fairfaxes and Culpeppers without question or dispute. Lee's unilateral action helped avert a potential crisis, as other planters that largely depended on the Lees for patronage followed suit. At this point, Lee not only found himself in the good graces of the two most powerful families in the Northern Neck, but he also won back the favor of the Crown. Lee traveled to Williamsburg, which had replaced Jamestown as the colonial capital, and swore an oath of loyalty to William and Mary. His reputation and personal honor were intact, and the royal government once again appointed him to the Council of State and restored him to his post as revenue collector for the Southern District of the Potomac.[12]

Nonetheless, as the seventeenth century drew to a close, these events had taken their toll. Before long, Lee resigned his seat on the Council, but he retained his role as revenue collector. He had tired of politics and now sought to expand his family's commercial interests. In his fifty-third year, Richard II began delegating more responsibilities to his sons. The war between England and France ended in 1696, and in the years following the conflict, he sent his oldest son, Richard III, to London to help his uncle Francis Lee run the family business in London. Soon after Richard III's arrival in England, the London Lee joined with young Richard's maternal uncle, Thomas Corbin, and launched a partnership by establishing the firm of Corbin and Lee.

Richard II then sent his second-eldest son, Philip, to Maryland, where he assumed control of the Lee estates in the neighboring colony. The third son, another Francis Lee, went to London, where he studied medicine before returning to Virginia and found a place as a physician. The two youngest boys, Thomas and Henry (ten and nine years old, respectively), moved to Williamsburg, where they began attending classes at William and Mary.

By 1711, Richard II began shifting more responsibilities onto Thomas and Henry. Both of his youngest sons lived with him at Machodoc and were well versed in handling the family's transatlantic affairs. As a third generation of Lees steadily took the helm of their commercial empire, animosities developed between the Lees and some of the neighboring families, most notably Robert "King" Carter of Corotoman. The rivalry turned personal in 1711, as "King" Carter lost an extremely lucrative post to a twenty-one-year-old Thomas Lee.[13]

Carter had managed the Fairfax lands in the Northern Neck for nearly a decade when Thomas Corbin quietly approached Lady Catherine Fairfax in London. Corbin suggested that her American lands should be earning more revenue then they were. These comments intrigued Lady Fairfax; she listened carefully and at the conclusion of their conversation agreed with Corbin that perhaps she should name a new, more qualified manager. Lady Fairfax named Edmund Jenings as "King" Carter's replacement. Jenings recently served as Virginia's acting governor and was a respected gentleman on both sides of the Atlantic. Additionally, Jenings conveniently had just signed on as another partner in the firm of Corbin and Lee. Jenings accepted the post but said he could not leave England. He asked if he could appoint his nephew, Thomas Lee, as his deputy. Lady Fairfax agreed, indicating that she still held Richard Lee II in high regard for his acknowledgement of the Fairfax proprietorship in the 1690s. However, this event generated a Carter–Lee rivalry that would last for well over a decade.

The fortunes of young Thomas Lee continued to grow. In 1713, Richard II, citing his declining health as the reason, asked Governor Alexander Spotswood to allow his son Thomas to assume the post as revenue collector for the Southern

District of the Potomac. Spotswood agreed to the request, and Thomas Lee now found himself with two exceedingly lucrative jobs that reinforced the Lees' transatlantic commercial interests as well.

Richard II died in 1715 at the age of sixty-eight. While the colony mourned the passing of a highly respected provincial leader and businessman, his sons steadily assumed control of their family's business.[14] Richard III remained in London, now a full partner; Philip remained in Maryland; and Francis moved into the Paradise estate in Gloucester County. Thomas and Henry shared Machodoc, where they assumed direct control over the Virginia side of the Lee family interests. Thus, a third generation continued the family traditions set by their grandfather, Richard Lee "the Emigrant."

III

By 1715 the Lee interests were soon threatened as several unexpected problems complicated the English end of their transatlantic commercial empire. Another war between England and France began in 1702, a conflict the colonists dubbed Queen Anne's War, and once again, the tobacco colonies had to face the economic consequences of a war denying them access to their single largest market for tobacco.

As the war entered its sixth year, Edmund Jenings, who then served as Virginia's acting governor, warned officials in England that planters were being forced to abandon tobacco production altogether. In an attempt to halt this disturbing trend, British officials sought to negotiate an end to the French monopoly system's governing tobacco and establish a relationship based on free trade. As the combatants prepared for the eventual end of Queen Anne's War, diplomats began incorporating such provisions into their drafts of peace treaties.[15]

Rumors circulated throughout the London merchant community that the French monopoly system was at an end. The number of London tobacco houses proliferated between 1710 and 1713; the war began tapering off; and ambitious merchants began preparing to take advantage of the new state of affairs as soon as the two governments signed the final treaty officially ending the war. The firm of Corbin and Lee now faced numerous competitors as planters and merchants on both sides of the Atlantic eagerly awaited the renewal of the tobacco trade between England and France.

Unfortunately, the rumors proved false, and the establishment of a free trade agreement between the two nations never emerged; as a result, several tobacco houses were forced to the verge of bankruptcy. Corbin and Lee was among the firms that teetered on the edge, and in 1716, the bottom finally fell out. Thomas Lee in Virginia received word that his oldest brother, Richard III, had disappeared. Apparently, Richard Lee was unable to pay the debts owed to creditors, and rather than face them, he fled London. Now, Thomas Lee had to make arrangements to leave Virginia and tend to the family crisis developing in London.

Soon after Lee arrived, he located his brother and convinced him to return to London and face his creditors. Thomas Lee worked with his brother and uncles to rebuild the family firm. Once the difficult work was behind him, Thomas Lee found time to tend to some personal business as well. While conducting a survey in the Northern Neck for the Fairfaxes along the shores of the Potomac River, he spied an outcropping of two majestic white cliffs. He began to make inquiries concerning the ownership of the property and learned that Nathaniel Pope owned the land; he also discovered that Pope had left the colony and returned to London. After Lee had tended to family matters, he located Pope and negotiated a price for what was known as the Clifts Plantation. Lee purchased 1,443 acres from Pope and then secured another 2,400 acres, which extended his holdings all the way to the river's edge, including the two white cliffs that first drew his attention to the area.

Thomas Lee remained in London for two years while he helped reestablish the family firm and purchase the Clifts Plantation, then he returned to Machodoc. Not long after his return to Virginia, more sad news arrived from London. Richard III died, and as a consequence of the death, the firm of Corbin and Lee had completely dissolved. The London end of the family's commercial interests now no longer existed. Lee began corresponding with his brother's widow, Martha Silk Lee, who announced her plans to remain in London. The question Thomas Lee needed answered concerned the Lee estate that he then occupied, Machodoc. Richard III had legal claim to the property, which he passed on to his wife according to the terms in his will. Martha Lee easily arranged for Thomas Lee to lease the property so that he could continue to use it as his primary residence in Virginia; yet, in the wake of his brother's death in London, Lee's position in Virginia remained tenuous at best. He had to contend with the reality that the London end of the family business was in shambles, and complicating matters further, Lee knew that Governor Alexander Spotswood was his only political patron in the colony. Unfortunately, the governor was at war with several prominent members of the Council of State and the House of Burgesses, and Robert "King" Carter led the faction discontented with Spotswood. Consequently, Lee had to shy away from his family's transatlantic interests and begin tending to political matters in Virginia in order to shore up the more immediate problems threatening to destroy all that the two previous generations of Lees had built.

IV

At this juncture, the rivalry between Thomas Lee and "King" Carter over the Fairfax land agency took on a new political dimension. As Lee entered his thirtieth year, he turned his attention toward seeking a place in the House of Burgesses representing Westmoreland County. Carter's enmity toward Lee had not abated over the decade since Carter lost his position as land agent to Thomas Lee in 1711. In many respects, the tensions between the Carters and Lees helped solidify the ties between Lee and Spotswood. Since the governor's arrival in 1710, he had to confront a growing clique in the Council and the burgesses that constantly tried to thwart his efforts to rule the colony. Spotswood remained convinced that his political enemies were always "stirring up the humors of the people" before elections and "tampering with the most mutinous members of the Burgesses" in attempts to prevent him from serving the Crown's interests in Virginia.[16]

As these problems persisted, Spotswood increasingly relied on those outside of the Council, yet he retained positions of rank and power in the colony while he occupied the governor's mansion in Williamsburg. This state of affairs explains the strong ties that developed between the Lees and Governor Spotswood—it also reinforces the pattern established by Richard Lee I of maintaining close ties with top colonial officials as the surest way of retaining royal patronage. Spotswood spoke warmly of Richard Lee II, describing him as "a gentleman of as fair character as any in the country for his exact justice, honesty, and exceptionable loyalty in all the stations wherein he has served in this government"; thus, the governor willingly extended open arms to Thomas Lee after Richard II's death in 1715.[17]

As a resident of Virginia's Northern Neck, several factors now put Lee at a distinct disadvantage over other planters living in the vicinity—with the enmity of "King" Carter certainly topping the list. In 1720, Lee launched his first bid for elective office by challenging his brother-in-law, Daniel McCarthy, for one of the Westmoreland County seats in the House of Burgesses. Lee won the election, and this victory proved significant not only to Lee but to Governor Spotswood as well because McCarthy also served as the Speaker of the House of Burgesses and was one of Carter's most powerful allies in the lower assembly. Lee's victory in the election dealt a devastating blow to Carter's dominance over provincial politics. Nonetheless, Lee prepared to move to Williamsburg and occupy his seat. Carter retaliated by launching a vicious assault on Lee, claiming that he had conducted a fraudulent campaign. He accused the master of Machodoc of rigging the election by allowing nonresidents to cast their votes in Westmoreland County. The scandal soon forced Thomas Lee to resign his seat and return to the Northern Neck. Complicating matters still further, Spotswood's political opponents pursued their growing list of grievances against the governor, and eventually the Crown could no longer afford to ignore them. Consequently, in 1722, Spotswood vacated the governor's office, and Thomas Lee lost his most influential patron.

Although his tenure in the House of Burgesses proved short, Lee made the most of what time he spent in Williamsburg. He enhanced his reputation among the Virginia gentry by hosting a ball attended by many of the wealthy planters living along the James River, many of whom were impressed by Lee's attention to detail. Additionally, he made frequent trips to Green Spring, the plantation home once owned by Sir William Berkeley but now inhabited by Philip Ludwell. During these visits, Lee courted Ludwell's daughter, Hannah, finally winning her hand in marriage. One year after their marriage, the couple returned to Machodoc and celebrated the birth of their first son, Richard Lee IV.

Not long after Thomas and Hannah had moved back to the Northern Neck, Daniel McCarthy died, opening another opportunity for Lee to pursue political office. Lee campaigned for the 1724 election and won; but upon assuming his seat in the House, he found himself in a perpetual battle with "King" Carter, as both men struggled to expand their personal empires in the Northern Neck. Earlier, Carter had won a crucial advantage in 1721, when he successfully lobbied the Fairfax family and was thereby reappointed as the Fairfax land agent. Now, Carter initiated a series of public charges, claiming that Lee was improperly claiming and withholding lands that rightfully belonged to the Fairfax estates. In the process, Carter made several veiled threats of legal action against Lee if he did not find "time to do me justice."[18] As the feud between the two planters raged on, Carter's attacks took on an increasingly personal nature by attacking the quality of Lee's tobacco. In one story that "King" Carter circulated, he claimed Lee attempted to ship "three black hogshead of tobacco" to London, which he went on to describe as the "most despicable stuff [he] ever saw in [his] life."[19] Accusations of this nature, if London merchants ever heard such stories, could have had devastating effects not only on his reputation within his community but on his credit as well. Yet, despite Carter's efforts, Lee successfully established himself as a prominent local planter and continued to cultivate a strong political base in the Northern Neck.

While Lee served in the House of Burgesses, his family continued growing, as did his responsibilities as a local leader in provincial politics. By 1728, Thomas and Hannah had two more children, a son they named Philip (after his maternal grandfather) and a daughter christened Hannah (after her mother) but whom they lovingly called Missy. Thomas Lee had also taken on additional positions within Westmoreland County while he was a member of the House of Burgesses. Lee took on the responsibilities of vestryman for Cople Parish and as a justice of the peace for Westmoreland County. As vestryman, Lee oversaw church repairs and managed the financial affairs relating to the religious life of residents living in Cople Parish; he also served on a local court that prosecuted and punished those convicted of moral offenses within the community.

In the years that followed, Thomas Lee's position within the colony continued to advance. In 1733, "King" Carter died, and Governor Gooch selected Lee to fill Carter's vacancy on the Council of State. The additional income that accompanied his promotion to the Council provided Lee with the needed funds to finally begin developing the Clifts property. In 1734, he filed a survey of this land and began purchasing other tracts in the vicinity. Four years later, construction started on a new home for the Lees that they would call Stratford Hall, no doubt after the London estate once owned by his grandfather. By 1740, workers completed the outer shell of the great house, and soon thereafter Thomas Lee moved his family into their new residence.

While building Stratford Hall, the Lee brood had increased by six. In addition to Richard Henry Lee, who was born in 1732, Thomas and Hannah had four more sons and one more daughter: Thomas Jr. (b. 1730), Francis (b. 1734), Alice (b. 1736), William (b. 1739), and Arthur (b. 1740). As the Lees moved into Stratford Hall, Thomas Lee had proven to be the most ambitious and enterprising of all of Richard Lee II's sons. Thomas Lee, like his father and grandfather before him, had successfully navigated Virginia's political and social system and steadily rose to prominence. His close ties with Alexander Spotswood and, later, William Gooch firmly established Lee among the most prominent men in the Northern Neck. Additionally, Lee was the scion of one of the colony's first families and the owner of more than 16,000 acres of land in his own right. Now, as the first master of Stratford Hall, Thomas Lee turned his attention to matters outside the political arena. He sought to protect and expand his vast holdings and promote the growing legacy that he would eventually pass on to his burgeoning family.

V

By the time Richard Henry Lee had celebrated his tenth birthday, the Lees had moved into these comfortable surroundings. As a boy, he was free to roam about the plantation grounds, making friends with the children of slaves living on the plantation, unfettered by parental supervision. Little evidence has survived concerning Richard Henry's early childhood experiences, and much that remains is at best anecdotal. As Richard Henry learned that he would soon be going to England to complete his education, he would arrange for boxing lessons with one of the "stout" slaves. One day, his father interrupted one such match and angrily asked Richard Henry, "What pleasure can you find in such rough sport?" Richard Henry responded that he "would shortly have to box with the English boys" and that he "did not wish to be beaten by them."[20]

Although little can be said specifically of Richard Henry's childhood with certainty, a tremendous amount of recent scholarship allows for an effective recreation of plantation life in the Georgian period.[21] Eighteenth-century parents allowed their children to socialize with younger slaves; however, such associations were discouraged by their early teen years. By that time, parents began to assign their children specific duties around the plantation. Other than this, fathers seldom concerned themselves with their preadolescent children. Thomas Lee, to a certain extent, represented an exception to this sort of generalization. Since he spent most of his time in the 1730s arranging for the construction of Stratford Hall, Lee could spend more time with his young children. When he had to leave and tend to matters of state, he always arranged to leave Williamsburg so he could be with Hannah as she gave birth to another child. Consequently, Lee had a luxury few planters could afford when it came to childrearing, and he thus devoted a tremendous amount of time and energy making sure his sons were prepared to assume their legacy when the time came.

The education of his children when they were between the ages of three and twelve remained one of Lee's primary concerns. He understood the importance of securing a formal education for his children. In the 1730s and 1740s, Lee hired three different tutors to educate his children. David Currie most likely instructed Philip and Missy; Alexander White took on the responsibility after Currie left Stratford and tutored Thomas Jr., Richard Henry, and most likely, Francis and Alice as well. The third one hired, known only as Mr. Craig, arrived at Stratford Hall in 1746, and he directed the studies of the two youngest boys, William and Arthur.[22] All three men had Anglican backgrounds, and all three returned to the ministry after leaving Stratford Hall. While employed by Thomas Lee, they provided instruction in reading, writing, mathematics, Greek, Latin, and religion. Frequently, close relationships would develop between teacher and pupil, and on occasion this turned into a lasting friendship. In 1758, long after Alexander White left Stratford, he wrote to Richard Henry Lee congratulating him on his recent election to the House of Burgesses; White referred to their "friendship so happily begun in [Richard Henry's] tender years."[23]

A tidewater education encompassed more than rudimentary academic skills. Parents frequently solicited instructors that could also introduce their children to the art of dance and music appreciation. Parents viewed dancing as a form of discipline and exercise, as well as a form of art. Consequently, they did not take matters concerning performance lessons lightly. Philip Vickers Fithian commented on the latitude dance instructors received when introducing their craft to children on the great plantations. Francis Christian, Fithian noted, was one of the most highly sought after dancing teachers in the Northern Neck. Fithian noted that Christian was both "punctual and rigid" as an instructor. During one class meeting, much to Fithian's astonishment, Christian actually "struck two of the young Misses for a fault in the course of their performance, even in the presence of the Mother of one of them!" Young men also frequently felt the sting of Christian's criticism. Fithian observed that the instructor once threw a young man out of the class because of his inability to keep up with other students. Fithian remarked afterward that he thought Christian's action was a "sharp reproof, to a young Gentleman of seventeen, before a large number of Ladies." Yet, the instructor's actions were tolerated and regarded as necessary in order for the young men and women to grasp the art of dance.[24]

Parents tolerated the demeanor of instructors like Francis Christian because dancing represented an extremely important aspect of plantation life and culture. The great families that resided along the James and Potomac Rivers gathered together at seasonal balls and festivals. These social events provided opportunities for parents and children to associate with their peers; all would feast and dance together and participate in a variety of games including horse and boat races. If a child of one of the great planters lacked the social graces, of which dancing was considered among the most important skills, the embarrassment could have had a devastating and lingering effect, lasting well into his adult years. The reason is that these social gatherings were frequently where young men and women met their future wives and husbands.

Festivals of this sort required extensive planning and preparation. When the Lees hosted such gatherings, slaves would roast an entire calf or hog for at least two days in the kitchen adjacent to the great house. Food prepared in this quantity would guarantee that the Lees' guests would never be in want of something to eat while attending such events at Stratford Hall. Frequently, these festivals would last several days, allowing for ample time for the hosts to ingratiate themselves with their neighbors and other visitors.[25]

Thomas Lee sponsored many such events and delighted in bringing guests to Stratford Hall. He was meticulous in matters concerning the appearance of his home, both indoors and outdoors. As a carriage bringing visitors to Stratford broke through a thick grove of trees, they would catch their first glimpse of the great house. The drivers steered their carriages around toward the eastern end of the house, thus allowing guests to pass by the beautifully sculpted gardens. The Lees would then greet their guests as they climbed out of their carriages. A brief glance northward afforded them a view of the Potomac River before they ascended the wide staircase that would take them into Stratford's great hall.

As host, Thomas Lee arranged for his guests to see the wonders of his home, and the festivities would culminate with a feast and a dance. Occasionally, Lee would move his guests down to Lee's Landing, where they would board a barge for a pleasure excursion down the Potomac River. Slave musicians generally provided the music for the dances, where fathers introduced their sons and mothers introduced their daughters. Men conducted business while the children made friends and found romance. At these events Richard Henry and his brothers established a lifelong friendship with their neighbor George Washington, while Gawain Corbin courted his future wife, Missy Lee.

Festivals of this nature had an effect on young Richard Henry, teaching him how to comport himself in the company of others. It imbibed in him a way of conduct that would remain with him throughout his adult life. Although Thomas Lee led an active life, both as a plantation manager and political leader, he made sure his boys learned how to present themselves to their peers. He divided his time between Williamsburg and Stratford Hall, returning home frequently to tend to his family's need. One anecdote from the 1740s related by the tutor Mr. Craig provides an interesting glimpse into the personal ties Thomas Lee established with his boys. One evening as the family gathered in the great hall before dinner, Thomas Lee lay sprawled on one of the sofas, resting. Richard Henry and his brothers soon filed in and saw their father dozing. On a nearby table, a servant had placed a pitcher containing a nutmeg drink forbidden to the children. The boys jostled for position as curiosity got the better of them, and they sought a taste of that "prohibited indulgence" while their father slept. As they neared the pitcher, they were startled by their father's urgent whisper telling them to "make haste boys, your mother will soon be here."[26] Thomas Lee proved he could be stern when necessary; but he also had the capacity to be a doting father as well, and all of his children were touched by his care and attention. As each of his sons reached the age of eleven or twelve, Thomas Lee assumed more direct control over their higher education. For a planter of Lee's stature, this generally meant making necessary arrangements to send them to England for additional schooling.

In 1738, Lee sent Philip to the prestigious English academy Eton, where he studied the works of classical authors, the language arts, geography, and advanced mathematics, including algebra and geometry. The younger Stratford boys remained at home for the time being but were assigned specific tasks around the plantation, helping to develop the practical skills needed to manage plantations of their own. As soon as Richard Henry learned how to ride and control a horse or how to handle a boat, he would be sent to deliver messages from his father to neighboring plantations. These excursions allowed him an opportunity to introduce himself directly to other prominent planters in a businesslike setting without being directly under the shadow of his father. Lee regarded his son's ability to handle these sorts of responsibilities as a crucial part of Richard Henry's overall education.

As his boys grew older, Thomas Lee gradually introduced them to the affairs of state as well. Philip, upon his return from Eton in 1743, received most of this type of instruction, but Lee's other sons would no doubt be included on varying levels. Thomas Lee regarded these matters seriously, especially as he groomed Philip Lee to become the second master of Stratford Hall. In 1744, Lee made preparations to represent Virginia at a series of negotiations with the Six Nations of the Iroquois in Lancaster, Pennsylvania. Governor Gooch selected Lee to lead a two-man delegation that included William Beverley. Lee also made additional arrangements for his seventeen-year-old son, Philip, to travel with him to the summit; he recognized the trip as an invaluable opportunity to educate his principal heir in the affairs of state. He no doubt had similar plans in mind for his other children as they grew and matured.

As Philip Lee returned to Stratford Hall, Great Britain and France once again declared war, and King George's War began. In many respects, the meeting at Lancaster was an attempt to garner some support for British imperial interests among the Iroquois and thus lessen French influence in the Ohio River Valley. Once the war began, however, the provincial government had to set many of these issues aside. Likewise, for Thomas Lee, he had to delay sending his boys Thomas Jr. and Richard Henry to England to complete their schooling until he could reasonably be assured of their safety while traversing the Atlantic Ocean. As King George's War dragged on into its fourth year, Thomas and Hannah recognized that they could no longer wait, and they made preparations to send their two sons to England. Although the war continued, news from the continent hinted that its end was near. As the tobacco ships began making their stops at the great plantations, the Lees realized that if they did not send Thomas Jr. and Richard Henry on board one of these vessels on its return voyage to England, their efforts to complete their schooling would be delayed for at least another year. Consequently, on that winter's morning in February 1748, Richard Henry left Lee's Landing along with his older brother, leaving their friends and family behind.

On that winter morning, Richard Henry was poised between two worlds. His familiarity with his family's history would allow him to recognize the similarities in the journey he was about to take and the adventure his great-grandfather had embarked on in 1639. He was also aware that as he completed his English education, he would have the opportunity to meet British merchants in London and elsewhere, which would allow him to make his own contributions to his family's commercial interests as part of a fourth generation of Lees. With these anxious thoughts crowding his mind, Richard Henry Lee boarded the tobacco ship and began his voyage across the ocean.

VI

As the tobacco ship moved through Chesapeake Bay, Richard Henry Lee caught a glimpse of Fort George as he sailed past Point Comfort. The fort was an imposing structure made of brick, with twenty-two mounted guns. Fort George represented one of several facilities designed to defend the principal waterways of Virginia from the intrusion of Spanish or French vessels and to protect the great tobacco plantations from the continual threat of pirates conducting raids up and down the North American coastline. Richard Henry was aware that Great Britain and France had been at war since 1744, which no doubt heightened his anxieties regarding the trip he was taking. Rumors abounded throughout the Chesapeake Bay area that seven French men-of-war, two of them with eighty guns each, were on their way to the tobacco colonies from Martinique. The French flotilla included, in addition to the gun ships, twenty-eight transports with an invasion force of 300 French soldiers. No one knew where the French would strike, but they were sure the enemy would arrive soon. Fort George, at least, offered some measure of security; if the French came bearing down on Virginia, the guns would let loose a volley sending the alarm to the residents living nearby. Richard Henry Lee, however, would still be a vulnerable target as his ship continued its trip across the Atlantic to Britain.[27]

In the winter of 1748, colonial defense was a topic on everyone's mind, including Richard Henry's. He was well aware of his family's concerns about his safety while traveling to England in the middle of a war. He was also cognizant of the threat posed by the French to his family's extensive interests in the Ohio River Valley—an area claimed by France as well as Great Britain. Since the first generation of Lees arrived in Virginia, his family had steadily pushed westward, seeking to maintain trade ties with the Native Americans and trying to secure fresh lands to grow tobacco. Now, several other families had followed, and Virginia's Northern Neck was heavily populated with planters turning wary eyes on French encroachments on their claims to the western lands.

In many respects, tobacco and western lands defined the dual nature of British–French relations in the seventeenth and eighteenth centuries. France remained Britain's single largest market for Chesapeake tobacco, and in order to maintain adequate levels of production, tobacco planters constantly vied for new land. Such needs drew a growing number of British colonists to focus their attention on western lands, following the rivers that stretched far into the interior of the continent. The French, on the other hand, sought to maintain their interests in the fur trade—initially with the Indians inhabiting southeastern Canada and later with the Iroquois, the Huron, and other tribes living in the Great Lakes region. By the 1730s and 1740s, French *cour de bois* began making their way further into the Ohio River Valley, bearing down on the edges of Britain's rich tobacco colonies. The competing interests between the British and the French kept tensions high, but planters and merchants always maintained a strong inclination toward peace to sustain normal trade relations. As these two European nations slipped back and forth between war and peace, the Ohio River valley increasingly became the focus of controversy. The Lees of Virginia and their allies were soon found at the center of these conflicts as they sought to secure British control over western lands in America, which would provide fresh lands for future tobacco production.

In 1748, as Richard Henry prepared to go to England and complete his education, his father began expanding his family's interests in the Ohio River valley by taking the lead in establishing the Ohio Company of Virginia. Through these efforts, Thomas Lee helped secure Britain's interests in North America from the French, and he promoted the Virginia planter elite's future interests in the tobacco trade. At this time, he turned his attention toward rebuilding his family's transatlantic empire. After Thomas's older brother Richard III died in 1720, he was not able to reestablish a merchant house in London to replace the defunct firm of Corbin and Lee, because his battles with "King" Carter prevented him from doing much of anything beyond consolidating his position in Virginia's Northern Neck.

In the interim, the Maryland Lees began taking up some of the slack through the marriage of Thomas Lee's niece to James Russell, who owned one of the more influential merchant houses in London. While the marriage facilitated transatlantic ties for at least one branch of the Lee family, Thomas Lee sought to reestablish the Virginia line with the same position and prominence they held earlier in the seventeenth century. To achieve this goal, he looked to his sons to help. So, as Richard Henry eagerly followed in the footsteps of his oldest brother, Philip, he joined the children of Virginia's first families, including the Amblers, the Nelsons, the Randolphs, and the Carters, all of whom were prominent families with personal and political ties to the Lees of Virginia. Richard Henry knew that a lengthy stay in England would allow him numerous opportunities to meet and acquaint himself with British merchants so that he could make his contribution toward furthering his family's transatlantic commercial interests.

VII

Before Richard Henry's ship left Lee's Landing in February 1748, his mother and father had arranged for an acquaintance, Martha Jacqueline, to meet their sons when their ship docked at an English port. In April, Jacqueline notified Edward and Jonathan Ambler that "two of Col. Lee's sons" had arrived and planned to attend classes with the Ambler boys at Wakefield Academy.[28] While enrolled in school, Richard Henry refined his rudimentary education he had received from Alexander White and sought opportunities to display social graces as he and his brother mingled with the families living in the surrounding communities. As soon as there was a break in school, Thomas Jr. and Edward Ambler left Wakefield to go on a walking tour of England and Scotland.[29]

While Thomas Jr. and Edward traversed the English countryside, Richard Henry remained in Wakefield, where he soon became romantically involved with the daughter of a prominent merchant with influential ties on both sides of the Atlantic, Edward Porteus of Rippon Hall. The Lees and the Porteuses had long-standing ties that extended back to the mid-seventeenth century. In the 1650s, a young man named Robert Lee, probably Richard Lee I's nephew, arrived in Virginia with his wife. Robert died soon after his arrival; his young widow married an Edward Porteus, and they had a son they named Robert. In 1693, Robert Porteus inherited a 692-acre plantation along the York River called New Bottle, which soon became a major tobacco producer. This property was most likely a gift from Richard Lee I to his nephew, and he simply allowed his widow to retain the property after Robert Lee's death.

After receiving his inheritance, Robert Porteus embarked on a successful career as a planter–merchant and became a highly respected political leader in Virginia. In 1713, Alexander Spotswood appointed Porteus to the Council of State; in 1720, recently widowed, he moved with his family back to England, citing his poor health and his desire to provide a better education for his children. Upon his return to England, Porteus moved to Yorkshire and married the daughter of Edmund Jenings, Thomas Lee's uncle, thereby further establishing the Lee–Porteus connection. Robert Porteus's last marriage produced several offspring, including Edward Porteus of Rippon Hall, whose daughter now attracted the attentions of Richard Henry Lee.[30]

As the romance blossomed between Richard Henry and Porteus's daughter, a marriage proposal seemed imminent; but before any arrangements could be made, tragic news arrived in Wakefield from Stratford Hall. Richard Henry learned that his mother passed away in January 1750; a few months later, he learned that his father had also died, in November. Consequently, in 1751, as a new year began, this information had significant ramifications for the Lee boys in England. Philip, as Thomas Lee's principal heir, began making the necessary arrangements to transfer all the Lee accounts to his name. Once the necessary changes had been made, Philip and Thomas Jr. began making preparations to leave England and return to America to begin settling their father's affairs in Virginia. Philip, of course, expected Richard Henry to follow suit. The youngest Lee, however, chose to stay in England and pursue his courtship of Edward Porteus's daughter—a decision that soon exacted a heavy, personal toll on Richard Henry.

Before Philip Lee left England to return to Stratford Hall, he displayed his apparent anger at his younger brother for refusing to leave by summarily breaking off the engagement between Richard Henry and the Porteus girl. The action caught everyone by surprise. After receiving word of Philip's decision, Edward Porteus, obviously dismayed by the news, wrote to Edward Ambler, hoping to stop Richard Henry before he left London. He wrote "Coll. [Philip] Lee writ us at our house about the affair between his Brother & my daughter." Porteus indicated how "surprised" he was to learn that the "affair between the two young peopell [was] at an end." He seemed to be at a loss to explain this turn of events. Porteus revealed the basis for Philip's decision, noting that the elder Lee stated he had great esteem for the young lady but that "he [could] not agree to the match which must be very bad for her, as his Brother's fortune [would] only maintain him alone."[31]

Edward Porteus pleaded with Ambler to return to Rippon Hall to console his heartbroken daughter. Additionally, Porteus revealed that his daughter was near and was begging Ambler, if he had the least value for her, to visit before going to London because his daughter had "something to say to you to tell [Richard Henry] Lee that she can not write him." Porteus hoped Richard Henry would remain in England long enough for his daughter's message to be relayed to him. As the distraught father concluded his letter, he added his daughter's plea: "You can not losse much time Miss Porteus begs so much to see you as the dear friend of [Richard Henry's]." He added with dismay: "I hardly know what to say that few young men [would] deny a young lady's request on an affair of such consequence to her."[32]

The tone of Porteus's letter to Ambler clearly reveals a desperate and confused quality, suggesting he was deeply disturbed by Philip Lee's abrupt decision to terminate the relationship between Richard Henry and his daughter. There is little reason to doubt that the young woman's grandfather Robert Porteus, then in his seventy-second year, was equally dismayed—especially over the notion that Richard Henry was an unsuitable match for his granddaughter. Another marriage tie between the Porteuses and the Lees seemed only logical, and both families stood to gain from such an arrangement. As prominent merchants in Yorkshire, the Porteuses would have naturally liked to secure a marriage tie with a wealthy and politically influential family in Virginia. Additionally, the heartrending, emotional outpouring exhibited by the young woman strongly suggests that an emotional bond had developed between the young couple.

Adding to the confusion was the need to find some plausible explanation for Philip Lee's actions. By the mid-eighteenth century, parents and guardians typically did not involve themselves in the marriage interests of their children, which made Philip's actions even more perplexing. We can only speculate on

Philip's motivations, and two possible and equally plausible explanations for Philip's behavior come to mind. First, as Philip Lee prepared to assume his position as the second master of Stratford Hall, he immediately became one of the wealthiest and most eligible bachelors in Virginia. Thomas Lee left Philip Stratford Hall and 4,000 acres surrounding the great house. Philip also inherited another 9,600 acres of Potomac shoreline property, two islands in the river, and 100 slaves. Coupled with these gifts of property, however, came the responsibilities of paying off his father's outstanding debts and caring for his younger siblings still living at Stratford Hall.

Thomas Lee's will included the injunction that the entire estate must be "kept together till all debts and Legacies be settled and Paid." Perhaps one reason why Philip broke off the engagement was that he could not condone the match, because if Richard Henry married Porteus's daughter, then Philip would have been compelled to release Richard Henry's inheritance before his father's debts had been paid. Consequently, the death of Thomas Lee and the injunction in the family will left Philip with no other option, and since Richard Henry would not end the engagement, Philip had to. Another possible explanation, one that reflects less favorably on Philip, would be that he viewed the match as unsuitable when Richard Henry's small fortune was compared to the vast inheritance Philip received. Perhaps Philip believed that he was a more suitable match for Porteus's daughter than his younger brother. The two families would still benefit from a marriage tie, but, clearly the emotional tie that existed between Richard Henry and Porteus's daughter made such an arrangement impossible. Either way, Philip believed, he would achieve his goal of forcing his brother to return to Virginia.

Unfortunately, evidence has not survived regarding Richard Henry Lee's perspective on these events. What is certain, however, is that he was not happy. Despite his brother's efforts, Richard Henry did not return to Virginia. He left London and embarked on a tour of the continent. It cannot be stated, with any degree of certainty, who may have traveled with him, but Lee remained in Europe for at least a year after Philip and Thomas had left England to return to Stratford Hall. After touring the continent, Lee boarded a ship and once again embarked on a voyage across the Atlantic. As he entered into Chesapeake Bay, Lee no doubt reflected on what had changed since his initial departure five years earlier. His mother and father were quietly resting in Burnt House Field. The sense of foreboding that filled his thoughts was reinforced as his ship sailed past Fort George. The once impressive structure now lay in ruins, a victim of one of the hurricanes that occasionally swept into the wide bay. Now, as his ship made its way into the Potomac River and anchored at Lee's Landing, Richard Henry Lee, now twenty-one years old, left the ship with anxious thoughts crowding his mind, and he made his way toward Stratford Hall.

NOTES

1. "English Education for Virginia Youth: Some Eighteenth-Century Ambler Family Letters," ed. Lucille Griffith, *The Virginia Magazine of History and Biography* 69 (January 1961): 7–27; William L. Sachse, *The Colonial American in Britain* (Madison, WI: The University of Wisconsin Press, 1956).

2. The following information regarding the life and career of Richard Lee is derived from the following: Ethel Armes, *Stratford Hall: The Great House of the Lees* (Richmond, VA: Garrett and Massie Incorporated, 1936), 1–12; Burton J. Hendrick, *The Lees of Virginia: A Biography of a Family* (Boston: Little, Brown, and Company, 1935), 3–26; Edmund Jennings Lee, *Lee of Virginia, 1642–1892: Biographical and Genealogical Sketches of the Descendants of Colonel Richard Lee* (Philadelphia: 1895), 49–65; Ludwell Lee Montague, "Richard Lee the Emigrant, 1618–1664," *The Virginia Magazine of History and Biography* 62 (January 1954): 3–49; Paul C. Nagel, *The Lees of Virginia: Seven Generations of an American Family* (New York: Oxford University Press, 1990), 7–16; and William Thorndale, "The Parents of Colonel Richard Lee," *National Genealogical Society Quarterly* 76 (December 1988): 253–67.

3. Daniel DeFoe, *A Tour through the Whole Island of Great Britain* (New York: Dutton Press, 1962), 46.

4. "The Will of Jane Hancock Lee Manning," in Thorndale, "The Parents of Colonel Richard Lee of Virginia," 262. Jane Lee married John Manning in 1629. Manning died in 1632, and Jane Manning remained a widow until her death in 1639.

5. Dyer, *The City of Worcester in the Sixteenth Century*, 88.

6. Craven, *White, Red, and Black: The Seventeenth Century Virginian* (Charlottesville, VA: The University Press of Virginia, 1971), 85–86. Richard Lee's acquisitions included much of the land near the present location of Washington, D.C., including 1,000 acres, which later became Mount Vernon. See Nagel, *The Lees of Virginia*, 13.

7. "The Navigation Act of 1651," in *American Colonial Documents to 1776*, ed. Merrill Jensen (New York: Oxford University Press, 1955), 353; Morgan, *American Slavery—American Freedom*, 147–48.

8. "The Will of Richard Heming Clothier of Saint Andrew Parish, Worcester, Worcestershire (Extract)," and "The Will of John Best," in "The Parents of Richard Lee of Virginia," 262–64.

9. W. J. Eccles, *The Canadian Frontier, 1534–1760*, rev. ed. (Albuquerque, NM: University of New Mexico Press, 1983), 124–25; Arthur Pierce Middleton, *Tobacco Coast: A Maritime History of Chesapeake Bay in the Colonial Era* (Newport News, VA: The Mariner's Museum, 1953), 171–74.

10. Richard Lee II quoted in Wilcomb E. Washburn, *The Governor and the Rebel: A History of Bacon's Rebellion in Virginia* (Chapel Hill: The University of North Carolina Press, 1957), 155.

11. Robert Beverley, *The History of the Present State of Virginia*, ed. Louis B. Wright (Charlottesville, VA: Dominion Books, 1947), 94; Warren M. Billings, John E. Selby, and Thad W. Tate, *Colonial Virginia: A History* (White Plains, NY: KTO Press, 1986), 119–20; Hendrick, *Lees of Virginia*, 42–45; David S. Lovejoy, *The Glorious Revolution in America*

(New York: Harper and Row, 1972), 53–69; Richard L. Morton, *Colonial Virginia: A History*, 2 vols. (Chapel Hill: The University of North Carolina Press, 1960), 1: 297–341; and Nagel, *Lees of Virginia*, 26.

12. Ibid.

13. On Thomas Lee's early life and contributions to his family's commercial interests, see Armes, *Stratford Hall*, 25–43; Jeanne Calhoun, "Thomas Lee of Virginia, 1690–1750: Founder of a Virginia Dynasty," *Northern Neck of Virginia Historical Magazine* 61 (December 1991): 4689–702; Hendrick, *Lees of Virginia*, 51–62; and Nagel, *The Lees of Virginia*, 33–48.

14. Richard II's brother, Francis Lee, died the year before in 1714, and Richard III consequently assumed a larger role in the family's London firm, Corbin and Lee.

15. Jacob M. Price, *France and the Chesapeake: A History of the French Tobacco Monopoly, 1674–1791, and of Its Relationship to the British and American Tobacco Trades*, 2 vols. (Ann Arbor, MI: The University of Michigan Press, 1973), 1: 524.

16. Morton, *Colonial Virginia*, 2: 415.

17. Nagel, *The Lees of Virginia*, 27, 33.

18. Robert Carter to Thomas Lee, July 5, 1721, *Letters of Robert Carter, 1720–1727: The Commercial Interests of a Virginia Gentleman*, ed. Louis B. Wright (Westport, CT: Greenwood Press, 1970), 107.

19. Dowdey, *The Virginia Dynasties*, 354.

20. Richard H. Lee, *Memoir of the Life of Richard Henry Lee*, 2 vols. (Philadelphia: William Brown, Printer, 1825), 1: 7.

21. See Jan Lewis, *The Pursuit of Happiness: Family and Values in Jefferson's Virginia* (New York: Cambridge University Press, 1983), 30–36; and Daniel Blake Smith, *Inside the Great House: Planter Family Life in Eighteenth Century Chesapeake Society* (Ithaca, NY: Cornell University Press, 1989), 25–54.

22. Armes, *Stratford Hall*, 61; Fischer, *Albion's Seed*, 344–49; Otto Lohrenz, "An Analysis of the Life and Career of the Reverend David Currie, Lancaster County, Virginia, 1743–1791," *Anglican and Episcopal History* 71 (June 1992): 142–66; Lohrenz, "The Reverend Alexander White of Colonial Virginia: His Career and Status," *Fides et Historia* 24 (Summer 1992): 56–75.

23. Alexander White to Richard Henry Lee, 1758, quoted in Lohrenz, "Alexander White," 57.

24. Fithian, "Journal Entry," December 18, 1773, 33–34.

25. Richard L. Bushman, *The Refinement of America: Persons, Houses, and Cities* (New York: Alfred A. Knopf, 1992), 100–130; Rhys Isaac, *The Transformation of Virginia, 1740–1790* (Chapel Hill: The University of North Carolina Press, 1981), 80–88; William Seale, "Past Presence: Interpreting Lifestyles through Material Culture," *Organization of American Historians Magazine* 9 (Summer 1994): 12–17. In addition to these sources, I would like to acknowledge the assistance of Dr. Jeanne Calhoun and the many tour guides at Stratford Hall Plantation and its environs. As a result of many tours and conversations, I am able to reconstruct this celebration at Stratford Hall.

26. Calhoun, "Thomas Lee," 4699.

27. Middleton, *Tobacco Coast*, 330–31.

28. Martha Jacqueline to Edward and Jonathan Ambler, April 28, 1748, "English Education for Virginia Youth," 14.

29. "English Education for Virginia Youth," 13.

30. The name of Edward Porteus's daughter is not mentioned in any of the sources that provide the evidentiary basis for this account. However, a Nancy Porteus lived with her father at Rippon Hall, and she was approximately the same age as Richard Henry. She also had close ties to Edward and Jonathan Ambler. The dearth of evidence prevents the cautious historian from stating that Lee's romance was, in fact, with Nancy Porteus, but perhaps a circumstantial case could be made.

31. Edward Porteus to Edward Ambler, October 19, 1751, "Education for Virginia Youth," 20–21.

32. Porteus to Ambler, "Education for Virginia Youth," 21.

Richard Henry Lee, Esquire

I

$\mathcal{U}$pon his return to Stratford Hall, Richard Henry Lee found the household in disarray. He suddenly found himself in the midst of a growing conflict between Philip and his younger brothers and sister, and he did his best to try to calm the growing storm. Thomas Ludwell Lee had remained in London and did not return to Stratford Hall until 1756.[1] Consequently, once Richard Henry arrived on the scene, his younger siblings turned to him for support. This mood marked the beginning of a somber and uncertain time for Richard Henry. Philip's reluctance to divide Thomas Lee's estate before all debts had been paid heightened tensions among the older siblings, and the atmosphere grew increasingly acrimonious. Several arbitrary decisions affecting the lives of the younger Lees—Francis, Alice, William, and Arthur—compounded an already difficult situation and served only to alienate them further from Philip. As these conflicts swirled about him, Richard Henry Lee once again took up residence in Stratford Hall and contemplated his future.

His English education prepared him for a career reading law, but he also understood that in order to protect his family's position and status, he would soon have to seek some sort of political appointment. In the interim, Richard Henry spent many of his days in Stratford Hall's library continuing his education by reading different books. Unfortunately, the continued squabbling in the household hampered his efforts. In 1754, he joined his brothers and sister in a lawsuit demanding that Philip immediately divide their father's estate in the manner described in the will. The suit eventually failed, but the younger Lees successfully arranged to have their cousin Henry Lee (1729–1787) named as their legal guardian, allowing them to live out from under the domineering shadow of their eldest brother.

While Richard Henry pondered his future, the second master of Stratford Hall pursued his parental role zealously. First, he determined that Francis was ideally suited to become a farmer, so he withdrew him from his formal schooling. Second, he decided that William would become the family's commercial agent and thus began making preparations for him to study business. Finally, he resolved to have Arthur, the youngest, study medicine, so he packed the young boy off to Eton to begin his training as a doctor. As Philip planned out the futures of his younger brothers, Richard Henry isolated himself in the family library and could fully sense the void left behind by the sudden deaths of his mother and father just a few years before. He penned a poem ruminating on the loss of his father, which was later inscribed on Thomas Lee's gravestone in Burnt House Field. As Richard Henry concluded the last verse, he asked "what limit can there be to our regret at the loss of so dear a friend."[2]

II

As Richard Henry Lee made preparations to go to England and complete his education in 1748, his father and his family had reached the pinnacle of power in Virginia. By 1747, Thomas Lee was appointed president of Virginia's Council of State. Two years later, Governor William Gooch died, and Lee was appointed as Gooch's replacement. As governor, Thomas Lee expressed a growing concern over French encroachments in the Ohio River valley, an issue that had occupied his attention since the moment he left Stratford Hall to attend the Lancaster conference five years earlier, in 1744.

At the beginning of King George's War, both Britain and France were vying for the dominant position in North America. As a tobacco planter, Thomas Lee was especially sensitive toward the need for continued access to western lands. Additionally, Lee viewed the continuation of trade between the English manufacturers and Native Americans as equally beneficial for long-term British imperial interests. Lee was not alone, because a growing number of British and Scottish merchants were also concerned about losing future profits if the king was not able to check French expansion in North America.

These concerns formed the foundation for Lee's decision to attend the Lancaster Conference, the third summit since 1685 between the Six Nations, Pennsylvania, and Virginia. Once the negotiations began, Lee and the Virginia delegation sought confirmation of Virginia's borders as stipulated in the 1612 charter, which included all of the land from "Point Comfort . . . all along the sea coast, to the southward two hundred miles, and all that circuit of land . . .

from sea to sea, west and northwest."[3] Lee received the confirmation he de-sired in the subsequent Treaty of Lancaster as well as an alliance between the British and the Six Nations. In exchange, the Iroquois secured access to a num-ber of valleys that their messengers used to maintain regular contact with var-ious tribes in the region.[4] After completing the negotiations, Thomas Lee re-turned to Williamsburg with a copy of the treaty. For Lee, the Treaty of Lancaster represented a new opportunity to further British imperial interests in North America and provide for the future expansion of Virginia beyond the Northern Neck. The only questions remaining concerned the best method of organizing the region so that Britain's interests could best be served. Unfortu-nately, not all Virginians shared the same goals.

Almost immediately after news of the Treaty of Lancaster arrived in Williamsburg, members of the Houses of Burgesses and Council sought ways to profit from the negotiations. In 1745, a group of prominent politicians, led by Speaker–Treasurer John Robinson, formed a speculative venture they ini-tially called the Greenbrier Company and later changed to the Loyal Land Company. They secured, by their own volition, a 100,000-acre land grant along the Greenbrier River and began making plans to sell the land. In addi-tion to approving their own grant, Robinson and his political allies also au-thorized another 100,000-acre grant to James Patton, who also attended the Lancaster conference representing Pennsylvania.[5]

These efforts on the part of Robinson and others in the colonial govern-ment quickly drew criticism from different quarters, and Thomas Lee and planters from the Northern Neck emerged as the most vocal critics. What con-cerned Lee the most was the formation of a company designed specifically to market the acreage. Lee understood that such a scheme could easily exacerbate tensions between Virginia and the Six Nations and thus allow France to gain a stronger presence in the region. In an attempt to counter the efforts of the Loyal Company, Lee petitioned Governor Gooch to approve a 500,000-acre grant north of the Ohio River, with the specific goal of settling families on the land as well as building forts and trading posts—all designed to strengthen Britain's claim to the territory. Gooch rejected Lee's petition, stating that he did not have the authority to make such a grant; but, in all likelihood, the governor did not approve the petition because he did not want to alienate the powerful speaker–treasurer of the House of Burgesses, John Robinson.

By the mid-1740s, provincial politics in Virginia had become factional-ized. Power within the colony bounced between two critical geographical regions—the Northern Neck and the James River. Thomas Lee led the for-mer, and Robinson led the latter, along with a growing number of planters from the developing Piedmont region. Members of the Robinson-led group had members who lived in the older, settled regions as well as members who lived in the recently settled areas. Those that lived along the James River lived in unproductive areas, at least as far as tobacco production was concerned. Consequently, they needed money to pay off debts and maintain their quality of life. Land speculation provided one of the surest ways for these men to raise capital. As for the newer planters from the Piedmont, they were drawn to the Robinson faction because of the influence the Speaker wielded and because they needed to secure the plantations they had recently established.

Lee and the Northern Neckers led an expansionist group looking to extend the British dominion deeper into North America.[6] While they hoped to earn profits, they directed their efforts toward trade and developing new lands for tobacco production—endeavors that offered potential profits for individuals but at the same time fostered British imperial objectives in North America as well. Gooch's rejection proved only to be a temporary setback. Lee appealed the governor's decision to the Board of Trade, who approved Lee's plans. In 1748, Lee established the Ohio Company of Virginia, after receiving a grant for 200,000 acres of land in the Ohio River valley. After the company settled 100 families and constructed a fort and trading post, the Board of Trade would add an additional 300,000 acres to the grant, thereby reaching Lee's original objective of 500,000 acres.

In many respects, the Ohio Company of Virginia resembled the original Virginia Company established in 1606 that led to the Jamestown settlement. Lee and the other Ohio Company shareholders cultivated ties with British merchants, who would ship English manufactures to America, which would then be sold to Native Americans or European immigrants who settled in the region. Through this process, the Ohio Company not only strengthened Britain's claim to North American territory, but it also helped create new markets for English-made goods. Preserving Britain's territorial claims remained the primary reason why the Ohio Company shareholders felt compelled to cultivate trade with the Native Americans in the contested region. As Lee observed, they had to "win the Indians' affections so they will not go to the French." Later, he noted in a letter to the Board of Trade: "If [the Indians] are not supplied with Guns, Ammunition, and Cloths by presents and trade, they must starve; soe they are obliged to cultivate a friendship with these yt will help them."[7] A distinguished group of gentlemen from the Northern Neck joined Lee in forming the Ohio Company of Virginia, including Lawrence Washington and his half brother, George; Robert and Landon Carter; and George Mason.

Thomas Lee's active interest in the development of western lands put him at odds with the Robinson-led faction. Upon learning of the Board of Trade's approval of the Ohio Company grant, Robinson marshaled his support in the House of Burgesses and the Council. The provincial government then authorized an 800,000-acre land grant for the Loyal Land Company, which remained simply a speculative venture without any obligations toward furthering Britain's imperial objectives. Although the grants did not overlap—the Ohio grant was north of the Ohio River, and the Loyal Company lands were located in present-day Kentucky—the brewing competition between the two land companies generated political divisions that affected provincial politics all the way until the colonies declared their independence from Great Britain in 1776. New members of the gentry from the Piedmont region, including Peter Jefferson and Edmund Pendleton, joined Robinson in promoting the Loyal Land Company's efforts. The shareholders in the Loyal Company simply could not bear the expense of constructing forts and trading posts, nor could they wait for the establishment of new settlements before extracting profits. However, Lee feared that the kind of rampant speculation Robinson sought would lead to an Indian war and thereby force them to abandon the British and side with the French. After William Gooch died and Lee assumed the responsibilities of provincial governor, his animosity toward Robinson increased, as did his suspicion of Pennsylvanian land speculators who were becoming more active in the Ohio Valley. At one point, Lee characterized the Pennsylvanians as "rascally fellows" who go "among the Indians by lyes and trechery and will be the Authors of much blood shed and in consequence give the French possession of the trade."[8]

At the time of his death in 1750, the Ohio Company of Virginia actively pursued the Indian trade and proved to be a thriving enterprise. Lee owned two full shares of Ohio Company stock. In his will he gave one share to his oldest son, Philip, and divided the remaining share between Thomas Ludwell, Richard Henry, and Francis. Since they were unproven, these young men lacked the steady hands and the fierce loyalty Thomas Lee cultivated. Both Richard Henry Lee and Philip recognized the importance of maintaining an active association in the Ohio Company as well as in provincial politics; but, in the absence of their father, the young men of Stratford had an uphill battle to wage—that they could only win if they cooperated with each other and if they set aside their personal differences. By the end of 1754, as he bided his time at Stratford Hall until an opportunity to engage in provincial politics presented itself, Richard Henry resolved to fight for the goals his father had set forth.

III

Thomas Lee's political opponents wasted little time before attempting to exploit the power vacuum created in the Northern Neck as a result of Lee's death. The men who comprised the James River faction under the direction of Speaker–Treasurer John Robinson now sensed an opportunity to decisively regain control of provincial politics. Lee and Robinson had battled each other frequently since the early 1730s, and much of the conflict involved colonial policies toward westward expansion. Lee and his Northern Neck allies strongly advocated an aggressive program solidifying Britain's claim to the Ohio River valley—most clearly manifested in Lee's active participation as a founding member of the Ohio Company of Virginia. Robinson and his group now sought ways to gain some of the ground they had lost during Thomas Lee's tenure as president of the Council and as acting governor of Virginia.

In one posthumous challenge, a controversy arose concerning Thomas Lee's position as a vestryman for Cople Parish. Typically, in order for a person to serve as vestryman, that person had to live within the parish borders. When Lee and his family occupied the Machodoc estate, the residency complied with this basic requirement. Once the construction of Stratford Hall had been completed and the Lees moved in to their new home, they lived outside the parish, yet Lee maintained his role as vestryman. In 1749 Lee was once again elected to the post, and a group of settlers from Cople Parish complained in a petition to the House of Burgesses, claiming the Lee's election as vestryman was illegal since he was no longer a resident. The petition did not mention Lee's name directly; however, the burgesses recognized that Lee was the obvious target, and since he was also serving as acting governor, the House quietly ignored the petition.

Four years after Lee's death, another complaint was issued concerning the matter. This time, the petitioners mentioned Lee by name and criticized what they regarded as the lingering influence to Thomas Lee, which they blamed as the cause for the continual election of a Lee to the Cople Parish vestry. As a result of this state of affairs, the petitioners requested that the House of Burgesses dissolve Cople Parish, thus allowing for the election of a new vestryman for the parish. Much to the chagrin of the Lees and their allies, the House complied with the supplicants' request and in May 1755 passed an act that dissolved Cople Parish.

The specific purpose of this measure remained unclear to many witnesses. Landon Carter, a Lee ally, participated in the debate and noted in his diary that the reasoning behind the legislation was a "great mistery," as far as he was concerned. Carter interpreted the bill as some sort of affront against the Lees, and his observations of the debate confirmed his opinions. He noted that the bill contained "all the Malice and venom that ever a Petition was stuffed with"; yet, despite this, Carter indicated that it was "vain to Oppose it." During the course of the debate, he attempted to show that the allegations made by the petitioners were "trifling," but his efforts were to no avail because his opinions "differed from a Certain Person who had in his day drank very large drafts of Rancour and Revenge against [Colonel Thomas Lee]."[9]

The "certain person" Carter alluded to was none other than John Robinson, who emerged as a major supporter of the measure calling for the dissolution of Cople Parish. Of course, we can only speculate why this petition drew such support and targeted Thomas Lee in particular, even though he had lain in his grave for nearly five years when the bill had passed. More than likely, the measure found support among the opponents of the Lees and other Northern Neck interests because it had the effect of weakening their influence in provincial politics as well as over local inhabitants in the Northern Neck. Any shift in power at these levels would also have the larger effect of benefiting the Loyal Company shareholders at the expense of the sponsors of the Ohio Company of Virginia.

Tension between the two competing land companies intensified in the months following Thomas Lee's death. Robert Dinwiddie arrived shortly after Lee died to assume the duties as governor of Virginia. Dinwiddie was attracted to the Ohio Company because of its expansionist tendencies that coincided neatly with the Britain's imperial objectives in North America. In 1752, Dinwiddie, with the support of Ohio Company shareholders, convened another conference with the Six Nations and other western tribes, at Logstown, Virginia. The resultant treaty confirmed the agreement reached at Lancaster eight years earlier, and it also extended the boundaries of Ohio Company lands to the southern side of the Ohio River, thereby threatening the claims held by the Loyal Land Company. Within a year of the Logstown Treaty, the Ohio Company began building a storehouse in its newly acquired territory, and the shareholders commissioned Christopher Gist to begin surveying the land for further development.

As Dinwiddie warmed to the Ohio Company group, an antagonistic relationship soon developed between the new governor and John Robinson. As tension increased between these two powerful men, other matters before the provincial assembly became embroiled in the growing dispute. The petition calling for the dissolution of Cople Parish represented but one example of process—any smear against Thomas Lee could possibly have the corollary effect of weakening the influence of the Lee family and, hence, the Ohio Company of Virginia as well. Unfortunately for Robinson and the James River faction, the measure dissolving Cople Parish had a galvanizing effect on the Lee family in general and the Stratford Lees in particular. Richard Henry Lee and his brothers set aside their differences with Philip Lee and came together to protect the larger interests of the family as a whole. They were not going to allow their squabbling destroy what their father had built.

IV

While tensions increased between the Lees and the Robinson faction over the dissolution of Cople Parish, a war between Great Britain and France for control of the Ohio River valley erupted in 1754; and before long, the military effort against the French became fatally linked to the partisan conflicts that had coalesced around the diverging economic interests between the leaders of the Ohio Company and Loyal Land Company.

As Christopher Gist conducted his surveys for the Ohio Company of Virginia, he came across evidence of French encroachments on territory claimed by Britain as a result of both the Lancaster and Logstown treaties. To address this new threat, Governor Dinwiddie in 1753 sent George Washington, who also worked as a surveyor for the Ohio Company, on a mission to order the French out of the Ohio River valley. After traveling 900 miles to Fort Le Beouf near the shores of Lake Erie with a message from Dinwiddie, the French rebuffed the young Washington and sent him on his way back to Virginia.[10] In response to this rejection, Dinwiddie authorized Washington to lead a militia force to the forks of the Ohio River, with orders to construct a military fort that would allow Britain to defend its claim to the territory. Washington left on this mission in July 1754 and soon discovered that the French and their Indian allies had already built a base of their own, which they named after the French governor of Quebec, Fort Duquesne. A few days later, there was a minor skirmish between the Virginia militia and a small detachment of French soldiers at a place now called Jumonville Glen, in southwestern Pennsylvania. Afterward, Washington pulled back and built a small fort, aptly named Fort Necessity. The young colonel soon realized that he was in an untenable situation and surrendered once an overwhelming force of French soldiers and their Indian allies arrived on the scene.[11] The war began.

Governor Dinwiddie now faced an uphill battle to try to get support from John Robinson and from the Speaker's sympathetic allies, both in the House of Burgesses and on the Council of State. Dinwiddie, and his expansionist allies like the Lees, recognized the strategic importance of the Ohio Valley for British imperial objectives and understood that much more was at stake than short-term profits through land speculation. The Ohio Company, from its inception, always placed British imperial objectives at the forefront. Profits for shareholders would only follow after the British crown successfully achieved its desired goals in North America. Governor Dinwiddie tried to make this abundantly clear in his communications with the Board of Trade after Washington's surrender at Fort Necessity. He warned that if the French presence went unchallenged, then British interests in the Indian trade would be lost.

While Dinwiddie attempted to garner support in Parliament, he had to face the more direct problem of securing immediate financial support from the House of Burgesses. Initially, Robinson publicly expressed his skepticism about the need for military action against the French; privately, he and his political friends were alarmed about the possible impact a war would have on their speculative ventures in the trans-Allegheny region. Viewing these events from the perspective of Robinson and the Loyal Land Company, a war between Britain and France in the Ohio River valley could prove to be an unmitigated disaster. The Loyal Land Company was founded without any tie to British imperial interests; participants relied on profits from quick speculative ventures that simply could not bear the costs of building forts and promoting settlements that were part and parcel of the Ohio Company's founding charter. The war threatened to bring unwanted attention to the region, and as a consequence, Robinson and his allies simply viewed these events as part of a private war between France and the Ohio Company of Virginia. Once Governor Dinwiddie realized that Robinson's support would be slow in coming, he turned to neighboring colonies, Pennsylvania and the Carolinas, for additional assistance; but they rejected Dinwiddie's appeals, refusing to contribute their resources to fight a war that seemed only to benefit the Ohio Company of Virginia. Dinwiddie now had to confront a situation where, at least until he received some form of support from the Crown, he would have to prosecute the war alone, only with a very narrow base of support found in Virginia's Northern Neck.

The auspicious beginnings of what would later be dubbed the "Great War for Empire" were caught up in competing visions of Britain's imperialistic designs for North America. The Northern Neckers of Virginia represented a sort of old school mentality toward empire building. This is evident in the manner in which they envisioned the Ohio Company of Virginia closely following the pattern set by the original Virginia Company in its heyday, under the direction of Sir Edwin Sandys. At that time, the Virginia Company represented a thorough mixture that promoted England's national interests through the use of private money in the form of investments from individual stockholders, who would receive profit-making opportunities in exchange for their financial commitments. The Ohio Company of Virginia based its organization on this model exactly. Provincial families like the Lees, the Washingtons, the Masons, and the Carters would provide necessary equipment to construct trading posts and forts that would help facilitate immigration into the unsettled areas. The benefits for Britain would be twofold. First, the increased settlements would solidify the Crown's territorial claims in North America; second, the new immigrants would create new markets for British manufactured goods and provide direct access to Indian tribes living further west. Provincial planter–merchants who purchased shares of Ohio Company stock worked closely with London-based merchants, like John Hanbury, who would ship a wide variety of British-made goods, which would then be traded to small planters in exchange for tobacco. Through this process, the Ohio Company furthered Britain's imperial designs in North America and, at the same time, afforded numerous opportunities for Ohio Company shareholders to personally profit from the efforts. As a result, prominent members of Parliament willingly assisted the Ohio Company and its expansionist endeavors. This sort of preferment annoyed many others in Virginia and in the other colonies who, for one reason or another, either lacked the resources to promote immigration or viewed such efforts as contrary to their immediate interests.

In Virginia, John Robinson and the Loyal Land Company represented the chief opposition to the Ohio Company interests. Others in league with Robinson included a growing number of new gentry men in Virginia's Piedmont region, such as Peter Jefferson, Thomas Walker, and Edmund Pendleton. These men opposed the type of immigration scheme central to the Ohio Company because they intended to hold the land for their own use as they expanded their land holdings in the region. Additionally, both the new aristocrats and the old ones associated with the Loyal Land Company simply lacked the capital to expend promoting immigration; consequently, they resented the Ohio Company and viewed its efforts as a threat to their immediate concerns.[12]

Merchant–speculators in other colonies such as Pennsylvania also feared the dominance of the Ohio Company because increased immigration into the region threatened their interests in the Indian trade in general and the fur trade in particular. For these reasons, Pennsylvania merchants frequently allied themselves with the Robinson faction in Virginia in a united effort to squelch Ohio Company activity in the area.[13] Consequently, these competing interests muted the French threat in the eyes of prominent colonial leaders in the southern and middle colonies and allowed them to easily characterize the war as an Ohio Company concern and nothing more.

Fortunately for Dinwiddie, the Board of Trade recognized the significance of the Ohio River Valley and made preparations to send British troops to America under the leadership of General Edward Braddock, whose mission was to lead an expedition against Fort Duquesne and force the French to abandon the Ohio River valley once and for all. The arrival of Braddock in Virginia electrified the Northern Neck, and many of the inhabitants of the region willingly stepped forward to volunteer their services to the British commander. Richard Henry Lee was among those willing to follow Braddock into the wilderness. He organized a group of Westmoreland County militiamen, who awarded Lee the rank of captain for his efforts and who offered to place themselves under Braddock's command. The general, however, viewed provincial volunteers with disdain and abruptly dismissed them. This relatively minor humiliation for Richard Henry soon proved to be a blessing in disguise, as Braddock's army suffered a massive defeat along the Monongahela River at the hands of the French and their Indian allies a few miles southeast of Fort Duquesne.

Before Braddock's arrival and subsequent defeat, provincial leaders like John Robinson had castigated the war effort, but following the disaster along the Monongahela, Virginia and Pennsylvania found themselves forced to wage a defensive war to preserve their frontier settlements from the French. At this juncture, Virginia's House of Burgesses and Council could no longer ignore the threat posed by the French presence in the Ohio Valley. Unfortunately, this change of heart came late, and dark days followed: The war flared along the frontier, and Dinwiddie's efforts to prosecute the war were still hampered by the acrimonious atmosphere that pervaded provincial politics at this time. The situation did not begin to change until 1757, when Dinwiddie acquired a determined group of political allies, led by none other than Richard Henry Lee, who were committed to a successful resolution of the war for both the sake of Virginia and the Ohio Company.

V

Since his return from England in 1753, with the exception of offering his services to General Braddock in 1755, Richard Henry Lee bided his time at Stratford Hall and worked to secure his portion of Thomas Lee's estate from his older brother. During this period, he waited for an opportune moment for him to enter into public service and continue promoting the uniform interests of the inhabitants of the Northern Neck. However, the small number of offices available limited his opportunities and forced him to stand by while his family's political opponents gained ground by trashing his father's reputation. Steadily, the situation began to change in the Lees' favor, and a new generation made preparations to take their place among the provincial elite.

In 1755, Philip Lee won election to the House of Burgesses, representing Westmoreland County along with Augustine Washington. The next year, Richard Henry launched his political career through his appointment as a justice of the peace in Westmoreland County—a minor post but one that was regarded as a crucial first step toward other elective offices. In the months that followed, Philip Lee began distributing the various lands left to his brothers in their father's will. Thomas Ludwell Lee left Stratford Hall and settled on his lands in Stafford County; Francis Lee soon followed, leaving the comforts of Stratford for his holdings in far-off Loudoun County. The dispersal of the Stratford Lees to their new residences further along the Potomac River set the stage for the Lees to reemerge as a significant political force during the 1757 elections. Their united opposition to the Robinson faction and their shared interests in the Ohio Company of Virginia allowed them to secure a powerful political patron in Williamsburg as well—Governor Robert Dinwiddie.

In 1757, a vacancy in the Council of State paved the way for Philip Lee to be promoted to that body, thereby leaving an open seat for the House of Burgesses in Westmoreland County. At that same time, Augustine Washington announced his intentions to retire from public service, thus creating another open seat. When election day arrived, Richard Henry Lee and his cousin Richard "Squire" Lee won places in the House of Burgesses, representing Westmoreland County. Thomas Ludwell and Francis Lee soon joined them in the House, each one representing Stafford and Loudoun Counties, respectively; and another cousin, Henry Lee, from Prince William County, soon joined them as well. Within one election cycle, the Lee family once again emerged as a powerful voting bloc in the House of Burgesses, especially when combined with their many friends and allies, like Landon Carter, who already held seats in the lower assembly.

Richard Henry Lee soon took his place as the spokesman for his family, as well as for the interests of the Northern Neck proprietors in Williamsburg. He served on several important committees, and in this capacity, he joined Governor Dinwiddie in a concerted effort to weaken John Robinson's hold on the House by demanding the separation of the offices of Speaker and treasurer.[14] Robinson had held these two positions since 1738 and had acquired a significant power base, which some suggested made him a more influential person than the governor of the colony.

John Robinson clearly recognized that any move along these lines represented a direct challenge to his role as a leader in provincial politics. By 1757, neither Robinson nor Dinwiddie had much use for each other. Almost since the day Dinwiddie arrived in Williamsburg, the two men constantly clashed over matters of politics as well as personal interest. The attempt on the governor's part to separate the offices of Speaker and treasurer simply signaled that Dinwiddie had had enough and now sought to break Robinson's hold over provincial politics. As the decade progressed, the hostility deepened, as did the ramifications of the struggle for power between Dinwiddie and Robinson. By 1757, the standoff had reached crisis proportions as the governor tried to wage a war against the French in the Ohio Valley with only reluctant support from Robinson and his allies in the House. Consequently, Dinwiddie began to rely heavily on the Lees and other sympathetic members of the lower assembly to prosecute the war against the French and lessen Robinson's strength among the burgesses.

Dinwiddie's efforts to separate the offices of Speaker and treasurer stagnated as the governor dispatched letters to the Board of Trade asking them to resolve the dispute once and for all. In the meantime, Richard Henry worked actively to continue the war against the French. Pursuant to his duties in the House, Lee monitored the progress of the British and colonial forces by maintaining a regular correspondence with General Adam Stephen, one of the highest-ranking officers in Virginia's colonial militia. Stephen kept Lee apprised of the tenuous state of affairs along the frontier. The general reported to

Richard Henry that he could not "help admiring the extensive views and great designs of the French," adding that "they are indefatigable in America."[15] Observations such as these served only to alarm Lee and his colleagues in the House of Burgesses. As a result, some Virginians began to openly question the validity of Britain's territorial claims to the Ohio River valley; but others, like Lee, began harboring resentment toward the Crown out of a sense of abandonment as the British shifted its main fighting force northward to Canada in the wake of Braddock's defeat.

Between 1757 and 1759, Lee devoted most of his time in the House of Burgesses to making sure that the militia remained in good order and well supplied. He introduced several initiatives to raise revenue for the militia; his efforts included supporting the printing of more paper money as a temporary expediency to pay for war-related expenses, sponsoring a measure raising the duty on African slaves imported into Virginia by 10 percent, and promoting a bill stipulating that any additional revenue collected by the provincial government should go directly toward financing the war effort. All of these initiatives solicited controversy and widened the gap between the Northern Neckers in the House, led by Richard Henry Lee, and the Robinson faction.

The war against the French forced Virginia to reluctantly turn to the practice of printing paper currency. Burgesses agreed to this sort of policy in 1754 only as a last resort because they understood that, without funds, they could not adequately defend their frontier settlements. Governor Dinwiddie found himself in an awkward position. On the one hand, he sanctioned the practice of printing paper currency because the war demanded it; but on the other hand, he expressed his concern that the effort might encourage "extravagance and idleness" and that, quite possibly, it might ruin Virginia's credit with British merchants. Initially, Dinwiddie tried to convince the Board of Trade to mint a special coin for the purpose of paying war-related expenses, but the lack of specie made such a scheme impossible.[16] As a result, Dinwiddie reluctantly agreed that the use of paper money was the only viable solution to Virginia's pressing financial problems.

The governor was not the only one with such concerns. Many of those involved in making this decision, including the Lees and their allies, recognized that this was only a temporary expediency. Advocates of the practice attempted to mollify Dinwiddie's apprehensions, as well as the concerns voiced by a growing number of British merchants, by pacing tax increases to currency emissions to allow the colonial economy to remain solvent. Yet, in spite of these precautions, paper money emissions had exceeded £250,000 by the end of the decade. The continuing military crisis along the frontier forced the provincial government to recognize paper currency as full legal tender and thus began accepting it as payment for taxes in order to get it out of circulation as soon as possible. Although the use of paper currency remained controversial, as the French and Indian War drew to a close, a growing number of Virginians defended the practice as vital for the stability of the provincial economy.

By January 1758, Governor Dinwiddie, jaded by his constant struggles with Robinson in the House of Burgesses, announced his intentions to leave his post and return to England. Although Dinwiddie proved victorious in many of his battles with the speaker–treasurer, few substantive changes ever resulted from these triumphs. For example, in the battle over the separation of Robinson's offices, the Board of Trade agreed with the governor that the combined position held by Robinson concentrated too much power in the hands of one individual; thus, the Board authorized the immediate separation of the two offices. The war and lingering problems he had with other members of the House of Burgesses made this a hollow victory at best for the governor and had little effect on his decision to vacate his office.

It was left to Richard Henry Lee and his allies to celebrate the news mandating the separation of Robinson's posts. Lee's former tutor Alexander White wrote to congratulate the young burgess on his victory. White expressed his surprise at how quickly Lee had challenged the established leadership in the House so soon after winning his first election. White commented: "Tis with great pleasure . . . that I already hear of your spirit and resolution as to the choice of a speaker." White voiced his criticism of the length of Robinson's tenure as speaker–treasurer, noting that "so much power lodged in one man's hands" seemed "inconsistent with the freedom and independency of the British legislature."[17] Lee's central role in the effort to separate the offices of speaker–treasurer helped establish the young representative from Westmoreland County as a leader in the House of Burgesses.

The victory, however, proved short-lived. With Dinwiddie's announced departure, not only did Lee lose an influential patron and powerful political ally, but the Robinson faction also remained entrenched. The speaker–treasurer decided to simply ignore the Board of Trade's ruling on the separation of his offices—at least until Dinwiddie's replacement arrived and occupied the governor's mansion in Williamsburg. Soon after Dinwiddie left, Francis Fauquier arrived to take on the duties as Virginia's new chief executive. As Fauquier settled into his new post, he quickly discovered that he would need Robinson's loyal support, and as a result, he urged the Board of Trade to set aside its decision calling for the separation of the offices held by Robinson. Fauquier informed his superiors on the Board of Trade that a division of the offices could not occur "without the most manifest prejudice to his Majesties Service," and any attempt to pursue the matter might "throw the Country into a Flame." Fauquier cast his lot with Robinson and his group, leaving Lee and the other Northern Neckers on their own.[18]

Fauquier recognized that he had to follow the path that would allow him to prosecute Britain's war against France, and the governor's decision had the effect of intensifying the conflict between the Lee and Robinson factions. The end result, however, made it even more difficult for the House to agree on a unified policy toward the war. When Lee stepped forward and sponsored a 10 percent import duty on African slaves imported into the colony as a means to raise revenue during the war, the House divided into two camps and reached an immediate impasse. New gentry men and small planters, predominantly from the Piedmont region, denounced the plan because it would force them to pay higher prices for their slaves to large planters who already had a surplus slave population residing on their plantations. Opponents to the measure criticized Lee by suggesting that his motivation was to increase his own fortune by selling his slaves without having to worry about competition from slave traders operating outside Virginia. Fauquier followed suit and fell in line with Robinson's group by agreeing with Lee's critics. In a letter to the Board of Trade, the governor summarized the dispute in the House of Burgesses as a "contest" between "the old settlers who have bred great quantities of slaves and who would make a monopoly of them by a duty which they hoped would amount to a prohibition."[19]

The proposed duty failed to pass the House, and the sort of characterizations set forth by Fauquier and the Robinson faction served only to intensify the hatred between the opposing factions in Williamsburg. Fortunately, not long after Fauquier took office, the war steadily turned in Britain's favor. By 1758, the main theater of fighting had shifted to Canada as British strategists determined to capture Montreal and Quebec. In addition, Britain sent General John Forbes to Virginia to begin making preparations to capture Fort Duquesne. Forbes's arrival pleased Virginia's provincial leadership, but his delay in launching an attack on the fort soon disillusioned Richard Henry Lee and many Northern Neckers.

Forbes hesitated because he was convinced that any attack on the fort would fail without the requisite number of Indian allies—clearly Forbes did not want a repeat of Braddock's disastrous march three years earlier. Northern Neckers took exception to Forbes's dalliances because they came to suspect that Forbes was in league with the Ohio Company's Pennsylvanian competitors. Their view was all but confirmed in August 1758, when Forbes notified Fauquier that he, along with a Pennsylvanian delegation, were going to meet with several Indian tribes in Easton, Pennsylvania. When Virginians associated with the Ohio Company learned of these plans, they protested. George Washington wrote to Governor Fauquier voicing his suspicion that Forbes had become a dupe "or something worse to [Pennsylvania's] Artifice." Washington was convinced that the apparent alliance between Forbes and Pennsylvanian merchant–speculators caused the delay in the British campaign against Fort Duquesne.[20]

Washington's suspicions, however, had little effect on the Easton meeting, which took place in October 1758. The subsequent Treaty of Easton established an alliance between Britain and several western tribes. Provisions in the treaty of this nature did not bother the men associated with the Ohio Company, but what did alarm Washington, Lee, and others were treaty stipulations such as ones that barred Pennsylvania from establishing any settlements in the Ohio River valley without first securing the express permission of the tribes in the area. This seemingly innocuous statement had the effect of expanding Pennsylvania's recognized border westward and tacitly abrogating Virginia's 1612 charter boundaries—not to mention its impact on the territory already awarded to the Ohio Company by Parliament. Governor Fauquier supported the terms of the Treaty of Easton for two reasons: first, it cleared the path for Forbes to attack Fort Duquesne; and second, because the concessions affected only the Ohio Company, not the Loyal Land Company, Robinson and his group had no objections to the treaty. By the end of November 1758, Forbes led an expedition and arrived at Fort Duquesne, only to discover that the French had abandoned the area and burned the fort to the ground before leaving.

General Forbes's conduct during the campaign against Fort Duquesne served only to increase the suspicions of Virginians like Richard Henry Lee and George Washington. They remained convinced that Forbes's delay was nothing more than a scheme to promote the interests of Sir William Johnson, Britain's superintendent of Northern Indian Affairs, and a combination of Pennsylvanians and Virginians actively involved in an attempt to derail the plans set forth by the Ohio Company of Virginia. As far as Richard Henry Lee was concerned, Adam Stephen confirmed Lee's worst suspicions when the general notified him in the summer of 1759 that he witnessed "the Pennsylvanians [sell] about £30,000 worth of goods to Indians at Pittsburg [formerly Fort Duquesne]."[21] It seemed the Pennsylvanians had wasted little time after the British capture of the fort to begin encroaching on the areas already claimed by the Ohio Company. Reports such as these from the frontier offered men like Richard Henry Lee little comfort, even as news arrived of France's surrender following Britain's capture of Quebec in 1760.

VI

As the French and Indian War drew to a close, Richard Henry Lee's eldest brother, Philip, worked diligently to establish Stratford Hall as a major center for transatlantic trade in the Northern Neck. Philip's political connections in the provincial government allowed Lee to arrange for the construction of a tobacco inspection warehouse at Stratford Hall. Planters who managed an inspection warehouse received a rent payment for every hogshead of tobacco brought onto their property, thus allowing these planters to profit substantially from such operations. Once Philip Lee secured the inspection warehouse, he made preparations to launch an even more ambitious building program.[22]

As more planters, both great and small, were drawn to Stratford Hall with their tobacco crops, the Lees recognized that the large, oceangoing ships that would transport the crops to British ports would soon follow. Consequently, Philip planned to build a large wharf that would become known as Stratford Landing, which could accommodate these large vessels. He constructed a pier two or three feet wide that stretched a "near ninety yards out into the Potomac River."[23] By the early 1760s, Stratford Landing had become its own community. In addition to the tobacco warehouse, the Landing also had its own shipyard for minor ship repairs, a storehouse for English imports, a cooper's shop, and a tannery. A portion of land near the wharf area was set aside for dockworkers to construct homes. Soon, Philip Ludwell began seriously considering expanding his interests to include shipbuilding, in addition to becoming the sole owner of *Mary*, a vessel with six sails, weighing ninety tons, with a crew of ten men.[24] By 1765, Stratford Landing had become an impressive commercial entrepot, far more extensive and impressive than what Richard Henry Lee had observed seventeen years earlier in 1748 as he prepared to go to England and complete his education.

As a result of these construction projects, Richard Henry Lee and his younger siblings had to set aside their differences with their eldest brother and work toward promoting the family interest. Despite the acrimonious feelings that characterized the Lee household at Stratford, they nonetheless worked together as partners. Philip employed William Lee as a clerk at Stratford Hall, where he assisted the family enterprise as a financial manager. Thomas Ludwell Lee and Francis Lightfoot Lee served in the House of Burgesses, where they defended the family's interests within that body; they also directed tobacco from Stafford and Loudoun Counties, respectively, to Stratford Landing—all for the purpose of fostering the greater good for the Lee family interest. Richard Henry Lee played a major role during this period as an emerging leader in the House of Burgesses and as the principal antagonist for Speaker–Treasurer John Robinson.

The Stratford Lees recognized the need for them to cooperate and support each other, although frequently they complained bitterly of Philip's attitude toward their financial needs. Despite these flare-ups, they all understood the pressing fiscal problems Philip had to confront. In 1758, the Hanburys of London lodged a lawsuit against the Lees demanding payment of £1,000 sterling. Circumstances forced Philip to acknowledge the debt and promise to pay the amount, but he could not do so. Consequently, the descendents of the Lees and the Hanburys battled each other in court until 1819.[25]

In 1757, Richard Henry Lee did finally receive the property in Prince William County left to him in his father's will, but he chose to remain living with his brother at Stratford Hall. Political expediency, of course, dictated this arrangement. Richard Henry won election to the House of Burgesses representing Westmoreland County; therefore, he had to maintain his residency. Since another family member, cousin Henry Lee, already lived in Prince William County and served as a delegate in the House, Richard Henry really had no other place to go; however, he could at least earn some income by leasing his Prince William land to tenants and further enhance the family fortunes by directing their tobacco to Stratford Landing. Nonetheless, this small degree of independency was, more than likely, not satisfactory as far as Richard Henry was concerned. These circumstances forced Lee to remain under the shadow of his older brother, sacrificing his own immediate self-interests for the sake of his father's legacy. As a new decade began, Richard Henry Lee sought to strike a balance between competing objectives—one that would allow him to maintain his position representing Westmoreland County in the House of Burgesses, and a second that freed him to carve an identity of his own and separate from his domineering brother.

NOTES

1. Jeanne Calhoun, "Philip Ludwell Lee of Stratford Hall," unpublished manuscript, 6. Jessie Ball Du Pont Memorial Library, Stratford Hall Plantation, VA.

2. Armes, *Stratford Hall*, 87.

3. "The Third Charter of the Virginia Company," March 12, 1612, *American Colonial Documents*, edited by Merrill Jensen (New York: Oxford University Press, 1955), 65. Hereafter cited as *American Colonial Documents*.

4. *George Mercer Papers Relating to the Ohio Company of Virginia*, edited by Lois Mulkearn (Pittsburgh, PA: University of Pittsburgh Press), 402–3. Hereafter cited as *Mercer Papers Relating to the Ohio Company*. Historian Francis Jennings called Lee's interpretation of the Lancaster Treaty into question. Jennings asserts that the Six Nations did not concede the territory in question to Virginia; instead, the Iroquois thought that they were simply negotiating mutual access to the Shenandoah Valley for the Six Nations, Pennsylvania, and Virginia. Jennings further noted that the Iroquois did not recognize Virginia's 1612 charter boundaries. See Francis Jennings, *The Ambiguous Iroquois Empire* (New York: W. W. Norton, 1984), 360–63.

5. Daniel M. Friedenberg, *Life, Liberty, and the Pursuit of Land: The Plunder of Early America* (Buffalo, NY: Prometheus Books, 1992), 113.

6. Marc Egnal, *A Mighty Empire: The Origins of the American Revolution*. (Ithaca, NY: Cornell University Press, 1988), 87–101. I have also utilized Professor Egnal's terminology distinguishing two separate camps in provincial politics as "expansionist" and "nonexpansionist." For additional clarification, see *A Mighty Empire*, xiii–xiv.

7. Paul C. Philips and J. W. Smurr, *The Fur Trade*, 2 vols. (Norman: University of Oklahoma Press, 1961), 1: 508–9.

8. Thomas Lee to Conrad Weiser, 1748, *Mercer Papers Relating to the Ohio Company*, 415.

9. Landon Carter, *The Diary of Landon Carter of Sabine Hall, 1752–1778,* 2 vols., ed. Jack P. Green (Charlottesville, VA: The University Press of Virginia, 1965), 1: 121. See also, Paul K. Longmore, "From Supplicants to Constituents: Petitioning by Virginia Parishioners, 1701–1775," *Virginia Magazine of History and Biography* 103 (October 1995): 421. Longmore presents an effective argument suggesting that the newly found support for the dissolution of Cople Parish represented an indicator of a larger trend as the House of Burgesses realized the changing role of petitioners and began viewing these freeholders as constituents. He indicated that this change began in the late 1740s and early 1750s, which could account for the Cople Parish petition's rejection in 1749 and its passage in 1755. Longmore, however, did not consider baser motives, such as revenge, political vindictiveness, or other such sentiments alluded to by Landon Carter in his diary entry.

10. Robert Dinwiddie to Jacques Legardeur de Saint-Pierre, October 13, 1753, *Letters from New France: The Upper Country, 1686–1783,* translated and edited by Joseph L. Peyser (Chicago: University of Chicago Press), 190–92.

11. "Washington Surrenders at Fort Necessity," *Letters from New France,* 196–208; for the most recent and most thorough discussion of Washington's efforts at the outset of the French and Indian War, see Fred Anderson, *The Crucible of War: The Seven Years' War and the Fate of Empire in British North America, 1754–1766* (New York: Alfred A. Knopf, 2000), 42–65.

12. Friedenberg, *Life, Liberty, and the Pursuit of Land,* 113–16.

13. Friedenberg, *Life, Liberty, and the Pursuit of Land,* 116–17.

14. Before 1723, the Speaker of the House of Burgesses did not receive any compensation for managing the affairs of the House. Rather than make the speaker's post a salaried one, the burgesses opted to merge the position with that of treasurer. This change allowed for the speaker to receive 4 percent of all revenue collected through the enforcement of provincial laws. In 1748, the burgesses raised this amount to five percent.

15. Adam Stephen to R. H. Lee, August 26, 1759, "Lee Papers," *Southern Literary Messenger* (December 1858): 433.

16. Ernst, *Money and Politics,* 48–49.

17. Alexander White to R. H. Lee, 1758, "Lee Papers," *Southern Literary Messenger* (August 1858): 117.

18. Francis Fauquier to the Board of Trade, April 10, 1758, *The Official Papers of Francis Fauquier, Lieutenant Governor of Virginia, 1758–1768,* 3 vols., ed. George Reese (Charlottesville: The University Press of Virginia, 1980), 1: 204. Hereafter cited as *Fauquier Official Papers.*

19. Fauquier to the Board of Trade, June 2, 1760, *Fauquier Official Papers,* 1: 372.

20. George Washington to Francis Fauquier, September 28, 1758, *Fauquier Official Papers,* 1: 81–82.

21. Adam Stephen to R. H. Lee, February 24, 1760, "Lee Papers," *Southern Literary Messenger* (December 1858): 434.

22. Calhoun, "Philip Ludwell Lee of Stratford," 16.

23. Jeanne Calhoun, "Semi-Annual Report on Research, Stratford Hall Plantation," unpublished manuscript, 3–7. Jessie Ball Du Pont Memorial Library, Stratford Hall Plantation, VA.

24. Calhoun, "Philip Ludwell Lee of Stratford," 16–18.

25. Calhoun, "Philip Ludwell Lee of Stratford," 8.

· 3 ·

Chantilly-on-the-Potomac

I

$\mathcal{A}$s Richard Henry Lee assumed his seat in the House of Burgesses, he had another reason to celebrate—his marriage to Anne Aylett on December 3, 1757. Nineteen years old, she was the daughter of William and Anne Aylett of King William County.[1] After the ceremony, Richard Henry and his bride returned to Stratford Hall, where the newlyweds made their home. As Lee resumed his duties in Williamsburg, Anne Lee no doubt became the mistress of Stratford Hall, since Philip Lee still remained unmarried. By the third year of their marriage, Richard Henry and Anne Lee had two sons: Thomas, born in 1758, and Ludwell, born in 1760. As his family grew, Richard Henry soon turned his attention to building a home of his own and leaving Stratford. After the birth of Ludwell Lee, Philip agreed to lease Richard Henry 500 acres of land adjacent to Philip's Westmoreland County properties for an annual rent amounting to 2,650 pounds of tobacco. Once the final arrangements had been made, Richard Henry selected a site to build his new home. Construction on the home took three years to complete, and in 1763, Richard Henry Lee left Stratford Hall once and for all. He moved his family into a handsome villa that Lee named after a home he once visited on the outskirts of Paris, France— Chantilly.

Richard Henry chose the location of his home very carefully. The main house was built on a high bluff overlooking Currioman Bay as it merged into the Potomac River. Lee's nephew, Thomas Shippen, once noted that Chantilly-on-the-Potomac commanded "a much finer view [of the river] than Stratford by reason of a large bay window into which the Potowmac forms itself opposite to Chantilly." Shippen spoke highly of the design and splendor of Lee's home, and he was enamored by the view of "a fine island called Blackstone's," which, Shippen noted, added a remarkable "finish to the landscape."[2] In addition to the bay, two other creeks bordered Chantilly on the northeastern and southeastern sides of Lee's home, Cold Harbor Creek and Currioman Creek. Lee constructed a modest dock system where these two creeks met, which he appropriately named Chantilly Landing. The location of the dock provided easy access to the Potomac River, but at the same time, the landing remained hidden from travelers unfamiliar with the terrain of the Potomac shoreline.

The location of Lee's home along the creeks branching off Currioman Bay and the Potomac River provided Lee with ample opportunities to indulge in one of his favorite pursuits—hunting. Each winter, as the geese arrived in the area on their annual migratory flight, Richard Henry would skulk among the rushes and reeds along the water's edge, hunting the majestic birds. In the winter of 1768, tragedy befell Lee: as he aimed at his target, the gun exploded in his hands. The accident cost Richard Henry all four fingers on his left hand. As friends and family rushed him back home to treat the wound, medical standards of the day dictated that the injury would first be cauterized by burning the area with a searing hot metal instrument. The burn would close off the wound, and the scar tissue that immediately began to develop stopped the bleeding. Afterward, Lee began a steady recovery. A few months after the incident, Lee only once referred to his "unhappy wound" in his correspondence.[3] After the injury healed, Richard Henry donned a black silk glove that concealed the ugly scar on his hand. Over time, Lee learned to use his gloved hand to maximum effect making his gestures all the more impressive when he addressed an audience.[4]

Chantilly-on-the-Potomac did share certain characteristics with Stratford Hall. As Thomas Shippen once observed, Chantilly was more "commodious than elegant," a complaint frequently uttered by Philip Lee regarding Stratford Hall.[5] Lee built a three-and-a-half-story frame building, with at least the first level made of brick. There were at minimum ten rooms inside the home in addition to a store and a cellar located in the basement. The downstairs portion of the house included a front hall to receive guests, a parlor, a nursery (which Richard Henry later converted into a library), and a dining room. The second story consisted of four large bedrooms for Richard Henry and Anne, as well as their older children. At the top of the first flight of stairs was one room that most likely served as a lookout, since a glimpse from the window provided an excellent view of Currioman Bay, the Potomac River, and Blackstone's Island. Lee placed twelve chairs near the window and kept at least two looking glass telescopes that guests could use to watch the tobacco ships and other vessels sailing past Chantilly—most likely on their way to Stratford Landing. During the War for American Independence, Lee and other prominent citizens living in the Northern Neck undoubtedly spent a considerable amount of time in this room monitoring British troop movements in the Potomac River. The third story had only one room that was most likely set aside as a schoolroom; along the third floor hallway, in addition to the schoolroom, Lee built a series of storage rooms and closets. Five outbuildings surrounded the house. These structures included a kitchen, a dairy, a blacksmith shop, stables, and a barn.

As guests arrived at Chantilly, they entered a richly furnished front hall containing a large round table, two square cherry wood tables, and twelve green armchairs on which to seat visitors. To the right of the front hall, a staircase rose leading to the upper floors; to the left, guests could enter either the dining room or the parlor. In the parlor, visitors would see one of the most characteristic features of Lee's home—a large bay window flanked by two large panel windows providing a panoramic view of the Potomac River. Bay windows were uncommon architectural features in provincial Virginia, but they were part of a standard design for many eighteenth-century European homes.[6] Although Chantilly did not rival Stratford Hall in size, such unique fixtures such as the bay window in Lee's parlor made Chantilly-on-the-Potomac one of the finest homes in Virginia's Northern Neck, surpassing the smaller and simpler frame structures that dotted the landscape along the Potomac River.[7]

When the time came to entertain guests at Chantilly, Richard Henry Lee spared little expense. Thomas Shippen observed that, when visiting Lee's home, guests had "everything that is most excellent in fish, crab, wild fowl, and exquisite meats—the best of liquors—and a most hearty welcome."[8] The dining room was twenty-four feet long and twenty feet wide, which provided ample room for entertaining, and the room contained several items that contributed to the lavish atmosphere—a large mahogany cabinet that housed a set of blue and white table china, a silver cup (valued at £30), silverware, and a set of wine glasses.[9] If, during dinner, a ship came into view of Chantilly, Lee always kept another looking glass—also made of mahogany—within easy reach so he and his guests could easily identify the vessel. Once his guests had finished dinner, visitors could take a stroll down the "great walk" that led to the edge of the bluff on which Chantilly rested. As they ventured down the path, guests would also view Lee's formal gardens decorating both sides of the walkway. A side path branched off that led down to Chantilly Landing, where Lee could take his guests on a dinner barge tour of Currioman Bay and perhaps venture into the Potomac River as well.

Lee clearly took pleasure in entertaining friends and associates, even to the detriment of his own health. Gout plagued Lee for most of his adult life, a condition most likely aggravated by his proclivity for wine and other spirits. The disease frequently caused serious discomfort resulting in arthritis and painful swelling of his lower extremities.[10] In his correspondence, Richard Henry Lee frequently complained about his "gouty" feet, and he relied heavily on his nephew, Thomas Shippen, to procure various items for him to ensure his physical comfort while he

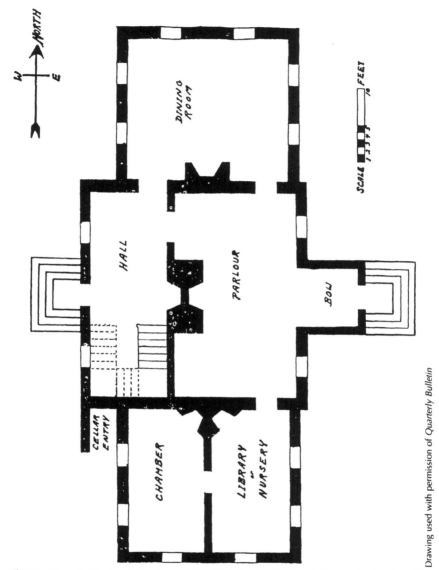

Figure 3.1. Conjectural drawing of the first level of Richard Henry Lee's Chantilly manor house. Chantilly-on-the-Potomac and its surrounding outbuildings are no longer standing, and no known drawing of the house as it actually appeared exists. In 1972, Jeffrey O'Dell excavated the Chantilly site, and based on his findings, developed the above illustration for the *Quarterly Bulletin*.

was a member of the Continental Congress. At one point, when he served as president of Congress, his affliction made his feet swell to the point that he could no longer wear his shoes. He described, in precise language, the type of shoes he needed his nephew to acquire—which, of course, emphasized both style and comfort. "The soles" had to be "made of thick but soft leather"; the "toes had to be round not sharp" and made of buckskin "stained black and lined with . . . fur."[11] After he made this request, Richard Henry's condition worsened. His pain became so intense that he had to arrange the purchase of a special chair so that he could fulfill his duties as president. Eventually, Lee had to take a month's leave of absence. He left New York City and went to Philadelphia, where he received medical care from his brother-in-law, Dr. William Shippen Jr., who had served as America's chief medical officer during the War for American Independence. Lee spent September 1785 in taking advantage of the medicinal springs located outside of Philadelphia, which finally allowed him to return to New York City with a "store of health . . . sufficient . . . to carry [him] triumphantly thro [his] Presidential year."[12]

Yet, despite his pain and discomfort, Lee's tastes for these indulgences never dissipated. Again, at one point during his presidency, as he prepared to receive the Spanish foreign minister Don Diego de Gardoqui, Lee arranged for a sumptuous feast consisting of "Black fish, Sheepshead, & Sea Bass," all of which were "numerous and fine." As for beverages, he secured ample provisions of "Champaign, Claret, Madiera, & Muscat." Afterward, upon surveying the evening's menu, Lee noted that cigars were the only item still lacking—and he hoped that Gardoqui would provide that particular treat. Lee wrote that "it will be unfortunate for us if Mr. Gardoque should not be a Smoker and so not be provided with Havana segars." Lee had acquired his taste for Cuban cigars from an earlier visit by Juan Miralles, who "used to supply us so copiously that he had occasioned us to lose all appetite for other smoking."[13] This pattern of Lee's behavior remained consistent down to time of his death. Richard Henry Lee kept his home stocked and ready to entertain. The inventory compiled after his death indicated that his cellar had "4 bottles of sweet oil, 28 bottles of port wine, 61 bottles of Virginia wine, and 7 bottles of gin."[14]

II

After moving out of Stratford Hall into Chantilly-on-the-Potomac, Anne Lee gave birth to two more children, both daughters: Mary (b. 1764) and Hannah (b. 1766). Although Richard Henry Lee maintained an active role in public service after moving his family into Chantilly-on-the-Potomac, his wife and children were never far from his thoughts. As Lee fought contentious battles against John Robinson and his allies in the House of Burgesses, Lee delighted in returning to Chantilly and spending time with young boys and girls.

Throughout his life, Richard Henry Lee found himself embroiled in numerous conflicts and controversies relating to provincial politics and imperial relations between Crown and colony. Events, on occasion, forced Lee to face the dilemma of choosing between his family and public service, and invariably, he chose his family every time. In December 1768, Lee notified his friend Landon Carter that he could not attend to public matters because "poor Mrs. Lee and my two sons [are] laboring under a severe Pluerisy and now so ill that [I do not know] what may be the issue of this night." His two sons recovered from their bouts, but just barely a week after celebrating their eleventh wedding anniversary, Anne Aylet Lee died. A few months after Richard Henry buried his wife, he had a monument constructed in her honor at Nominy Church and penned the following dedication:

> *Sacred to the memory of Mrs. Anne Lee, wife of Col. Richard H. Lee. This monument was erected by her afflicted husband in the year 1769.*

> *Reflect dear reader on the great uncertainty of human life, since neither esteemed temperament nor the most amiable goodness could save this excellent Lady from death in the bloom of life. She left behind her four children, two sons and two daughters, Obitt 12th December, 1768, aet. 30.*

> "*Was then so precious a flower*
> *But given us to behold it waste,*
> *The short-lived blossom of an hour*
> *Too nice, too fair, too sweet to last.*"[15]

Dark days followed the death of Anne Lee. The prospect of raising his young family all by himself put Richard Henry Lee under tremendous pressure. His two boys, Thomas and Ludwell, were now age eleven and nine, respectively, and Richard Henry now had to consider their higher education as they finished their studies at their in-home school. He undoubtedly found solace in the way his family came together and was aided by his older brother, Thomas, and Thomas's wife, Mary, who helped tend to Richard Henry's young daughters.[16] Eventually, the situation steadily improved for Lee and his children. By June or July 1769, Richard Henry met and married a recent widow, Anne Gaskins Pinckard. He wrote his younger brother, William, then residing in London, about his "great happiness" that his new wife proved to be a "most tender, attentive and fond mother to my dear little girls."[17]

After his marriage to Anne Pinckard, the Chantilly brood continued to grow. Richard Henry and the second Anne Lee had another five children—two sons and three daughters—between 1770 and 1782, and Richard Henry proved to be a doting father to all of his children. As Lee tended to public business in Philadelphia as a delegate in the Continental Congress, he would take the time from his duties and purchase lottery tickets for himself and his daughters—then he would meticulously record the numbers on the tickets by the name of each daughter in the journal he always carried with him in his vest pocket.

Even during the War for American Independence, Lee's children were never far from his thoughts. At one point in 1778, a correspondent wrote Lee asking when would he return to his political duties. He wrote back, saying he would return to Williamsburg as soon as he could "quit the entertainment of [his] prattling fireside." Only after he "heard every little story and settled all points" with his children would he return to his public duties.[18] As British ships launched an invasion of the Potomac in 1778 and 1779, Lee had to frequently abandon Chantilly and seek refuge at a plantation once inhabited by George Washington's mother, Epping Forest. During one of these flights, Anne Lee gave birth to a son they named Cassius, and with a slight touch of humor, Richard Henry notified his friend Samuel Adams of his son's birth and commented on the infant's temper. Lee indicated that already at the age of five months, Cassius Lee had already proven that he "would be no Lover of Tyrants."[19]

Because of the tumultuous times in which he lived, Richard Henry Lee had to spend much of his time away from home tending to affairs of state. He frequently left his wife alone to tend with matters relating to the management of Chantilly-on-the-Potomac, but he thought of her often as well. While Richard Henry served as president of the Continental Congress in 1785, he informed his nephew, Thomas Shippen, that "my Mrs. Lee writes me that she must & will have a handsome Bread Tray for serving bread to Table, also a basket proper for holding clean plates and for foul plates." Lee quickly added that "this demand comes from too high Authority for me to venture neglecting it," indicating that he had better not return to Chantilly without these items in tow.[20] Richard Henry's duties as president of Congress frequently required him to entertain guests in the home provided for him by Congress. Three times a week, Lee would receive as guests members of Congress and visiting dignitaries; but, since his wife was not present to act as hostess, Lee did not invite ladies to these affairs. There is little doubt that Richard Henry loved each of his wives dearly. As he prepared his own last will in testament, he recorded his dying wish:

> I desire to be decently, privately, and frugally buried in the family burying ground at the burnt House as it is called, and as near to my late ever dear wife as 'tis possible to place mine without disturbing her remains, and upon her left, so that my present dear Mrs. Lee may be laid, when she dies, on my right; and so my body be placed between those of my dear wives.[21]

Throughout his life, Richard Henry Lee demonstrated his tender love and affection for his wives and children, and they returned the same feelings in kind, which in large part, explains the inscription on his gravestone—"We cannot do without you."

III

With a family as large as Richard Henry Lee's, one of the most pressing matters that weighed on his mind concerned providing a suitable education for all nine of his children. From 1763 until 1786, the nursery on the first floor of Chantilly-on-the-Potomac remained occupied, as did the schoolroom on the third floor. He, like his father before him, most likely hired a tutor to provide his children with a rudimentary education, although there is no record of any specific individual employed for that purpose. Lee did, however, indicate in his journal that he hired Francis Christian to teach his children to dance in February 1781.

To further the education of his children while they lived at Chantilly, Richard Henry Lee built a rather impressive library consisting of almost 100 titles. It seems as if Lee had a particular affinity for books on historical topics and biography, including Edward Gibbons's *Decline and Fall of the Roman Empire*, David Hume's *History of England*, Catherine McCauley's *History of England*, and even David Ramsey's *History of the American Revolution*. Among the biographical studies, Lee owned copies of *The Life of Henry II*, *The History of Charles V*, and *The Life of Mahomet*. In addition to these works, Lee's library included several different scientific, theological, and philosophical studies, plus a wide selection of various literary works including William Shakespeare, John Milton, Jonathan Swift, and Laurence Sterne.[22]

Richard Henry Lee's children no doubt used these volumes to supplement their education while living at Chantilly. Once his sons reached the ages between ten and twelve, however, Lee had to turn his attention to their additional schooling. The expense of providing a suitable education for his children placed a tremendous economic burden on Richard Henry. In 1772 he wrote to his brother William about his need for "a profitable employment" indicating that he had "five children already . . . with a teaming little wife." All combined, Lee regarded his financial situation as "sufficiently alarming" as he considered the costs of raising such a large family.[23] Yet, in spite of these problems in the summer of 1772, Lee began making preparations to send his two oldest sons to England so they could complete their education. Richard Henry Lee did have less expensive alternatives, but he noted that, after "great reflection, aided by observation, and my own experience," he remained convinced that an

English education would be the most beneficial for his sons. He briefly considered sending Thomas and Ludwell to the College of William and Mary but soon rejected the notion because "so little attention is paid either to the learning, or the morals of boys that I never could bring myself to think of William & Mary."[24]

Richard Henry Lee used his own experiences to guide him in determining the best education suited for his two boys. His family was already well connected with London's tobacco interest, primarily through Richard Henry's younger brother, William, who operated a tobacco merchant house of his own in London, and also through James Russell, who had married into the Lee family via the Maryland line. Consequently, Lee did not feel compelled to direct his sons into the merchant profession. He determined that his oldest son, Thomas, would become a minister.[25] Once Richard Henry had determined the areas of study for Thomas, he asked William Lee to introduce Thomas to the Reverend Beilby Porteus, who then served as the bishop of London. Richard Henry had apparently maintained a good relationship with the Porteuses after his plans to marry Beilby's niece had fallen through in the early 1750s. As for Ludwell Lee, Richard Henry had other plans. Ludwell was to study and become a lawyer. Lee estimated that it would take eleven years for Ludwell to complete his education; he expected that by age fifteen, Ludwell would attend the Inns of Court and begin studying law by the age eighteen "so that he may return with the Gown at 21."[26]

Once these decisions had been made, the only remaining problem was the cost of providing an adequate education for Thomas and Ludwell, and financial matters of this sort weighed heavily on Richard Henry's mind. Lee informed William that he could not afford anything above "£30 sterling apiece for Board[,] clothing, and education." For this reason, securing additional income to handle these expenses remained a top priority for Lee. He applied for a position as a Westmoreland County clerk. He contacted James Steptoe, a friend in a neighboring county who had already worked as a clerk, and he asked him to put in a good word for him. Richard Henry stated his situation honestly to his friend, informing Steptoe that with his "two Sons going this summer to England, [it] added to the heavy charge of supporting so many here"; thus, it made it necessary for him to gain the clerkship.[27] His efforts, however, were of no avail, and Lee failed to secure the desired employment. As a result of failures such as this, Lee's personal financial situation remained precarious, despite the fact that he lived in comfortable surroundings. (These circumstances also forced Richard Henry Lee to maintain Chantilly-on-the-Potomac as a viable profit-making entity, allowing him to meet a variety of expenses.)

IV

Debt was a persistent problem that plagued all tidewater planters, and maintaining accessibility to credit, whether from merchants or fellow planters, was a matter of constant concern. Managing his debt while trying to maintain the expenses that came along with raising a large family weighed heavily on Richard Henry Lee.[28] All planters, great and small, were either indebted to one another or to a merchant or some other factor in Great Britain. The Lees of Virginia were uniquely situated, and they managed their extensive holdings through a centralized location, Stratford Landing. Independently, Chantilly-on-the-Potomac could not sustain the level of income the planter Richard Henry Lee needed to meet for the expenses of raising a family and maintaining his standard of living. Lee's extensive family in tidewater Virginia alleviated many of the problems that undermined the success of other tobacco planters in the region.

On the 500 acres Richard Henry leased from his older brother, he grew tobacco—most of which went toward his annual rent, wheat, and corn. Additionally, he raised some livestock at Chantilly. The produce he grew on his plantation primarily took care of the immediate needs for his burgeoning family. The transactions at Stratford Landing represented the main business enterprise that occupied much of Richard Henry's time and attention. He assisted his larger family's interests by working as a business agent for his older brother as they collected tobacco from several other plantations owned and operated by members of their extended family. The business interests of the Lee family were facilitated by the fact that Richard Henry leased all of his inherited land to several tenants—all of whom grew tobacco that eventually found its way to Stratford Landing as well. In conjunction with all this activity, Lee recorded in his journal numerous occasions when he took tobacco from a variety of other small planters in the vicinity. The Lee family operated in a fashion similar to a modern corporation: as they would gather tobacco from various sources, they would arrange for shipment across the Atlantic, where it would be received by either William or Arthur Lee in London, the associates of their cousin, James Russell, or some other trading house.

As for managing day-to-day expenses, Richard Henry Lee, like many other great planters, tried to maintain a "pay-as-you-go" system for as many items and services as possible.[29] Yet, in spite of such efforts, most planters could not avoid borrowing money from merchants, friends, or family. Lee was more fortunate than most other tidewater planters because of his large, extended family. Richard Henry would frequently share his possessions with his brothers and sister, and he would borrow freely from them as situations developed. His nieces and nephews would arrive at Chantilly and stay for days and weeks at a time; likewise, it would not have been unusual for his children to visit their uncles and aunts at different plantations throughout the Northern Neck.

The practice of sharing was not limited to household products—it extended to slaves as well. Richard Henry Lee inherited forty slaves in 1750 from his father, and that number increased to sixty-three by the time of Lee's death in 1794. Although little evidence has survived regarding the African-American experience at Chantilly, ample evidence suggests that the Lee family's slaves were frequently transferred back and forth from Stratford, Chantilly, Hannah Lee Corbin's home, Pecketone, and Thomas Ludwell Lee's home, Bellvue in Stafford County. Richard Henry recorded this sort of activity in his journal on numerous occasions. He once noted that "a yellow Negro girl (property of Col. P. L. Lee's estate) named Grace, the child of Abraham and Letty . . . was sent to Bellview by Miss Mitilda Lee."[30] Additionally, according to Philip Lee's 1782 estate list, two slaves employed as ship carpenters appeared, Osman and Edmund, and they were valued at £120 and £100, respectively. Twelve years later, both Osman and Edmund resided at Chantilly, still working as ship carpenters, and both men were appraised at £100 each.[31] Another example of the transference of slave property from one Lee family home to another is found with a slave named Harry, who frequently entertained the Lees by playing the fiddle at Stratford Hall. In 1787, when Richard Henry's niece visited Chantilly, Lucinda Lee recorded in her journal that "dinner is just over. Harry the Fiddler is sent for, and we are going to dance."[32]

There were occasions when a slave would run away from Stratford Hall, only to show up at one of the other Lee plantations. One of Philip Lee's slaves named Sawney fled and ran to Pecketone, but Philip's sister, Hannah Lee Corbin, soon discovered his presence on her plantation. She confronted Sawney and demanded an explanation. Sawney recounted how Philip came upon him one day and found him resting and smoking his pipe. In response, Sawney said Philip "whacked him." Consequently, Sawney determined that he would rather reside at Pecketone than Stratford. Hannah confronted her brother with this account, suggesting that, if true, she would keep Sawney. Philip defended his actions, declaring that Sawney had "never been touched above twice . . . and then very gently."[33] What actually happened to Sawney after this exchange between brother and sister remains uncertain.

Although the evidence remains scant, certain observations can be made regarding the relationship between master and slave at Chantilly-on-the-Potomac.[34] A clear sense of community developed between Richard Henry Lee and the slaves residing on his plantation. The "Chantilly Inventory"[35] and entries in Lee's journal indicate that he kept track of individual slaves, their parentage, their families, as well as their physical conditions. Lee mentions "compensating" field hands by sharing corn and wheat harvested from Chantilly fields. On another occasion, Richard Henry paid one of his slaves two shillings more than he owed the slave so that he could have two dozen partridges the slave had trapped.[36] At the time of Lee's death in 1794, meticulous records show that of the sixty-three slaves in Lee's possession, six were with "children in arms," and one slave named Abigail was described as "past labor."[37] Chantilly slaves performed a variety of duties around the plantation as indicated by the examples of Osman, Edmund, and Harry. Additionally, Richard Henry Lee noted in his journal that another slave, named Congo, "worked 13 1/2 days . . . whitewashing." Lee also hired slaves out to perform tasks off the plantation as well. At one point in 1781, for example, Lee arranged for Congo to work "at the court house for about 5 months in the Spring, Summer, and Fall."[38]

Lee, like other tidewater planters, probably provided his slaves with the minimum provisions needed for their survival. Included among these items, according to one observer, were "coarse clothing; a Negro quarter residence, or a private house."[39] Richard Henry Lee, more than likely, provided for his slaves much to the same degree his brother Philip did at Stratford. The homes for field hands were generally small, cramped, one- or two-room structures that housed anywhere from eight to twenty-four persons. Typically, the size of a standard slave quarter at Stratford Hall varied between twelve-by-sixteen feet to twelve-by-twenty feet, and they were spaced anywhere from 30 to 100 feet apart. Of course, we can only speculate about the conditions experienced by Chantilly slaves, but it seems reasonable that circumstances on Richard Henry's plantation would not be much different than those found at Stratford Hall.[40]

Richard Henry Lee's actual views toward the institution of slavery represent another area of critical interest that remains elusive to the historian. For the most part, documentation regarding Lee's opinions on slavery has not survived over the years. It is quite obvious that Lee was not averse to owning slaves, but he was highly critical of the slave trade. During the French and Indian War, when Lee sponsored an effort to impose a 10 percent duty on all African slaves brought into Virginia to help finance the war, he delivered a speech before the House of Burgesses denouncing the practice—but he did not do so for humanitarian reasons. Lee commented on how Virginia seemed to develop at a slower pace in comparison to those colonies that did not rely so heavily on slave labor, and in Lee's mind, there was a connection. He stated that other colonies "with their whites . . . import arts and agriculture, whilst we, with our blacks, exclude both."[41]

One of the primary factors that shaped Richard Henry Lee's opposition to the slave trade was his growing fear of a slave rebellion, should the importation of Africans continue unabated. He referred to the internal threat posed by the institution and how an uprising was a constant threat because the slaves "observe their masters possessed of liberty which is denied to them, whilst they and their posterity are subjected for ever to the most abject and mortifying slavery." As far as Lee was concerned, these conditions made slaves "natural enemies to society, and their increase consequently dangerous."[42]

Although Virginia did not experience a violent slave rebellion until Nat Turner's uprising in 1831, planters in Virginia, especially those residing in the Northern Neck, could not dismiss the possibility of such an occurrence. In the area of Virginia resting between the Potomac and Rappahannock Rivers, between 40 and 50 percent of the population were enslaved; in Westmoreland County, the slave population outnumbered the free white population by 600.[43] Consequently, many eighteenth-century Virginians voiced similar opinions as those expressed by Lee.[44]

Despite his concerns over the effects of the slave trade and the possibility of a slave rebellion, Lee never spoke openly of abolishing slavery; at one point, he even attempted to engage in the slave trade as a means of securing some additional income to provide for his growing family. In July 1772, Lee wrote to his brother William about securing some slaves for consignment to Virginia. He was hopeful that this transaction would prove profitable, "as the planters are nearly out of debt and Negroes [had] become valuable here." The deal fell through because the two brothers could not agree on financial terms of the arrangement, and Richard Henry was unable to secure his desired margin of profit on the transaction.[45] Although his fear of a rebellion was real enough, Lee most likely only experienced nonviolent episodes of slave resistance—similar to those encountered by his brother Philip at Stratford Hall.[46] In the final analysis, Lee, like many of his contemporaries, expressed contradictory views toward slavery, expressing their hatred of the institution yet refusing to abolish it because he and other planters needed slave labor to run profitable tobacco plantations.

V

Throughout his adult life, Richard Henry Lee found it increasingly difficult to sustain the needs of his family by growing tobacco alone. Consequently, he constantly had to seek new opportunities to secure additional income, and he also had to diversify his crop production at Chantilly to accommodate wheat and corn as well as tobacco. Richard Henry understood that producing a quality crop of tobacco required a tremendous amount of time and effort, and the fluctuating price of tobacco created a constant state of economic uncertainty for tidewater planters. Yet, despite these concerns, Lee and numerous others continued to grow tobacco because of the high demand for the crop in European markets. With a moderate degree of success, ambitious planters like the Lees continued operating their own ships, which would transport the tobacco they produced as well as that grown by smaller planters throughout the Northern Neck. The Lees would collect their annual crops and ship them across the Atlantic in ships they either owned or co-owned with William Lee or James Russell, both of whom represented the family's interests in London.

As a successful planter, Richard Henry Lee understood the problems with which tobacco growers had to contend. In 1768, he wrote a brief pamphlet titled "The State of the Constitution of Virginia." Lee provided the intended English audience a comparison of the British system of government to that found in Virginia; then he lapsed into a full discussion of Virginia's most valuable crop—tobacco. Lee's purpose for writing this pamphlet was clearly political in nature; he hoped to secure preferential treatment for the tobacco colonies in matters relating to imperial economic polices. In the course of his commentary, Lee introduced readers to the unique tobacco culture of Chesapeake communities, and he highlighted the many difficulties in producing a successful crop. Lee's pamphlet illustrated the extent to which tobacco permeated the daily life of the planter, from the beginning of the planting season (either in late December or early January) until the tobacco ships arrived to take the annual crops to London merchants. Tobacco required the constant attention from planters and their slaves, and men like Lee understood that they could never take a successful yield for granted. He initiated his presentation with an overview describing how tobacco production occurred in four separate stages, each one demanding skill, judgment, and luck on the part of the planter.[47]

The first stage began with sowing seeds in tobacco beds, carefully covered with tree branches protecting the seeds from frost damage. Frequently, because of the risks involved with unpredictable winter weather, the prudent planter would plant ten times more tobacco than he could use since few plants actually survived the winter months. The second stage began in early spring by transplanting tobacco seedlings from the beds into the main fields. At this juncture, planters hoped for frequent rains so that the seedlings could be easily removed from their beds without damaging their root systems. During this stage, whenever a good shower poured down, slaves—and occasionally the planters themselves—would rush to the seedbeds and begin moving the crop while the rain came down. The second stage kept slaves on tobacco plantations busy for several months and typically did not end until late May or early June.

At this juncture, planters and their slave laborers waged a constant battle against weeds until they spotted anywhere from eight to twelve tobacco leaves on the stems of the plants. Now the third stage began. This phase of the tobacco cycle, known as the "topping process," consisted of removing flowers from the plants so that more of each plant's energy was directed into its leaves. Once slaves had completed topping the plants, the fourth and final stage began in late September, as slaves started to cut off tobacco leaves. This final phase required careful attention because an entire crop could easily be ruined. Less experienced planters often relied on established growers, like Richard Henry Lee, to tell them when the cutting process should begin. Lee told them to cut the leaves when they were "ripe," as indicated when "brown spots appeared on the leaf," but he cautioned them by warning that there were no exact measures. If immature leaves were cut, then the quality of the entire crop could be compromised.[48]

Once planters had finished the cutting process, the leaves had to be cured, or dried. This task was difficult as planters tried to produce a leaf that was neither too dry nor too moist. Excessive wetness sometimes caused the shipment to rot while en route to England. If the leaves were too dry, they could become brittle and disintegrate on the voyage across the Atlantic. The successful planter had to strike the middle ground by producing a leaf that was pliable, but not moist; and dry, but not brittle. Occasionally, planters would start small fires in their drying sheds if too much rain fell during the drying season. Thomas Jefferson, who also frequently gave advice to less experienced planters, warned those who started such fires to exercise "great care . . . as [tobacco] is very inflammable, and if it takes fire, the whole crop, with the house, consumes as quickly as straw would."[49]

After the drying process had concluded, planters began "stemming" their crops. Slaves would remove all of the stems from the leaves so that they could be more easily packed into barrels, called *hogsheads*, for shipment. The average weight of one hogshead ranged from 300 to 1,800 pounds. On average, one hogshead of tobacco from Chantilly-on-the-Potomac weighed between 1,000 and 1,200 pounds.[50] Planters frequently competed with one another to see how much they could press into one hogshead. Planters, of course, had a practical reason to participate in this sort of gamesmanship. Shippers charged planters by the barrel, not by the pound. As a result, planters who packed more tobacco into each hogshead paid less money in shipping costs.[51]

When the time came to bring the barrels of tobacco from the drying sheds to the docks for loading on the tobacco ships, large planters like Richard Henry Lee had to rely upon gravity to facilitate transportation. The hogsheads would be turned on their sides, and slaves would begin pushing them down the "rolling roads"—flattened dirt paths connecting the tobacco fields to dockyards. Planters that lived further inland would load their hogsheads onto barges and follow the navigable creeks and streams to the Potomac River. The tobacco ships would begin arriving between February and June, sailing up Chesapeake Bay into the Potomac River, picking up consignments of tobacco along the way. By the time the ships arrived, planters had another crop in the ground, and another production cycle was well underway.

The potential profits from a successful crop made the ordeal well worth the effort; as one contemporary observer noted, "the greatest advantages attending the culture of tobacco was the quick, easy, and certain method of sale."[52] The fragility and the uncertainty of the process proved to be a constant source of worry and concern for planters. The unpredictable weather and insects could ruin a planter.

Weather conditions often hampered the success of tobacco producers, frequently preventing planters from getting their crops to market. Richard Henry informed William that "during the whole Winter, until this fortnight[,] the Waters have all been bound up in Frost [so] that Capt. Brown has not been able to do anything in the way of getting tob[acco] on board."[53] Lee also commented on how flooding had made it impossible for planters to navigate the streams; as a result, many growers kept their crops on their plantations, rather than risk losing it in transit.[54] Richard Henry Lee warned his readers about a "small fly that eats the plants" while they were still in the seedling beds. Later, planters had to maintain a vigilant eye for a "large worm that devours the [tobacco plant's] leaves."[55]

VI

Because of the risks involved with tobacco production, planters like Lee believed that tobacco colonies like Virginia deserved special consideration in respect to colonial policy. Such provisions would include cooperative efforts to ease the burden of debt, as well as continued access to new lands beyond the Appalachian Mountains, which would allow planters to continue producing tobacco in the future.[56] These were justifiable requests in Lee's mind because of the high demand for Chesapeake tobacco in European markets and because of the vital role tobacco played in the imperial economy. Between 1761 and 1776, the British colonies in North America shipped an annual average of fifty million pounds of tobacco to English ports, and in return, the British government collected a rather substantial amount of revenue through trade duties.[57]

American tobacco planters like Richard Henry Lee were not the only ones supporting special dispensation for the Chesapeake colonies in the mid-eighteenth century, as well as guaranteed access to western lands. John Mitchell, a British agricultural expert who traveled throughout the American colonies in the 1750s and 1760s, echoed the sentiments expressed by Lee and numerous other planters. Mitchell presented his conclusions in two separate treatises, *The Contest in America between Great Britain and France, with Its Consequences and Importance* (1757), and *The Present State of Great Britain in America* (1767).

In the first of these two works, Mitchell clearly advocates an aggressive policy toward the French in the Ohio River valley, for economic reasons based on the importance of tobacco to the imperial economy. Mitchell noted that the "want of fresh lands for planting tobacco" made it crucial for the British crown to guarantee access to the region beyond the Appalachians. He made an even stronger case in the second volume by observing that the only fresh acreage left in British America that could sustain tobacco production were the rich lands along the Mississippi and Ohio Rivers. Mitchell concluded that "whoever were possessed of these [lands] must soon command the tobacco trade, the only considerable branch of trade in all of North America, and the only one [Britain] has left."[58]

Other contemporary commentators reinforced Mitchell's observations. In 1775, another traveler published an account describing the agricultural practices and conditions in America, titled *American Husbandry*. In this particular volume, the author observed that "there is no plant in the world that requires richer land or more manure than tobacco; it will grow on poorer fields, but not yield crops that are sufficiently profitable to pay expenses." He noted that the only way to address this particular problem was to acquire new lands because "such land will, after clearing, bear tobacco many years without any change, [and] prove more profitable to the planter than the power of dung can do on worse lands." The author urged his readers to look westward to the Ohio River valley for the solution. He described that the region is "well watered by several navigable rivers, communicating with each other" and that the "river Ohio is at all seasons of the year navigable for larger boats," which allowed for the transportation of "bulky articles," like tobacco at half the cost of overland routes.[59]

John Mitchell and the author of *American Husbandry* did not contribute anything new to the general body of knowledge held by planters like Richard Henry Lee, but they did confirm their worst fears concerning the future of the tobacco trade. Lee's presence at Chantilly-on-the-Potomac allowed him to raise his children and contribute to his family's business interests while maintaining his residency in Westmoreland County, thus letting him retain his seat in the House of Burgesses. His ability to keep a position of political influence became increasingly important due to the precariousness of his financial situation and the increasing burden of his growing family. The conclusions presented by Mitchell in his two treatises, in large part, help explain Lee's strong support for waging war against the French in 1757, once he took his seat in the House of Burgesses; from this time forward, Lee maintained a vigilant eye toward preserving Virginia's interests in the Ohio River valley. He found his efforts frustrated by his political opponents in Virginia and his economic competitors in England and neighboring colonies; thus, he looked toward his own uncertain future with a nascent hostility toward British policies in America as he struggled to preserve and maintain the society his family helped create.

NOTES

1. Lee, *Lee of Virginia*, 172, 206.

2. Thomas Shippen to William Shippen Jr., September 29, 1790, Shippen Family Papers, Library of Congress, Washington, D.C. Photostat copy, Research Department, The Colonial Williamsburg Foundation.

3. R. H. Lee to "A Gentleman of Influence in England," March 27, 1768, *The Letters of Richard Henry Lee, 1762–1794*, 2 vols., ed. James Curtis Ballagh (New York: Macmillan, 1911–1914), 1: 27. Hereafter, cited as *Lee Letters*.

4. Oliver Perry Chitwood, *Richard Henry Lee: Statesman of the American Revolution* (Morgantown, WV: West Virginia University Library, 1967), 223.

5. Chitwood, *Richard Henry Lee*, 223. See also, Calhoun, "Philip Lee of Stratford Hall," 29. Reconstructing Lee's home is a difficult task since the structure is no longer standing; consequently, I have drawn on a variety of sources to present this portrayal of Chantilly-on-the-Potomac. Edmund Jennings Lee provides an excellent description of Chantilly-on-the-Potomac in *Lee of Virginia*, 205–6. As for the furnishing and other details regarding the interior of Lee's home, see the "Chantilly Inventory," a document compiled after Lee's death in 1794. Scholars have long since believed the "Chantilly Inventory" to be lost, but, in actuality, it remains among the Lee papers in the Jessie Ball Du Pont Memorial Library at Stratford Hall Plantation. This document has provided vital information regarding the contents and interior of Chantilly-on-the-Potomac. For additional information and insight, see also George William Beale, "Chantilly: The Home of Richard Henry Lee," *Old Dominion Magazine* (July 1871): 421–24; Jeffery O'Dell, "1972 Excavation at the Chantilly Manor House Site, Westmoreland County Virginia," *Quarterly Bulletin: Archeological Society of Virginia* 28 (September 1973): 1–21; Camille Wells, "Social and Economic Aspects of Eighteenth Century Housing on the Northern Neck of Virginia," (Ph.D. diss., The College of William and Mary, 1994), 210–17.

6. O'Dell, "1972 Excavation of the Chantilly Manor House," 15. O'Dell commented on the rarity of bay windows in provincial Virginia and noted that only one other home, Thomas Jefferson's Monticello, contained a similar feature. Consequently, O'Dell characterized Chantilly as the "Paladian predecessor to the revolutionary Monticello."

7. I am indebted to Carl Lounsbury of the Colonial Williamsburg Foundation for this observation, made in a personal letter to me.

8. Thomas Shippen to William Shippen Jr., September 29, 1790, Shippen Family Papers.

9. Thomas Shippen to William Shippen Jr., September 29, 1790, Shippen Family Papers.

10. A. McGhee Harvey and Victor A. McKusick, eds., *Osler's Textbook Revisited: A Reprint of Selected Sections with Commentaries* (Baltimore: Johns Hopkins University School of Medicine, 1968), 163–64.

11. R. H. Lee to Thomas Shippen, May 22, 1785, *Lee Letters*, 2: 361.

12. R. H. Lee to [?], October 10, 1785, *Lee Letters*, 2: 387–88. It is true that, since an excess of uric acid in the bloodstream causes gout, large quantities of water ingested with a modified diet (and no alcohol) could relieve the painful symptoms of gout. Once the treatment ended, however, the disease would recur after a period of temporary relief. *Osler's Textbook Revisited*, 173.

13. R. H. Lee to Thomas Shippen, June 4, 1785, *Lee Letters*, 2: 368.

14. "Chantilly Inventory" (see note 5).

15. Lee, *Lee of Virginia*, 206; Armes, *Stratford Hall*, 107.

16. This sort of assistance remains undocumented but cannot be discounted because of the simple fact that Thomas Ludwell Lee and Richard Henry Lee married two sisters—Mary and Anne Aylett.

17. R. H. Lee to William Lee, December 12, 1769, *Lee Letters*, 1: 40–41.

18. R. H. Lee to William Whipple, November 29, 1778, *Lee Letters*, 1: 454.

19. R. H. Lee to Samuel Adams, January 18, 1780, *Lee Letters*, 2: 171.

20. R. H. Lee to Thomas Shippen, October 14, 1785, *Lee Letters*, 2: 393.

21. Lee, *Lee of Virginia*, 202.

22. "Chantilly Inventory" (see note 5).

23. R. H. Lee to William Lee, October 23, 1772, *Lee Letters*, 1: 78.

24. R. H. Lee to William Lee, July 12, 1772, *Lee Letters*, 1: 70–71.

25. R. H. Lee to William Lee, July 12, 1772, *Lee Letters*, 1: 70–71.

26. R. H. Lee to William Lee, July 12, 1772, *Lee Letters*, 1: 70, 73

27. R. H. Lee to James Steptoe, July 4, 1772, *Lee Letters*, 1: 68.

28. For discussions on debt and its impact on the daily lives of tidewater planters, see T. H. Breen, *Tobacco Culture: The Mentality of the Great Tidewater Planters on the Eve of Revolution*, with a new preface by the author (Princeton, NJ: Princeton University Press, 2001); and Herbert E. Sloan, *Principle and Interest: Thomas Jefferson and the Problem of Debt* (Charlottesville, VA: The University Press of Virginia, 1995).

29. See Sloan, *Principle and Interest*, 13–49.

30. R. H. Lee, "Journal Entry," November 8, 1781. *Richard Henry Lee's Journal and Memoranda Book*. Huntington Library, San Marino, CA. Hereafter cited as *R. H. Lee's Journal*.

31. "A List of Negroes," in "Chantilly Inventory" (see note 5).

32. Lucinda Lee, *Journal of a Young Lady of Virginia, 1787* (Richmond, VA: Whittet and Shepperson, 1976), 52.

33. Jeanne Calhoun, "The African American Experience at Stratford: 1782," unpublished manuscript, 2–3. Jessie Ball Du Pont Memorial Library, Stratford Hall Plantation, VA.

34. For more information and a broader perspective on this particular topic, see Philip D. Morgan, *Slave Counterpoint: Black Culture in the Eighteenth-Century Chesapeake and Low Country* (Chapel Hill: The University of North Carolina Press, 1998), 257–437.

35. A document compiled after Lee's death in 1794. See note 5.

36. Morgan, *Slave Counterpoint*, 364.

37. "Chantilly Inventory."

38. R. H. Lee, "Journal Entry," 1781.

39. William Tatham, *William Tatham and the Culture of Tobacco*, ed. G. Melvin Herndon (Coral Gables, FL: University of Miami Press, 1969), 104.

40. Calhoun, "The African American Experience at Stratford: 1782," 8; Mechal Sobel, *The World They Made Together: Black and White Values in Eighteenth-Century Virginia* (Princeton, NJ: Princeton University Press, 1987), 110.

41. Richard H. Lee, *Memoir of the Life of Richard Henry Lee and His Correspondence*, 2 vols. (Philadelphia: William Brown, Printer, 1825), 1: 17–18.

42. Lee, *Memoir of the Life of Richard Henry Lee*.

43. Sylvia R. Frey, *Water from the Rock: Black Resistance in a Revolutionary Age* (Princeton, NJ: Princeton University Press, 1991), 9; Louis K. Koontz, *The Virginia Frontier, 1754–1763* (Baltimore: 1925), 166.

44. David Brion Davis, *The Problem of Slavery in the Age of Revolution, 1770–1823* (Ithaca, NY: Cornell University Press, 1975), 164–212; and Charles Royster, *The Fabulous History of the Dismal Swamp Company: A Story of George Washington's Times* (New York: Alfred A. Knopf, 1999), 21–25.

45. R. H. Lee to William Lee, July 12, 1772, *Lee Letters*, 1: 75–76.

46. Calhoun, "The African American Experience at Stratford: 1782," 2–3.

47. R. H. Lee, "The State of the Constitution of Virginia," Lee Family Papers, Virginia Historical Society, Richmond, VA. Mssl L51 f378. See also, *American Husbandry*, ed. Harry J. Carmen (New York: Columbia University Press, 1939), 157–68.

48. R. H. Lee, "The State of the Constitution of Virginia," Lee Family Papers.

49. Thomas Jefferson, "On Tobacco Culture," *The Papers of Thomas Jefferson*, 50 vols. (to date), ed. Julian P. Boyd et al. (Princeton, NJ: Princeton University Press, 1950–), 7: 211.

50. R. H. Lee, "The State of the Constitution of Virginia."

51. R. H. Lee, "The State of the Constitution of Virginia."

52. *American Husbandry*, 171.

53. R. H. Lee to William Lee, March 2, 1774, *Lee Letters*, 1: 103.

54. R. H. Lee to William Lee, April 15, 1774, *Lee Letters*, 1: 105.

55. R. H. Lee, "The State of the Constitution of Virginia."

56. For more on the importance of western lands and how tobacco planters looked westward to secure their future interests, see Breen, *Tobacco Culture*, 182–86.

57. "Statistics on Colonial Trade," *American Colonial Documents*, 410.

58. *American Husbandry*, 206–7.

59. *American Husbandry*, 164, 203–4.

· 4 ·

The Making of a Radical

I

$\mathcal{A}$s Richard Henry moved his new family into Chantilly-on-the-Potomac in 1763, news arrived in Virginia announcing a peace agreement between Great Britain and France, thereby officially ending the French and Indian War. Richard Henry Lee and other planters welcomed the end of hostilities. As he managed his various enterprises at Chantilly-on-the-Potomac, he also continued his association with Philip by monitoring activities at Stratford Landing. By the end of the 1760s, his business experience provided him and his extended family with unique training often denied to most planters—knowledge pertaining to the technical aspects of commerce and the tobacco trade. The Lees of Virginia had successfully reestablished the transatlantic kinship network that allowed the first generation to prosper, and it extended to them opportunities for profits that few planters could enjoy.

Richard Henry and Philip, using Stratford Landing as their primary base of operations, worked in close partnership with William Lee's London-based trading house. The Lees sent the tobacco grown at Stratford and Chantilly, and other Northern Neck plantations, to William in London; this process contributed to their overall prosperity because they did not have to deal with middlemen when shipping their tobacco consignments. Planters that could not afford to maintain this type of transatlantic tie, out of necessity, shipped their tobacco on consignment to British merchants who in turn extended them credit to purchase goods shipped back to Virginia from London. As long as tobacco prices remained high and everyone profited, few tobacco planters questioned this process. By the early 1760s, however, tobacco prices began a steady decline, thus making the relationship between planters in Virginia and British merchants increasingly strained. The Lees remained largely above this because of their interfamilial links across the Atlantic Ocean.

Yet, in spite of his role as Philip's business associate, Richard Henry's relationship with Philip remained tenuous at best. Although questions and concerns over Thomas Lee's estate remained unaddressed, the two brothers relied heavily on each other. Richard Henry needed to rent land from Philip so that he could retain his residency in Westmoreland County and his seat in the House of Burgesses. Likewise, rather than live on his inherited lands in Prince William County, Philip depended on his younger brother's assistance in managing Stratford's vast tobacco operations.

Nonetheless, Richard Henry Lee would not hesitate to pursue new opportunities for himself, if there were some promise of shifting away from the complete dominance of Philip and a means of securing additional income to support his family. In 1762, Richard Henry learned of a pending vacancy on Virginia's Council, so he initiated a deliberate campaign to secure that seat. He contacted Virginia's resident agent in London, James Abercrombie, and made additional appeals to other influential men in Virginia, hoping to secure a promotion to the Council.[1]

The unpredictable nature of the tobacco trade and the financial burdens brought on by his growing family led Lee to seek the seat on the Council. As a member of the House of Burgesses, he received a ten shilling per diem, not a regular salary. These arrangements made maintaining a seat in the House a financial burden on many individuals. Lee no doubt shared the sentiments expressed by his friend and colleague George Washington, who noted that office holding was an onus "attended with a certain Expense and trouble without the least prospect of gain."[2] This was not the case for members of the Council, as each member received an annual salary of £1,000 per year.

Lee's pursuit of this office failed largely because Philip already had a seat on the Council. The Council provided direct representation at a high level for the most powerful families in the colony, and since one Lee was already present, to appoint another seemed a bit excessive. Considering the number of Lees that also maintained seats in the House, some men of influence feared that promoting Richard Henry would afford his family too much power in the colonial government. The disappointing results of his campaign annoyed Lee. He believed he should have been allowed a seat on the Council, unless there were a "previously established want of virtue in the brothers, which may lead them to coalesce in schemes destructive to their country."[3] He criticized the decision against him, stating that his ambition to join the council stemmed only from an "ardent desire to serve [his] country"; and considering the "time and application already employed in service of the public," he believed he had earned an appointment to the Council.[4]

Although his efforts had failed, Richard Henry continued to ignore convention, so he waged a private campaign for a seat on the Council. Rather than bide his time and work his way through the established hierarchy, he attempted to maneuver around the accepted procedures. His relationship with the leadership of the House of Burgesses no doubt influenced his decision on this matter. Lee already regarded Speaker–Treasurer John Robinson as corrupt, and this view tainted his assessment of all those who remained loyal to the speaker; in addition, because of the close ties between Robinson and Governor Francis Fauquier, Lee felt he had but one course of action—to initiate his own direct contacts with members of Parliament who might facilitate a political promotion for Lee in Virginia.

As his efforts to secure political advancement were frustrated and as tobacco prices continued to decline, Richard Henry followed his father's lead and looked westward for new opportunities in trade and land speculation. The end of the French and Indian War seemed to open the way for new ventures in the West. The Ohio Company of Virginia now held few opportunities for the Lees, for essentially two reasons. First, the Ohio Company had not yet fully recovered from the recent war with the French. Second, the ongoing lawsuit between Philip Lee and John Hanbury dampened much of the passion for the Ohio Company the Lees once possessed. Richard Henry Lee now saw a chance to capitalize on the void by organizing a land company of his own. George Washington with Richard Henry and his brothers, with the exception of Philip, joined together to form the Mississippi Land Company in 1763. They described themselves as a "Body of Adventurers . . . with a view to explore and settle some tracts of land upon the Mississippi and its waters." The company limited membership to fifty stockholders and guaranteed "every single member" an equal share of 50,000 acres of land.[5]

The organizers of the Mississippi Company planned to secure a grant of 2.5 million acres of land in the Mississippi River valley that fell within the watersheds of the Wabash, Ohio, and Tennessee Rivers. They understood that Parliament's support for this sort of venture was absolutely critical for their success, so they designed the company with the same mission as the original Virginia Company and Ohio Company—as an effort designed to promote the larger interests of the British Empire in North America. In the petition Lee and his associates sent to London, they promised to settle 200 families on the land granted by Parliament, helping to secure Britain's hold on the territory won from France in the recent war. Additionally, to help secure parliamentary allies, the organizers of the Mississippi Company also reserved a portion of their stock exclusively for members of Parliament who were willing to approve the company request for land. The Mississippi Company employed Arthur Lee as their agent in London and authorized him to distribute shares of company stock at his discretion. Other factors, however, soon intervened and thus delayed the effort of the Mississippi Company to profit from new opportunities in the West.[6]

Legend:
— Proclamation Line, 1763
▓ Spanish Possessions
▓ Thirteen Colonies
□ British Possessions

LAKE SUPERIOR

CANADA

LAKE HURON

LAKE MICHIGAN

LAKE ONTARIO

LAKE ERIE

St. Lawrence R.

NOVA SCOTIA

MAINE DISTRICT (MASS.)

NEW HAMPSHIRE

Boston

Providence
RHODE ISLAND
CONNECTICUT

NEW YORK

New York

PENNSYLVANIA
Philadelphia

NEW JERSEY

Baltimore

DELAWARE

MARYLAND

VIRGINIA

Wabash R.

Ohio R.

RESERVED FOR INDIANS

Ohio R.

NORTH CAROLINA

Cumberland R.

SOUTH CAROLINA

N

Tennessee R.

Tombigbee R.

Alabama R.

GEORGIA

Charleston

ATLANTIC OCEAN

Savannah

0   100   200   300 Miles

Chattahoochee R.

WEST FLORIDA

EAST FLORIDA

GULF OF MEXICO

Map reprinted with the permission of James K. Martin.

Figure 4.1.   North America after the Treaty of Paris, 1763.

II

The Mississippi Company was only one of several companies petitioning Parliament for western lands. In addition to the already established Loyal Land Company and Ohio Company of Virginia, Parliament also heard from the Connecticut-based Susquehanna Company, the Maryland-based Illinois-Wabash Company, and the Pennsylvania-based Indiana Company. The attraction to western lands stemmed from several sources; notably, colonial Americans knew that they could obtain vast amounts of land for a very small investment of capital. If land speculators had to provide any initial funding up front, seldom was it more than a penny-per-acre; once they had possession of a title to this land, they could sell the acreage at prices ranging from five shillings to one pound per acre. If they opted not to sell the land, speculators could rent plots to tenants who could develop the land by clearing forests and building houses, fences, and barns. In addition to selling and leasing real estate, merchants were drawn to this sort of activity in order to foster new opportunities for trade with Native American tribes that still inhabited the region.[7] Parliament, unfortunately, soon dashed all of the American speculative ventures targeting western lands and began to send forward its own independent initiatives designed to reorganize Britain's newly acquired North American empire.

After signing the Treaty of Paris of 1763, Parliament had to confront a variety of issues relating to the recent war. The British government was disturbed by reports received during the conflict that American merchants persisted in their trading efforts with various Native American groups. This sort of activity had the unhappy effect of inadvertently providing arms and other supplies to the native allies of the French. Consequently, some members of Parliament resolved to prevent situations like this from developing in the future. Initially, parliamentary action along these lines occurred in a piecemeal fashion. First, Parliament confirmed the terms of the 1758 Treaty of Easton, which had the effect of forbidding future settlements along the Ohio River. Next, Parliament turned its attention toward establishing a comprehensive policy regarding the newly acquired territory in North America. Parliament's efforts suddenly gained a new sense of urgency, however, in the spring of 1763, when Pontiac, an Ottawa chief, launched a series of attacks on colonial settlements along the North American frontier. Within a short period, Pontiac and his followers captured thirteen forts that the British had captured from the French. Although the main thrust of Pontiac's uprising lasted only about six months, sporadic fighting continued on through to 1765.[8]

Pontiac's uprising galvanized Parliament and fostered a heightened demand for a policy designed to prevent further outbreaks of violence. In October 1763, the king finally took action by issuing the Proclamation of 1763, which prohibited all colonial settlements beyond the Appalachian Mountains. The Proclamation reserved all territory west of the mountains for the Indian tribes that inhabited that region, and it declared that no royal official could "upon any pretence . . . grant warrants of survey, or pass any patents for lands beyond the bounds of their respective governments." The pronouncement also prohibited the direct purchase of land from native inhabitants after the authors expressed their concerns regarding fraudulent acts committed by colonial merchant–speculators and the role such events played in promoting tension between Indians and colonists. Promoters of this policy, however, could not ignore the importance that the Indian trade played in the imperial economy. Consequently, they announced their intention to begin regulating the trade—primarily with an eye toward preventing the kind of illicit trade conducted during the French and Indian War. In pursuance of that goal, the Proclamation declared that "trade with the . . . Indians shall be free and open to all subjects . . . provided that every person who may incline to trade with the said Indians, do take out a license for carrying on such trade."[9]

The issuance of the Proclamation of 1763 generated concern in America on several fronts. Investors in the Philadelphia-based Indiana Company opted toward demanding compensation for losses sustained during Pontiac's uprising. They began referring to themselves as the "Suffering Traders" and sought to establish alliances with supporters at the highest level of the British government. George Croghan of Pennsylvania worked closely with his friend and business associate Benjamin Franklin, who then resided in London working as Massachusetts's colonial agent to secure these objectives. In the months that followed the announcement of the Proclamation of 1763, the "Suffering Traders" joined with other Philadelphia merchants, like Samuel and Thomas Wharton, and began forming new coalitions with interested parties involved with the Maryland-based Illinois-Wabash Company.[10]

Governor Fauquier in Virginia, once he was notified about the Proclamation, expressed reservations about the validity of the plan. He wrote to the Board of Trade, informing his correspondents that there were "some difficulties relating to his Majestys Proclamation arising from the present State of this Colony." He provided the Board with a list of land grants dating back to 1746 and asked how he was to proceed on these matters.[11] The response from the Board of Trade effectively brought the end of all speculative ventures involving western lands. The new policy abrogated all preexisting agreements across the board, equally affecting the Ohio Company of Virginia and the Loyal Land Company. Additionally, the new comprehensive policy squashed the goals and desires of the nascent Mississippi Company as well.

Few Virginians could accept this sort of sweeping announcement. Some, like Thomas Walker of the Loyal Land Company, simply ignored the Proclamation and continued conducting business as usual. Richard Henry Lee more than likely shared the sentiments of George Washington, who later expressed the opinion that he could "never look upon the Proclamation in any other light . . . other than as a temporary expedient to quiet the Minds of the Indians." He confidently asserted that the policy "must fall of course in a few years especially when the Indians are consenting to our Occupying the Lands."[12] Lee, like his friend and business partner, decided the best course of action was to bide time and wait for Parliament to revise its policy, rather than antagonize sponsors of the plan and risk further action by the Crown regarding western lands. In the meantime, however, Richard Henry still had to secure additional income to provide for his family and allow him to fulfill his duties and responsibilities as a public servant.

III

Richard Henry Lee's relatively passive acceptance of the Proclamation of 1763 indicated a recognition shared by his father and grandfather—that his most immediate interests were served by working within imperial guidelines. Since the Ohio Company was, for all practical purposes, defunct, and since the Mississippi Company never progressed further than the planning stages, Lee still had reason to believe that other opportunities would soon present themselves for him to advance his own personal goals. Although he was upset about his failure to win a seat on the Council, he attributed his loss to his political enemies at the provincial level, not the Crown. Lee soon found such an opportunity when it seemed apparent that Parliament intended to levy a stamp tax in America unless the colonies could find some other means of raising revenue independent of Parliament's intervention. Although he disputed assertions that alleged Parliament had "a right to tax subjects" in America "without the consent of [their] representatives," he viewed his role primarily as one to "prevent unreasonable impositions on the people" he represented in Virginia's House of Burgesses.[13]

By November 1764, Lee had learned from a friend in London that, if Parliament did in fact levy a stamp act in the colonies, a stamp distributor would be appointed by the Crown for each colony. As compensation, the stamp distributor would receive a percentage of the total revenue collected from the tax. In anticipation of these events transpiring, Richard Henry sent an inquiry to a friend in London asking his correspondent to advance his name for consideration as Virginia's stamp distributor. If he could secure this appointment, it would more than make up for being denied a seat on the Council; unfortunately, his action would soon come back to haunt him. Shortly after Lee dispatched his letter to his London friend, he resumed his duties in the 1764 session of the House of Burgesses; the possibility of a stamp act was the topic of several angry conversations in Williamsburg. In December, Lee found himself on a committee that drafted a memorial to the King George III warning of potentially dire consequences if Parliament posed direct taxes on Virginia. Once the burgesses had finished this work, they adjourned, setting May 1, 1765, as the date for their next gathering.[14]

Lee returned to Chantilly-on-the-Potomac and tended to plantation business. Before the House met again, news had arrived that Parliament had enacted the Stamp Act in March 1765. As May 1 arrived, Lee remained at home and did not attend the new session, and a new member of the House of Burgesses, Patrick Henry, dominated the debates against the Stamp Act. News finally reached Virginia that the Crown had appointed George Mercer as stamp distributor. Lee notified his London friend and gave thanks "for helping [him] to that collection"; however, he added that "it is very well that the appointment has passed me, since, by the unanimous suffrage of his countrymen [Mercer] is regarded as an execrable monster, who with parricidal heart and hands, hath concern in the ruin of his native country."[15]

While Richard Henry remained in Westmoreland County, he launched a protest of his own against the Stamp Act in September 1765. Lee led a procession to the county court house in Montross that consisted largely of his own slaves from Chantilly. Together, they paraded effigies of Mercer and George Grenville, who then served as Britain's lord of the treasury. Later, Lee published Mercer's "dying words" in the *Virginia Gazette*:

> for it is true that with parricidal hands I have endeavored to fasten chains of slavery on this my native country, although, like the tenderest and best of mothers she had long fostered and powerfully supported me. But it was the inordinate love of gold, which led me astray from honour, virtue, and patriotism.[16]

As these events transpired, Mercer arrived in Virginia to assume his role as stamp distributor, after spending several years in London representing the interests of the Ohio Company of Virginia. After Mercer arrived in Williamsburg, an angry crowd quickly gathered and forced him to resign the position. Governor Fauquier indicated in a letter to the Board of Trade that he would have called the gathering a mob had it not been "composed of Gentleman of property in the Colony some of them at the head of their Respective Counties, and the Merchants of the country."[17]

Initially, Fauquier refused to accept Mercer's resignation. As he later described his quandary to the Board of Trade, the governor noted that if he allowed Mercer to step down from his appointed office, he would have to appoint another; yet, he knew no one else would accept. Fauquier's resolve, however, had no bearing on Mercer's decision, and he turned to the crowd and announced that he would not carry out the duties of the office bestowed upon him by the Crown. The governor's fears were realized as no one stepped forward to assume the duties of stamp distributor; as a result, Mercer's resignation effectively ended the effort to implement the Stamp Act in Virginia.[18] Yet, for leaders of the opposition against the Stamp Act, until Parliament took official action, the legislation remained in effect, and some colonists vowed that they would obey the law in spite of Mercer's resignation.

One of Richard Henry Lee's neighbors in Essex County, Archibald Richie, was one of those who publicly proclaimed his intention of obeying the letter of the law until Parliament indicated he should do otherwise. Lee, and others who joined him in opposing the Stamp Act, realized if Richie succeeded in his endeavor, others might follow, but their protests would prove to be of no avail. Richard Henry and a coterie from Westmoreland County took the initiative by forming the Westmoreland Association in February 1766. Members drafted a set of articles of agreement providing the logic behind their efforts. One surviving draft, written in Lee's hand, stated that

> the Birthright privilege of every British subject, (and of the people of Virginia as being such) founded on Reason, Law, and Compact; that he cannot be legally tried but by his peers; and that he cannot be taxed, but by the consent of a Parliament, in which he is represented by persons chosen by the people. . . . The Stamp Act does absolutely direct the property of the people to be taken from them without their consent.

Consequently, members of the Westmoreland Association were determined without "regard to danger or death . . . to prevent the execution of the said Stamp Act in any instance whatsoever within this Colony." Richard Henry Lee and all of his brothers, with the exception of Philip and Arthur, signed the document along with an additional 110 signatories, vowing to fulfill the goals and objectives of the Westmoreland Association.[19]

Archibald Richie was the Association's first target. Four hundred men from Westmoreland and surrounding counties descended on Richie's plantation, Hobb's Hole. The crowd demanded that Richie issue a public apology for supporting the Stamp Act. If he refused, the crowd threatened to strip him to the waist, tie him to a cart, and parade him through the surrounding communities. Richie would then be strapped to the pillory for at least an hour—and if these actions still did not secure Richie's signature on the apology, he would be thrown into the Leeds Town jail to await further punishment. As he had to confront the hostile crowd, Richie's confidence and resolve withered away, and he read the following statement drafted by the Westmoreland Association:

> Sensible now of the high insult I offered the Country . . . I do most submissively in the Presence of the Public . . . shew my deep remorse for having formed so execrable a Design; and I do hereby solemnly Promise and Swear on the Holy Evangels, that no Vessel of mine shall sail Cleared on Stampt Paper, and that I never will on any Pretence make use of, or cause to be made use Stampt Paper, unless the Use of such Paper shall be Authorized by the General Assembly of this Colony.[20]

Richard Henry Lee and his fellow associates savored their victory over Archibald Richie, even more so as in the weeks that followed the incident at Hobb's Hole, news arrived that Parliament had conceded the point and repealed the hated Stamp Act.

Richard Henry Lee's role during the Stamp Act controversy in Virginia fueled much debate about his motivations among his contemporaries. In the months following the repeal of the Stamp Act, George Mercer's relatives publicly attacked Lee in the newspapers, revealing how he had applied for the stamp distributorship and charging him with leading the protests only because he failed to win the appointment. The editorials were most likely penned by John Mercer, and he signed the pieces with the telling pseudonym "An Enemy of Hypocrisy."[21] Within a week after these editorials appeared in the *Virginia Gazette*, Lee drafted his rebuttal in which he claimed that he had realized the error of his ways within days after submitting his application for the stamp distributorship, and from that day forward, he vowed to oppose any attempt to implement a stamp tax in Virginia.[22]

Richard Henry's defense, upon initial consideration, seems disingenuous at best; but, after careful assessment of Lee's commentary within the context of other events that were contemporaneous with the Stamp Act controversy, his explanation becomes more plausible. In the years immediately following the end of the French and Indian War, Parliament initiated several measures as part of a larger effort to more effectively manage Britain's imperial interests, and three of these measures presented specific challenges to Virginians like Richard Henry Lee and his associates.[23] The Proclamation of 1763 was among the first example, followed roughly two years later by the Stamp Act, which went into effect in August 1765. In between these two measures, Parliament introduced another piece of legislation as part of an attempt to address an infinitely more complex problem relating to the imperial economy—the Currency Act of 1764. The impact of this legislation was utterly devastating to planters like Lee, especially when taken in conjunction with the Proclamation of 1763 and the Stamp Act. These three measures, taken together, are crucial components that explain how Richard Henry Lee went from being a loyal advocate of British imperial interests to an American revolutionary leader. Within this milieu we can truly witness the making of a radical.

IV

The genesis of the Currency Act of 1764 came about as a result of growing pressure applied by British merchants on Parliament due to their growing concern over the unchecked emissions of paper money in the American colonies.[24] The fears expressed by the merchants intensified as the price of tobacco continued to plummet, which directed more scrutiny to tobacco-producing colonies like Maryland and Virginia. Ever since the first emission of paper money in Virginia in 1754, British merchants had lodged complaints in Parliament concerning the possibility that their American debtors would attempt to pay their outstanding sterling debts with colonial treasury notes. Virginians who advocated the use of the notes tried to alleviate the fears of British merchants, assuring them that they had levied enough taxes to cover the amount of money printed. Each emission of currency stipulated that once local authorities had collected the revenue through taxes, the paper money would be gathered and burned. Yet, in spite of these attempts to reassure the merchants, the Board of Trade generated a brief panic in February 1763 in Virginia when members announced that they were considering a plan to abolish all of Virginia's existing currency, a move that many Virginians feared would have the effect of destroying their local economy.

The reason the concerns expressed by British merchants were unabated was due to the persistent rumors that Speaker–Treasurer John Robinson, the man responsible for destroying redeemed currency, was quietly putting the money back into circulation in the guise of discreet loans to his friends and political allies. Stories along these lines had circulated for a number of years. In 1757, in an attempt to address the rumors, Virginia's Council of State mandated the immediate removal of all paper money from the treasury upon redemption. The Board of Trade, however, repealed the measure by determining that the Council had infringed upon the authority of the House of Burgesses as the originator of all money bills. As a result, the rumors continued unabated.

Members of the Council that supported the attempt to monitor currency redemption now had to rely on their like-minded colleagues in the lower assembly; at this juncture, Richard Henry Lee once again emerged in center stage. Each year, from 1760 to 1762, Lee and his allies in the House pressured Speaker–Treasurer Robinson to open his account books to examine Robinson's handling of paper currency. The speaker complied, albeit reluctantly, to these demands and selected a committee to survey the accounts. Robinson, of course, loaded the investigative body with close friends and allies, but for appearances sake, he did put Lee on the committee. Each year, however, the committee's formal report consistently ruled that there were no irregularities in the treasurer's books; yet, the rumors persisted.

The stakes in the controversy rose as the Board of Trade leaned more adamantly toward acquiescing to the demands of British merchants in 1763. If the Board took the extreme step of abolishing all of Virginia's paper currency as it indicated it might, the economic effects would prove devastating. The absence of specie in Virginia left the local economy completely dependent on paper currency. If the Board eradicated these funds, planters throughout the colony would go bankrupt. With this sort of threat hanging over their heads, planters in the House of Burgesses had to take decisive action and address these rumors to alleviate the concerns of British merchants and prevent the Board from taking action on this matter.

Richard Henry Lee was an obvious candidate to lead this clique of planters in the House, since he certainly was not a friend of Robinson's; and more important, since his family was actively involved in the tobacco trade on both sides of the Atlantic, he had unique insight regarding the fears expressed by British merchants relating to paper money. In May 1763, Lee gave an impassioned speech before the House in which he expressed a sympathetic voice to the fiscal worries of London tobacco merchants, stating that equating a debt of £10 sterling to £10 worth of paper money was in no way appropriate; but, Lee added, it would "be an act of the highest injustice, now to pass a law" banning the use of paper currency as legal tender in Virginia. Richard Henry defended the use of treasury notes during the French and Indian War and again emphasized that the House had levied taxes sufficient to retire the emissions in due order. At this point, Lee noted that disturbing discrepancies in the handling of Virginia's currency more than justified the concerns voiced by British merchants. He confirmed that the last five collections of paper money had revealed a disparity of £65,000 between the amount of currency collected by the treasury and the amount destroyed. Lee now demanded an accounting for the difference. He wanted to know the precise location of the money, and he insisted that Robinson explain why he had not completed his assigned task of destroying the currency as the law stipulated. Richard Henry dryly observed that a careful investigation would most likely reveal that the missing money would be found in circulation.[25]

Considering the gravity of the charges he had levied against the Speaker–Treasurer, Lee's speech justifiably generated a stir in the House. Lee's motivations for launching the attack have often been regarded as result for Lee's personal hatred for Robinson. The timing of the speech, however, makes it more likely that Lee's fear that the Board of Trade might actually end the use of paper money spurred him to action at that particular time. Recall that Richard Henry had participated in at least three investigations of Robinson's conduct, and each time, the committee exonerated the Speaker. Since these earlier investigative bodies were stacked with Robinson's allies, Lee's dissenting voice could have easily been muted. This may explain why Lee went public with his charges, because the committee system in the House had failed; and with the genuine threat to wipe out Virginia's currency possibly becoming real, Lee and his allies may have felt compelled to take some sort of action. As Lee noted in his speech, the "enormous deficiency [was] sufficient to alarm not only the merchants of Britain . . . but every thinking person."[26]

In May 1764, John Robinson appointed a committee of three, consisting of Richard Bland, Benjamin Harrison (both of whom were strong supporters of the speaker), and Richard Henry Lee. At this point, no one in the House could simply ignore the problem, which had apparently been the preferred course of action in the past. When the committee issued its final report, it confirmed the existence of a £40,000 shortfall in the treasurer's account books— but the committee, no doubt at the behest of Bland and Harrison, exonerated Robinson, blaming the discrepancy on minor officials.[27] The May 1764 report represented a last-ditch effort on the part of the House to stave off Parliamentary intervention, but their attempt came too late: Parliament enacted the Currency Act in April, a month before the latest investigating committee began its business. The measure forbade all emissions of paper money as of September 1, 1764, and through this sort of legislation, Parliament hoped to appease British merchants and ensure a more equitable foundation for trade between Britain and her American colonies.[28]

Initially, Richard Henry Lee accepted the Currency Act as a rational compromise that did have some beneficial effects for him, his family, and their transatlantic interests, especially since the measure did not affect paper money's current standing as legal tender in relation to public debts. The act stipulated that planters had to pay their private debts in specie. Lee had reason to believe that some of the more stringent aspects of the legislation regarding the printing of paper money might be alleviated if colonial legislatures could prevent abuses like those Robinson allowed. Soon after the Currency Act went into effect, Lee and many of his colleagues united and began issuing strident denunciations of the measure. What made the difference for men like Richard Henry Lee was that, about the time of the issuance of the May 1764 report on Robinson's conduct, he began to realize the full implications of the Proclamation of 1763. Lee and his partners in the Mississippi Company were still hoping to launch the business venture in the trans-Appalachian west and, by selling land to immigrants, still have a means of earning specie to pay off their outstanding debts. Once Lee began to understand the combined effects of the Proclamation of 1763 and the Currency Act, his animus toward Parliament's actions grew. Richard Henry expressed his temperament in one letter in which he observed "many late determinations . . . seem to prove a resolution to oppress North America with the iron hand of power."[29]

Lee's immediate reaction, however, was not to challenge Parliament's authority but to pursue Robinson with greater vigilance as if to prove that Virginia could take care of this sort of excessive abuse and lessen the need for Parliament's intervention in such matters. His problem at this point was that the House remained rigidly divided between those who remained loyal to Robinson and those opposed to the Speaker–Treasurer. Burgesses like Peyton Randolph, Edmund Pendleton, Carter Braxton, and Benjamin Harrison now closed ranks, displaying their support for Robinson. In exchange for their resolute loyalty,

Robinson continued making illicit loans to these men with paper money earmarked for destruction. Between 1764 and 1766, Robinson doled out another £20,000 in currency slated for burning.

As the 1766 session of the House of Burgesses began, Richard Henry Lee joined with friends from the Northern Neck—like George Mason, Landon Carter, and others—who did not share in the largesse of Speaker–Treasurer John Robinson. Lee and his allies steadily began building an anti-Robinson coalition that hopefully would break his hold on the House of Burgesses. Lee networked with other disgruntled planters, both large and small, through his involvement in the Westmoreland Association during the Stamp Act controversy. When the 1765 session of the House of Burgesses began, he broadened his base by connecting with Patrick Henry, a political firebrand who established his reputation in May 1765 by promoting a series of strongly worded resolutions denouncing the Stamp Act. Lee launched his new challenge against Robinson, first, by challenging the May 1764 report that exonerated the speaker from any wrongdoing, and then, by pressing other members of the House to demand another investigation of Robinson's conduct. This time, a new committee was established that consisted of eleven members led by Richard Henry, his younger brother, Francis Lightfoot Lee, and Patrick Henry. John Robinson's friends in the House now understood that they could no longer prevent the disclosure of the discrepancies in the treasurer's accounts. Soon after the inquiry began, Robinson became ill and died. The House named Robert Carter Nicholas as interim treasurer until new elections could be held. In an attempt to stave off a hostile report of Lee's committee, Nicholas produced an independent report that detailed a shortage of more than £100,000 in treasury notes, directly attributable to mishandling of public funds by John Robinson.[30] This massive debt now had to be absorbed by the late Robinson's estate, and it remained Edmund Pendleton's task, who served as the executor of Robinson's last will and testament, to collect the money from those who received loans from the speaker.

The disclosure generated a scandal of massive proportions as it revealed that several of Virginia's leading men had essentially taken illegal loans from Robinson using currency that was supposed to be destroyed. A list of names and the amounts they owed soon began circulating. William Byrd III, a member of the Council and one of the wealthiest men in the colony, owed the treasury £14,921. Others, such as Carter Braxton and John Mercer, also owed large sums of money that could only be paid if they liquidated portions of their estates, and since this information was in the public domain, they could no longer avoid public scrutiny and had to pay their arrears.[31]

In the midst of the Robinson scandal, John Mercer began publishing his editorials under the pseudonym "An Enemy of Hypocrisy," revealing Richard

Henry Lee's application for the position of stamp distributor back in November 1764. Mercer had several reasons for launching his newspaper war against Lee. One reason was certainly to exact some revenge for Lee's personal attack on his son George Mercer during the protests Lee led against the Stamp Act in Westmoreland County. Another reason most likely looked forward to the upcoming election for a new speaker–treasurer. Since Lee would be a likely candidate for the office, Mercer and his friends hoped to impugn Lee's integrity; perhaps they could even break Lee's association with Patrick Henry and others in the House that Governor Fauquier once described as the "hot, young, and Giddy Members."[32] Although Mercer's attack did temporarily put Lee on the defensive, in the end, his editorials had no effect on the election of a new speaker–treasurer.

Governor Fauquier watched these events unfolding in the House of Burgesses very closely. He informed the Board of Trade that Richard Henry Lee and Peyton Randolph, who then served as the colony's attorney general, were the two leading candidates for the post of speaker–treasurer, but others vied for the vacant seat, including Richard Bland and Robert Carter Nicholas. Fauquier made it known to the Board that he clearly favored Randolph over Lee and the others. He described Randolph as a person who "always used his endeavors to induce the Assembly to concur with me in all measures."[33] As Lee's prospects for winning the seat dwindled, he withdrew his name from consideration and endorsed Richard Bland; but his efforts were to no avail.[34] In the fall of 1766, the House of Burgesses elected Peyton Randolph to the Speaker's chair. Upon learning about Bland's defeat, Lee immediately revived the effort to separate the offices of Speaker and treasurer that he had launched in 1757 after winning his first election to the House. The bill that Lee sponsored to this end called for awarding the Speaker of the House an annual salary of £500 as compensation for the lost income that would follow the separation. The measure passed, and Lee now hoped to win the office of treasurer; however, he was disappointed once again as the House simply confirmed Robert Carter Nicholas as the new treasurer. The election results following the Robinson scandal angered Lee. From his perspective, those who were involved in the corruption were not only exculpated but rewarded by winning elections to higher offices.

Although Lee retained his seat in the House, these events nurtured a growing radical spirit in Lee that led to a greater willingness to challenge governmental authority—initially at the provincial level and later at the imperial level. The passages of the Proclamation of 1763, the Currency Act of 1764, and the Stamp Act in 1765 contributed to Lee's nascent radicalism. The evidence suggests that each of these measures taken alone did not bother Lee, but the combined effects proved devastating, not only to him but many other Virginians as well. Richard Henry's actions after the passage of the Proclamation of

1763 indicates a level of certainty that the measure would be temporary at best; consequently, it did not become problematic until after Parliament instituted the Currency Act. Even then, Lee still willingly accepted the Currency Act because he thought it applied only to private debts contracted between planters and merchants—an action that proved beneficial to the Lee family with their transatlantic commercial interests. It was only after Lee learned that the Currency Act also applied to public debts, such as taxes paid to imperial authorities, that put planters like Lee in an impossible situation; and the passage of the Stamp Act then proved to be the catalyst for action.[35]

Richard Henry Lee's role during the Stamp Act crisis was regarded by many of his contemporaries as paradoxical and hypocritical, that his public defense of his actions rang hollow. A careful examination proves that Lee's comments in the *Virginia Gazette* were a logical as well as accurate assessment of his situation in 1764 and 1765. When Lee submitted his application for the stamp distributorship in November 1764, he understood that he would no longer be able to earn specie through land speculation; yet, he needed the coin to pay the private debts he owed to British merchants because the Currency Act had already gone into effect. When Lee first heard rumors that Parliament might implement a stamp tax in the American colonies, Lee was still under the impression that he could pay taxes in paper currency since it was still regarded as legal tender. If he won the position of stamp distributor, then he would be able to earn specie as a result of fulfilling the duties of his office and continue paying his private debts. In the weeks that followed, Richard Henry realized that the terms of the Currency Act applied equally to private and public debts. At that point, the firebrand was ignited, and a political radical emerged: Lee assumed a very public role denouncing the Stamp Act after it went into effect in August 1765.

Initially, Richard Henry Lee attributed the reckless efforts of speculative ventures like the Loyal Land Company and their Pennsylvanian cohorts, who promoted their private interests at the expense of imperial objectives for the passage of the Proclamation of 1763. Additionally, Lee blamed the Currency Act on the financial abuses by those who recirculated paper money earmarked for destruction. Speaker–Treasurer John Robinson and his loyal supporters on the Council and in the House of Burgesses represented the common link between the two Parliamentary measures that had potentially devastating consequences for men like Richard Henry Lee. These factors explain the vehement attacks Lee launched as he led the efforts to dislodge the Robinson clique from power in 1766. Since Richard Henry failed in his attempt, he had to face the realization that he now had no hope of gaining any favors or patronage from Virginia's colonial governor because, as far as Lee was concerned, Fauquier was enmeshed in the scandal as much as the others. As a result, a sullen Richard

Henry Lee left Williamsburg, filled with invective and bitterness toward the provincial assembly, and returned to Chantilly-on-the-Potomac.

V

As a new year began, Richard Henry Lee sought new ways to establish the financial security he needed to provide for his immediate family and promote the transatlantic interests of his extended family that remained a powerful force in the politics and economy of Virginia's Northern Neck. The reality of the world in which Lee lived mandated that, without the patronage and support of prominent individuals, genuine opportunities were few and far between. Unfortunately for Richard Henry, he had burned too many bridges in Virginia as he took on leading roles during the Stamp Act crisis and the Robinson scandal. Since he could not find the desired help from his fellow Virginians, he began looking across the Atlantic to like-minded Englishmen, especially those who shared his opinions on the Stamp Act and Parliament's ability to tax the American colonies.

In June 1767, Lee began corresponding with Charles Pratt, Lord Camden—a prominent member of Parliament who delivered several speeches denouncing the Stamp Act. Lee lauded Camden as the "Patron of [America's] liberty" and asked if he would agree to sit for portrait that would serve as a "memorial to posterity."[36] Richard Henry began soliciting contributions from citizens of Westmoreland County to pay for the painting. Once he had collected approximately £100, Lee contacted his cousin Edmund Jenings, in London, to schedule an appointment for Lord Camden to sit for the portrait. Lee hoped that Jenings could secure the renowned portraitist Benjamin West as the artist, but by August 1768, the project had collapsed. Jenings informed Lee that he "had taken much pains . . . to obtain Lord Camden's portrait." Although Camden had apparently agreed to the terms, he failed to show when the scheduled day arrived, and he failed to set an alternative appointment as well.[37]

Undaunted, Richard Henry drafted another request, this time asking Jenings to try to arrange for William Pitt, Lord Chatham, who, like Camden, many colonists held in high regard for his public opposition to the Stamp Act. Jenings complied with Lee's request, but since Benjamin West was unavailable, he hired Charles Willson Peale as the artist, who was a young American painter then residing in England. Unfortunately, Pitt now lived isolated, refusing to speak or see anyone, including Peale.[38] The young artist, however, was unwilling to lose his commission, so he contacted a friend who once had an opportunity to sculpt a likeness of Chatham. Peale drew a sketch based on his friend's sculpture and used it as a model for Chatham's portrait.

Peale's finished portrait eventually became known as "The Allegorical Mr. Pitt," and when it arrived in Westmoreland County, a dramatic, if some-what comical, controversy ensued. Peale depicted Pitt dressed as an ancient Roman consul holding a copy of the *Magna Carta* in his left hand and point-ing to a statue of "Lady Liberty" with his right hand. Pitt's likeness appeared in the Banqueting House of Whitehall Palace—the same room that King Charles I had passed by on his way to the scaffold back in 1649. Those who viewed the painting recognized the allusions as an indication of what happens to monarchs who ignore the rights of their subjects. Lee received the painting of Chatham in May 1769 and sent a note to his cousin in England that it had "arrived in fine order, and [was] very much admired"; he did not, however, speak for everyone in the county.[39] Richard Henry had every intention of dis-playing the portrait in the Westmoreland County Court House in Montross. Unfortunately, the portrait stood eight feet tall and was too large for the build-ing, which conveniently provided those alarmed by the controversial allusions with a reason to tell Lee to take the painting away.

Richard Henry brought the portrait back home. When Philip saw the painting, he immediately demanded that it hang in Stratford Hall—a request that served only to antagonize the residual hostility that still existed between the two brothers as a result of ongoing disputes over Thomas Lee's estate. Richard Henry argued that since he led the effort and made the collections that funded the portrait, it should rightfully be displayed inside Chantilly-on-the-Potomac. The two brothers finally agreed to let the collective membership of the West-moreland Association decide the issue, and they agreed that Richard Henry and Chantilly should have the painting—but only with the stipulation that Stratford Hall would acquire the portrait at Richard Henry's death.[40]

Lee's efforts first to secure a portrait of Lord Camden and, later, Lord Chatham represented an attempt on his part to gain some sort of personal recognition in the eyes of these two powerful and politically connected men. Ideally, Richard Henry could secure their patronage and support as he sought to promote himself within Britain's imperial system, since in the aftermath of the Robinson scandal, he had no hope of new opportunities at the provincial level. Since Camden refused and since Pitt never actually sat for his portrait, Richard Henry failed to achieve his desired objectives, which served only to compound his frustrations; without patronage, he would have to be content as a member of the House of Burgesses. Lee was not satisfied with this state of af-fairs because he needed a salaried position so he could provide for his grow-ing family. His sense of desperation undoubtedly grew in the dark days he suf-fered through in 1768, as he had to deal with the injury to his left hand while hunting, the near deaths of his two sons, and the death of his wife of eleven years. In the wake of these events, Lee's interest in gracing courthouse walls with the portraits of distinguished Parliamentarians waned and his frustrations grew, but now his attention was increasingly turning toward the imperial government as well as Virginia's provincial assembly.

VI

The American victory celebrations that followed Parliament's repeal of the Stamp Act in March 1766 were short-lived. Within a year, Parliament instituted another series of taxes collectively referred to as the Townshend Duties, named after Charles Townshend, who briefly served as Britain's chancellor of the exchequer from August 1766 until his death in September 1767. These duties taxed glass, lead, painter's colors, tea, and paper imported into the American colonies. They were designed to collect £40,000 annually, which was to be used to pay military expenses in North America, including the full implementation of the Proclamation of 1763 as well as the fixed salaries of royal officers residing in the colonies. In Virginia, as tobacco prices continued on a downward slide, planters like Richard Henry Lee struggled to survive financially and still comply with the terms of the Currency Act. Lee emerged as a critic of the Townshend Duties, describing them to one correspondent as "oppressive . . . arbitrary, unjust, and destructive of that mutually beneficial connection [between Crown and colony], which every good subject would wish to see preserved."[41]

Colonists throughout North America shared the sentiments expressed by Richard Henry Lee. Soon after the Townshend Duties went into effect, John Dickinson from neighboring Pennsylvania authored what proved to be the strongest denunciation of the revenue measures, titled *Letters from a Farmer in Pennsylvania*. Dickinson's pamphlet won over a wide audience, and copies appeared in all of the American colonies. As the letters arrived in Virginia, Richard Henry read them with delight and quickly arranged for the publication of a Williamsburg edition of the letters. Lee wrote the preface to this edition, in which he took the opportunity to lambaste the economic relationship between Britain and America as an inherently unfair situation. He wrote that the combined effects of Britain's "exclusive trade to these colonies, and from the manner in which she [has] tied up our manufacturing hand," British merchants received all of the mercantile benefits, leaving colonists like Lee wallowing in debts that they can never pay off.[42] Lee's commentary provided only a brief hint of the level of his frustration, and as tobacco prices continued to decline, Lee became an active supporter of nonimportation agreements as a means to force Parliament to address their grievances.

After reading Dickinson's *Letters from a Farmer in Pennsylvania*, Richard Henry sent the Pennsylvanian a letter proposing the establishment of "select committees" dedicated to the facilitation of correspondence "between the lovers of liberty in every province."[43] Lee's suggestion, however, did not excite many people, including Dickinson. In the absence of formal committees of correspondence that Richard Henry advocated, he joined his fellow Virginians and assisted in efforts to launch an economic boycott of British-made goods in May 1769. Once the boycott went into effect, the verbal attacks leveled at the Townshend Duties were transformed into concrete action. The goal that supporters of the boycott strived to reach was the unequivocal revocation of all of the taxes initiated by Charles Townshend two years earlier. Northern Neckers like Richard Henry Lee, George Washington, and George Mason emerged as the more prominent advocates of nonimportation in Virginia. The boycott included all British manufactures, tea, and slaves from Africa and the West Indies, although small planters simply ignored the ban on slaves and surreptitiously evaded that provision of the nonimportation agreements.[44] Advocates of the boycott had both political and economic motivations. Politically, if the plan went according to schedule, Parliament would relent and repeal the hated Townshend Duties. Privately, the boycott gave those planters heavy with debt a good reason to reduce their spending while at the same time promote the growth of colonial manufactures. In the process, the large planters who also rented property to small tobacco growers hoped they could alleviate the burden of debt with which their tenants had to contend.[45] At this same time, Lee began writing the draft of his unpublished pamphlet titled "The State of the Constitution of Virginia," which not only offered advice on how to grow tobacco but also provided an argument to grant the tobacco colonies special dispensation in respect to British policies because of the important role tobacco played within the imperial economy.

Although the nonimportation agreements proved successful by securing the repeal of all the Townshend Duties, with the exception of the tax on tea in April 1770, planters like Richard Henry Lee had to suffer through dire economic times brought on by natural disasters. In August 1769, just a few months after the boycott had gone into effect, "a most dreadful hurricane" swept into the Chesapeake Bay, cutting a wide path of destruction. Contemporary accounts of the storm described it as the worst hurricane to hit the vicinity in over a century. The wind and rains leveled homes; demolished mills, tobacco storage, and inspection warehouses; washed out roads; and ruined entire fields of tobacco. Both Chantilly-on-the-Potomac and Stratford Hall sustained damage during the storm—Stratford Landing and its outbuildings in particular were almost completely destroyed. In December 1769, as an indication of the losses suffered by Richard Henry and his brother Philip, the House of Burgesses entertained a motion calling for the discontinuation of tobacco inspections at Stratford Landing, "where the warehouses have been lately entirely destroyed."[46] The House temporarily set the motion aside and did not render a vote. In May 1770, proponents of the measure had it reintroduced. This time, the House voted to allow time and public funds to facilitate repairs on Stratford Landing so that tobacco inspections could continue being conducted at that location.[47]

The Lees were obviously pleased to learn how the vote transpired in the House and, no doubt, worked hard with their political friends and allies in the assembly to maintain tobacco inspections at Stratford. Soon after the House resolved the issue, Richard Henry Lee took a leave of absence from his public duties and returned to his family at Chantilly-on-the-Potomac.[48] He did not resume his seat in Williamsburg until after the 1771 session. During his absence from the House, Lee most likely spent his time repairing the damage Chantilly sustained during the 1769 storm and helping Philip oversee the rebuilding of Stratford Landing. All the while, as a member of the Westmoreland Association, he maintained a vigilant eye monitoring the progress of the nonimportation agreement he and so many Northern Neckers endorsed. Although there is little reason to doubt that Lee was pleased to hear news announcing the repeal of the Townshend Duties, he had neither the time nor the inclination to celebrate. As he set himself to the task of rebuilding both his home and family in the months following the storm, as well as his marriage to Anne Gaskins Pinckard, he found his desired objectives increasingly at odds with the agenda for North America set forth by British imperial officials.

NOTES

1. R. H. Lee to James Abercrombie, August 27, 1762, *Letters*, 1:1.

2. George Washington to James Wood, July 1758, *The Writings of George Washington*, 39 vols., ed. John C. Fitzpatrick (Washington D. C.: Government Printing Office, 1931–1944), 2: 251–52. Hereafter cited as Washington, *Writings*.

3. R. H. Lee to [?], 1762, *Letters*, 1: 4.

4. R. H. Lee to Thomas Cummings, August 27, 1762, *Letters*, 1:2.

5. "The Mississippi Land Company Articles of Agreement," June 3, 1763, *The Papers of George Washington: Colonial Series*, 7 vols., ed. W. W. Abbot, Dorothy Twohig, et al. (Charlottesville: The University Press of Virginia, 1990), 7: 219–220. Hereafter cited as *Washington Papers*.

6. Royster, *The History of the Dismal Swamp Company*, 69–71.

7. Aubrey C. Land, "Economic Behavior in a Planting Society: The Eighteenth Century Chesapeake," *Journal of Southern History* 33 (November 1967): 481–82.

8. Gregory Evans Dowd, *A Spirited Resistance: The North American Indian Struggle for Unity, 1745–1815* (Baltimore, MD: Johns Hopkins University Press, 1992); Alvin M. Josephy, "The Wilderness War of Pontiac," *The Patriot Chiefs: A Chronicle of American Indian Resistance* (New York: Viking Books, 1968), 97–128; Howard H. Peckham, *Pontiac and the Indian Uprising* (Princeton, NJ: Princeton University Press, 1947), 92–110.

9. "The Proclamation of 1763," *American Colonial Documents*, 642–43.

10. Friedenberg, *Life, Liberty, and the Pursuit of Land*, 116–28.

11. Fauquier to the Board of Trade, February 13, 1764, *Official Papers*, 3: 1076–84.

12. George Washington to William Crawford, September 21, 1767, *Washington Writings*, 2: 468–69. For a more general, albeit brief, discussion of the reaction to the

Proclamation of 1763 in Virginia, see Eugene Del Papa, "The Royal Proclamation of 1763: Its Effect upon Virginia Land Companies," *Virginia Magazine of History and Biography* 83 (October 1975): 406–11.

13. R. H. Lee to [?], May 31, 1764, *Lee Letters*, 1: 5–7.

14. Merrill Jensen, *The Founding of a Nation* (New York: Oxford University Press, 1968), 97.

15. R. H. Lee to [?], July 4, 1765, *Lee Letters*, 1: 9.

16. Chitwood, *Richard Henry Lee*, 37–38.

17. Fauquier to the Board of Trade, November 3, 1765, *Official Papers*, 3: 1292.

18. Fauquier to the Board of Trade, November 3, 1765, *Official Papers*, 3:1292–96.

19. Chitwood, "The Association of Westmoreland," *Richard Henry Lee*, 239–40.

20. John Carter Matthews, "Two Men and a Tax: Richard Henry Lee, Archibald Richie, and the Stamp Act," *The Old Dominion: Essays for Thomas Perkins Abernathy*, ed. Darrett B. Rutman (Charlottesville, VA: The University Press of Virginia, 1964), 96–108.

21. "An Enemy of Hypocrisy," July 12 and 18, 1766, *Virginia Gazette*.

22. "To the Editor of the *Virginia Gazette*," July 25, 1766, *Lee Letters*, 1: 16–18.

23. In addition to the three measures mentioned, Parliament also passed the American Duties Act, better known in America as the Sugar Act in 1764; although this measure had important ramifications in New England and mid-Atlantic colonies, its impact on Virginia in comparison to the Proclamation of 1763, the Currency Act of 1764, and the Stamp Act was negligible. For more on the origins and implementation on the American Duties Act, see Anderson, *Crucible of War*, 572–80.

24. See Marc Egnal, *A Mighty Empire*, 215–26; Joseph A. Ernst, *Money and Politics in America, 1755–1775: A Study of the Currency Act of 1764 and the Political Economy of Revolution* (Chapel Hill: University of North Carolina Press, 1973); Jack P. Greene, *The Quest for Power: The Lower Houses of Assembly in the Southern Royal Colonies, 1689–1776* (New York: W.W. Norton, 1963), 245–49, 387–98; Bruce A. Ragsdale, *A Planter's Republic: The Search for Economic Independence in Revolutionary Virginia* (Madison, WI: Madison House Publishers, 1996), 43–68.

25. "Speech before the House of Burgesses," May 1763, "Selections and Excerpts from the Lee Family Papers," *Southern Literary Messenger* (February 1860): 134.

26. "Speech before the House of Burgesses," *Southern Literary Messenger*, 134.

27. Ernst, *Money and Politics*, 74–75. For the political ties between Robinson, Harrison, and Braxton, see Alonzo T. Dill, *Carter Braxton: Virginia Signer and Conservative in Revolt* (New York: University Press of America, 1983), 25–32; and Howard W. Smith, *Benjamin Harrison and the American Revolution* (Williamsburg, VA: The Virginia Independence Bicentennial Commission, 1976), 8–29.

28. "The Currency Act of 1764," *American Colonial Documents*, 649.

29. R. H. Lee to [?], May 31, 1764, *Lee Letters*, 1: 5–7.

30. Ernst, *Money and Politics*, 177–84. The 1765 audit of treasury accounts revealed that between 1755 and 1757, Robinson had loaned out approximately £20,000 in paper money slated for burning. Later, Robinson continued this activity, giving out an additional £60,000 by the end of 1763. The auditors covered up their discovery, and the shortage did not become public information until after Robinson's death in May 1766.

31. For a substantial but sympathetic discussion of the Robinson scandal and its aftermath, see David John Mays, *Edmund Pendleton, 1721–1803: A Biography* (Cambridge, MA: Harvard University Press, 1952).

32. Fauquier to the Board of Trade, June 5, 1765, *Fauquier Official Papers*, 3: 1250.

33. Fauquier to the Board of Trade, May 11, 1766, *Fauquier Official Papers*, 3: 1359.

34. Ernst, *Money and Politics*, 185–92.

35. Ragsdale, *A Planter's Republic*, 52–53.

36. R. H. Lee to Lord Camden, June 1, 1767, *Lee Letters*, 1: 22–23. For Camden's opposition to the Stamp Act, see *The Debate on the American Revolution, 1761–1783*, 3rd ed, ed. Max Beloff (Dobbs Ferry, NY: Sheridan House, 1989), 119–24.

37. Edmund Jenings to R. H. Lee, August 17, 1768, *Lee Memoir*, 1: 50–51. For Pitt's opposition to the Stamp Act and defense of colonial protests against the measure, see *Debate on the American Revolution*, 92–96 and 100–105.

38. Jeremy Black, *Pitt the Elder* (New York: Cambridge University Press, 1992), 273–76. For additional information regarding Peale, his painting, and his relationship with Benjamin West, see Kenneth Silverman, *A Cultural History of the American Revolution: Paintings, Music, Literature and the Theater in the Colonies and the United States from the Treaty of Paris to the Inauguration of George Washington, 1763–1789* (New York: Thomas Y. Crowell Company, 1976), 118–33.

39. R. H. Lee to Edmund Jenings, May 31, 1769, *Lee Letters*, 1: 51.

40. Eric Langford, *The Allegorical Mr. Pitt* (Montross, VA: Lawrence-Allen, 1976), 9. The portrait remained at Chantilly until Lee's death in 1794, when the executor's of his estate transferred it to Stratford Hall in compliance with the terms set in 1769. In 1821, the owners of Stratford Hall, who were no longer Lees, arranged to have the painting sent to the Montross Court House, which had a new building and could accommodate its large size. Today, visitors can view the portrait inside the Westmoreland County Historical Museum in Montross, Virginia.

41. R. H. Lee to "A Gentleman of Influence in England," March 27, 1768, *Lee Letters*, 1: 27.

42. R. H. Lee, "Introduction to the Williamsburg Edition of John Dickinson's *Letters from a Farmer in Pennsylvania*," *Writings of John Dickinson*, 2 vols., ed. Paul L. Ford (Philadelphia: 1895), 1: 292.

43. R. H. Lee to John Dickinson, July 25, 1768, *Lee Letters*, 1: 29.

44. Woody Holton, *Forced Founders: Indians, Debtors, Slaves and the Making of the American Revolution in Virginia* (Chapel Hill: University of North Carolina Press, 1999), 90–92; Ragsdale, *A Planter's Republic*, 69–109.

45. Holton, *Forced Founders*, 79–90.

46. *Journal of the House of Burgesses, 1766–1769*, edited by John Pendleton Kennedy (Richmond, VA: 1906), 322.

47. *Journal of the House of Burgesses, 1770–1772*, edited by John Pendleton Kennedy (Richmond, VA: 1906), 46.

48. *Journal of the House of Burgesses, 1770–1772*, 85.

The Decision for American Independence

I

$\mathcal{D}$eclining tobacco prices in the late 1760s heightened Richard Henry Lee's level of anxiety as he continued pondering the injury to his hand, the death of his wife, and his increasingly difficult financial straits. In May 1769 a despondent Richard Henry told his brother William of how he had been "so covered with affliction this past winter" that he "thought of little but his own unhappiness."[1] These problems were compounded as Lee also had to contend with the ongoing feud with his provincial political rivals in the colonial assembly, the threat of British taxation, and the additional burdened heaped on him and his family by Lee's active support of the nonimportation agreements made in the wake of the Townshend Duties.

II

During that contentious period in the late 1760s, Richard Henry and several other planters from the Northern Neck once again turned toward western lands for salvation during these desperate times. Ever since the Proclamation of 1763 had gone into effect, Lee shared the sentiments expressed by his friend George Washington that the pronouncement would be a temporary measure at best. Events in 1768 seemed to confirm this impression of British intentions regarding the future development of the trans-Appalachian region. Virginians readily received word that Sir William Johnson, one of Britain's deputy superintendents for Indian affairs, began a series of talks to renegotiate the boundaries of the lands claimed by the Six Nations of the Iroquois, and other tribes inhabiting the Ohio River valley at Fort Stanwix. More than 3,000 Native Americans attended the convocation with the intention of clarifying the borders between their lands and those claimed by Great Britain and her subjects. Johnson surreptitiously, however, also allowed a group of Pennsylvanian merchant–speculators to attend the conference, which arranged for the purchase of 2.5 million acres of land from the Iroquois at Fort Stanwix in direct violation of the stipulations found in the Proclamation of 1763. Samuel and Thomas Wharton of Philadelphia soon emerged as the chief financial backers of the Pennsylvania group. After the negotiated treaty at Fort Stanwix had been signed, Samuel Wharton left the colonies and traveled to London to secure parliamentary approval for the treaty in general and the land purchase in particular. News of the treaty and Wharton's arrival quickly sparked a flurry of activity and once again excited the interests of several resident agents representing American land companies.

Two agents in particular took interest in Wharton's arrival: George Mercer and Richard Henry Lee's youngest brother, Arthur Lee. After the Stamp Act protests forced Mercer to resign his commission as Virginia's stamp distributor, he returned to London, where he continued to work as the Ohio Company of Virginia's agent. Arthur Lee had taken on a similar role for the Mississippi Company. Before long, several different interested parties began rapidly moving in, hoping to capitalize on opportunities found through investing in American western lands. When Lord Hillsborough, Britain's secretary for American affairs, suddenly found his office besieged by so many competing and conflicting claims, he quickly announced a firm policy adhering to the terms of the Proclamation of 1763 and rejected all proposals and petitions submitted by American land companies. Once he learned about Johnson's complicity and how he allowed for the purchase spearheaded by the Whartons, Hillsborough flew into a rage denouncing Johnson's conduct. He wrote Johnson and told him that "obtaining so large an additional tract of land in that part of the continent" based only on "political and commercial principles" in the end would only serve to disadvantage and embarrass Parliament and the Crown.[2]

Hillsborough's wrath fell hard and fast on the hopeful prospects of the American land companies. In the end, he recognized the new territorial boundaries negotiated at Fort Stanwix, but he refused to sanction the land purchase; he followed this action by rejecting all of the petitions submitted by American speculators and by refusing to discuss the matter any further. Arthur Lee realized the futility of trying to get Hillsborough to reconsider his decision. He dispatched a letter notifying Richard Henry that the "Mississippi affair rests entirely, and must do so until the present ministry [is] removed." He added that, whenever Hillsborough vacated his office, he would resume his duties as land agent for the Mississippi Company as well.[3] Richard Henry Lee and other interested Virginians, however, refused to abandon their efforts to new financial opportunities in the American West. In December 1769, the House of Burgesses adopted a petition asking for the Crown's permission to annex Kentucky and all of the land north of the Kanawha River.[4] The Crown rejected their petition, and soon thereafter, Lee began agitating for the House to take more decisive action in promoting Virginia's interests in western lands. In June 1770, he sponsored a motion urging the provincial governor Norborne Berkeley, Lord Botetourt, to take independent action and negotiate an extension of Virginia's borders without involving imperial officials. The House, however, did not take action on Lee's motion, and Governor Botetourt communicated the mounting concerns of planters like Lee to Lord Hillsborough but did little beyond taking those steps. Consequently, the anger and frustration felt by Lee and his compatriots in the Northern Neck grew, and they soon began steadily chipping away at their allegiance to the British Crown.[5]

III

Samuel Wharton and his growing number of parliamentary allies proved to be the biggest source of consternation for Richard Henry Lee. After Hillsborough's decision to effectively shut down American land companies, Wharton adopted a somewhat innovative approach toward salvaging his interests in western lands. First, he approached influential members of Parliament and steadily began building a coalition, determined to bring an end to the Hillsborough ministry. He found that both Thomas Walpole, a prominent London merchant–banker, and Charles Pratt, Lord Camden, would stand with him as willing accomplices. Wharton won these two men over to his camp by liberally dispensing with several shares of stock in a new land company formed by Wharton and his Philadelphia investors—the Grand Ohio Company. Once Walpole and Camden signed on as shareholders in the new venture, they began increasing their influence among other members of Parliament as well as prominent leaders among London's merchant community. As a result of the combined influence organized under Wharton's direction, they were able to force the resignation of Lord Hillsborough, thereby clearing their path of a major obstacle that had prevented them from realizing their desired goal in the American West.

The next problem Wharton and his friends had to surmount was the strict wording of the Proclamation of 1763 barring American settlements and land purchases west of the Appalachian Mountains. Lord Camden now proved to be an indispensable colleague in the Grand Ohio Company's designs. Camden resurrected an old opinion he helped write back in 1757 in partnership with one of his old friends, Charles Yorke. The document concerned the distribution of territory the British had gained control over on the subcontinent of India during the course of fighting the Seven Years' War, and it soon became known as the Camden–Yorke Opinion. The missive stipulated that "in respect to such places, as have been or shall be acquired by treaty or grant from the Grand Mogul or any of the Indian princes or governments, your Majesties letters patents are not necessary, the property of the soil vesting in the grantees by the Indian grants." Camden now brought this document to the attention of William Trent, one of Wharton's American associates in London. Camden urged Trent to reprint the old Camden–Yorke opinion and omit the reference to the Grand Mogul. Since Yorke was already dead, Camden felt relatively safe in promoting this sort of manipulation of the document's language. Now, with the revised opinion supporting the Grand Ohio Company's desired objectives, Wharton and his compatriots felt they could now begin the process of purchasing land directly from Native American tribes with impunity, since Hillsborough's ministry had recognized the Treaty of Fort Stanwix back in 1768.[6]

As Wharton continued cultivating his associations with prominent parliamentarians, he also took another innovative step that entailed buying out his other American competitors. In 1770, Wharton began approaching George Mercer, who still resided in London and represented the interests of the original Ohio Company. He suggested that the two competitors merge their interests; Wharton also made the additional offer of giving all of the shareholders working with the Virginia-based land company two shares of Grand Ohio stock, and Mercer would receive a third share in recognition of his cooperation in setting up the proposed merger. Mercer readily agreed to these terms and joined Wharton's group. He felt more than justified in taking this action for several reasons; first and foremost, he genuinely thought he was acting in the best interests of the Ohio Company shareholders, since it seemed unlikely that abandoning the claims of the old Ohio Company in deference to Wharton's more organized group remained the only logical course of action to take.[7]

After Mercer had signed on with the Grand Ohio Company, by all accounts, Samuel Wharton had achieved a formidable corporation, one that was amply prepared to emerge as a dominant force in the transatlantic commercial traffic. On the American side, Wharton, in addition to his brother Thomas, had a litany of Philadelphia's most prominent merchants and community leaders. The list included Benjamin Franklin; Robert Morris and his partner, Thomas Willing; John Dickinson; and Joseph Galloway. Additionally, the Wharton group reached into Virginia and allied with the old James River faction once led by the late John Robinson. Men such as Benjamin Harrison and Carter Braxton, who were still in debt due to the fallout from the ruinous Robinson scandal of 1765–1766, joined William Trent and Patrick Henry, all of whom sought commercial opportunities beyond the mountains.

On the English side, Wharton found other powerful friends outside the halls of Parliament, as well as inside.[8] John Sargent II and his circle of merchant friends emerged as dominant members of the Grand Ohio group. Sargent inherited a prominent dry goods company from his cousin in 1751. He devoted much of his energy cultivating commercial ties on the continent in Germany and Portugal, but after 1763, Sargent and his friends joined with other prominent London merchants toward investing in the North American lands won from the French. At this time, Sargent and others like Richard Oswald became increasingly interested in American lands. Oswald had already tried his hand at operating a plantation in Florida, but that venture failed. By the early 1770s, he had his eye on opportunities in Nova Scotia; however, he also had struck a close friendship with Benjamin Franklin, who no doubt kept Oswald apprised of similar opportunities in the Ohio River valley.

The group of London merchants represented by men like Jonathan Sargent II and Richard Oswald were the remnants of the first English mercantile efforts dating back to the formation of the first charter companies in the mid-sixteenth century. As England reached outward toward the European continent for new commercial ties through the formation of the Muscovy Company, and later the Levant Company, those prominent merchants invested their personal fortunes to help secure for England an overland trade route to Asia. The failure of the Muscovy Company and the tight controls imposed on participation in the Mediterranean and Turkish trade by the men in charge of the Levant Company prompted other ambitious English merchants to seek new opportunities in the Americas. Thus, the Virginia Company came into existence. The wealthiest and most powerful English merchants, without hesitation, sought to exploit their commercial interests in America, Europe, and Asia; but as the expense of maintaining the American plantations increased while showing few prospects for profits between 1607 and 1624, many of the wealthiest merchants withdrew their investments from the Virginia Company and concentrated on their interests in the Mediterranean, the Levant, and India.

By the mid-eighteenth century the London merchant community had become increasingly interested in the transatlantic trade, initially through their active promotion of the African slave trade and, later, as the result of almost continuous warfare between Britain and France, as these merchants provided food, supplies, and other stores to the growing number of British soldiers fighting in North America between 1700 and 1763. By the time Britain had achieved its decisive victory over France in the Seven Years' War, merchants like Sargent and Oswald now hoped to extend their influence and dominate the tobacco trade as well. They planned to secure their objectives by establishing plantations in British America and by cultivating a mutually beneficial partnership with the already well-entrenched colonial–merchant community most heavily concentrated in Philadelphia. Once these London merchants could effectively dominate the tobacco trade on the American side, they also hoped to extend their influence into France—the single largest market for Chesapeake tobacco—by working closely with French Huguenot émigrés who still had commercial contacts on the continent. In contemporary language, merchants like Sargent and Oswald hoped to achieve the backward integration of the transatlantic trade. They would use their wealth and political connections to steadily increase their influence over the tobacco and slave trades; in essence, they would steal away the infrastructure that colonial families like the Lees of Virginia had taken generations to build. Sargent and Oswald found accomplices who were more than willing and able to help them in the guise of Samuel Wharton and his Philadelphia coterie.[9] The remaining difficulty, however, lay in the realization that there were many American planters and merchants who would not easily surrender their suzerainty and the commercial interests that they had developed over the course of the last century. As these two separate groups battled for control in the early 1770s, the contest soon blossomed into a test of allegiance either to the British Crown or an independent America.

IV

Richard Henry Lee had maintained a close association with other planters from the Northern Neck interested in Virginia's exclusive claims to western lands. As far as Lee was concerned, the terms of the 1612 charter remained inviolate and intact, which meant that Virginia retained undisputable title to the Ohio River valley. After he had learned about the duplicitous negotiations at Fort Stanwix and then experienced the failure on the part of the House of Burgesses to at least secure Kentucky, Lee became increasingly agitated. Since his father's death in 1750, Richard Henry had maintained a limited partnership with the Ohio Company of Virginia. Thomas Lee owned two full shares of stock; at his death, he left one full share to Philip and divided the one remaining equally among Thomas Ludwell Lee, Richard Henry, and Francis Lightfoot Lee. The Lees renewed their focus on Ohio Company interests as an entity that would allow them to retain at least a vestige of Virginia's claim to western lands in the wake of the actions taken by the Philadelphia-based merchant–speculators.

The situation grew more intense in August 1771, when George Mercer notified George Mason of Gunston Hall, who then served as the Ohio Company's treasurer, of his decision to merge the Ohio Company of Virginia with the Grand Ohio Company.[10] The news outraged Mason, who immediately began conferring with Richard Henry Lee's cousin Richard "Squire" Lee; the two men began leading the effort to nullify the merger. In July 1772, "Squire" Lee lodged a formal complaint against Mercer before Virginia's Council, noting that Mercer "had undertaken without their consent or Authority to make an Agreement of Copartnership" between the Ohio and Grand Ohio Companies. Richard Henry joined in with the efforts to defend the Ohio Company's interests. While Mason and "Squire" Lee dealt with the Council, Richard Henry sought additional information from his brothers William and Arthur, both of whom still resided in London. Later, Richard Henry expressed his frustration to William about his inability to "get further authentic intelligence about the [Grand Ohio] company."[11]

At the heart of the matter, as far as Lee and his compatriots were concerned, was their fear that, if Wharton and the Grand Ohio interests succeeded, then Virginia would lose its exclusive claim to western lands. Such a scenario, if realized, would prove devastating to Virginia's provincial economy on several levels. For great planters like the Lees, the loss of western lands would potentially wrest control of the tobacco trade out of their hands and place it in the hands of merchants in Philadelphia and London. Additionally, large planters in Virginia also sought to protect the interests of small planters, making it possible for them to continue growing the crop and allowing the merchant–planters to continue their active interests in the transatlantic trade. Without access to new western lands, men like Richard Henry Lee genuinely believed they would lose their entire way of life, a life carved out of the wilderness by their predecessors.

The instability of tobacco prices, however, made the agenda of Richard Henry Lee and other great Northern Neck planters harder to maintain. One central complication resulted from the reality that few planters had commercial contacts on both sides of the Atlantic, as the Lees had. Consequently, these planters found it increasingly difficult to get their tobacco to London merchants who would sell the crop on consignment. As the price of the plant fluctuated, the number of indebted tobacco planters who were so deeply in debt believed that they had little choice but to begin reaching out to prominent merchants in neighboring colonies for assistance. Men like Benjamin Harrison and Carter Braxton found willing accomplices in Philadelphia—most notably, Robert Morris who, by the early 1770s, had emerged as one of the most influential colonial merchants based in Philadelphia. The legacy of the Robinson scandal of 1765–1766 complicated matters still further. The financial crisis that men like Harrison and Braxton had to contend with resulted from the revelations made by Richard Henry Lee nearly a decade before, as both men found that they had to pay their outstanding debts to the Robinson estate; as a consequence, their animosity toward Lee continued unabated.

The developing alliance between a growing number of Virginians and the merchant–speculators of Philadelphia had the effect of further isolating Lee and his Northern Neck friends. As Richard Henry Lee became more alarmed about the threat posed by the Grand Ohio interests, the growing factional splits within Virginia prompted him to start reaching out to other disaffected individuals and groups in the colonies as a means to strengthen the position held by him and his associates. In February 1773, Lee initiated a correspondence with Samuel Adams of Massachusetts. Richard Henry's youngest brother, Arthur, worked as Massachusetts's colonial agent, and through this connection, Lee had learned of Adams's long struggle against perceived abuses of royal authority in that colony. As far as Lee was concerned, Adams seemed to be a likely candidate to help revive Lee's effort, beginning in 1768, to establish committees of correspondence.

Lee wrote to Adams inquiring about a group of rioters in Rhode Island who attacked and burned a British naval vessel, the *Gaspee*, in June 1772. Richard Henry's account, however, lacked sufficient detail, so he asked Adams to fill in the gaps. Lee commented on how "at this distance . . . we may never perhaps . . . receive a just account of the affair," so he requested that Adams write a brief description of the episode and send it to the House of Burgesses. He then expressed the hope that the assemblies in Massachusetts and Virginia would maintain a regular correspondence so that everyone in their respective colony could be informed of the latest news.[12] Two months later, Lee sent a similar request to John Dickinson in Pennsylvania, again expressing his hope that "every Colony on the Continent will adopt these Committees of correspondence and enquiry."[13] These letters clearly suggest that, as Lee learned that his provincial rivals in Virginia were reaching out to like-minded folk in neighboring colonies, he realized he had better do the same; and, at least with one of these correspondents, Samuel Adams, we can mark the beginning of what would become a formidable political alliance.

V

The Grand Ohio group, now known in London circles as the Walpole Company because of its strong identification with Thomas Walpole, was undaunted by the opposition to their agenda managed by George Mason and the Lees of Virginia. As the Grand Ohio Company consolidated its organization in London and Philadelphia, nothing seemed capable of stopping the juggernaut. In addition to men like Walpole and Lord Camden, Grand Ohio shareholders included prominent members on the king's Privy Council, members of the Pitt family, and Sir George Colebrook, who then served as the director of the British East India Company. The Walpole Company clearly had won the distinction as a global business enterprise in an advantageous position to effectively manage the commercial integration of the whole British Empire—a goal sought by imperial policy makers since the days of Cromwell and Charles II, when the first Navigation Acts were enacted by Parliament.

Once Wharton and his American friends and the British shareholders lined up, they began to more clearly define their objectives in North America. The Walpole Company petitioned the Crown for twenty million acres of land (adjusted later to thirty million acres), for which they would pay £10,460 sterling. If the Crown agreed to these terms, the goal of the Walpole Company sought to establish a new colony in America that they would call Vandalia. The Ohio River would be the proposed colony's northern border, the Cumberland Mountains and the Greenbrier River represented its southern border, and the Scioto River marked Vandalia's western boundary. The city of Pittsburgh would serve as the gateway into this new colony, as it stood at the northeastern corner of the Walpole Company's grand scheme. As the principal players hammered out these details, Samuel Wharton kept busy shoring up other American competitors, like George Mercer, thus removing the last vestiges of opposition to the designs of the Walpole group.[14]

The concentration of political and financial power found within the Walpole Company's organization, in many respects, represented a necessary adaptation to the reality of the transatlantic tobacco trade. Since the mid-seventeenth century, France represented the single largest market for Chesapeake tobacco.[15] As a means of promoting France's mercantilist interests, the French king Louis XIV awarded a monopoly on tobacco sales to prominent French merchants who demonstrated the necessary talents that would allow France to maximize its interests in the American trade. The resultant system led to the establishment of a single purchasing agent, who would reside in London and buy all of the tobacco at wholesale, which would eventually be sold at retail in France. Consequently, the French buyer effectively had the power to set the price of tobacco, and as the number of London merchants dealing in tobacco proliferated in the eighteenth century, the price of Chesapeake tobacco went on a roller-coaster ride—more often than not, to the detriment of the American planters.

As the number of wars between Britain and France increased, tobacco planters and the London creditors consistently held out the hope that France would abandon its monopolistic system of purchasing tobacco; but they were disappointed every time. Since the end of the War of the Spanish Succession in 1713, British merchants began to realize that the only way to effectively combat the French monopsonistic system was to develop a similar organization. When France lost its North American empire as a result of the Seven Years' War, even French tobacco interests had to marvel at the impressive degree of organization found within the Walpole Company, as indicated in 1769 when France appointed Thomas Walpole as the person responsible for buying the tobacco for the French market. If Walpole and his associates now succeeded in establishing the Vandalia colony, then they would effectively control the tobacco trade entirely—from planting all the way to sales and distribution, which had the effect of shutting out all of the remaining competition in the transatlantic tobacco trade.

VI

As Richard Henry Lee and his Northern Neck friends slowly realized the impact that the Walpole Company had on their livelihood, their efforts to prevent its success became more strident. The absence of reliable information was a constant source of frustration for those trying to block the Walpole Company's designs in America. Thomas Ludwell Lee dispatched an angry letter to James Mercer demanding answers to questions he had had about the Grand Ohio Company. He asked: "What benefits do the Grand Ohio Company propose to themselves? What progress have they made in the attainement of those ends? Have they actually obtained the grant from the crown?" The intense tone of the letter hinted at the degree of concern Thomas Ludwell had about the Grand Ohio Company. As he concluded the letter, he observed "a set of wealthy men acting in England upon a large scale, might very quickly exhaust the slender finances of a Virginia fortune."[16]

Thomas Walpole maintained an arrogant and dismissive tone toward the concerns expressed by Lee. Earlier, as he first began hearing rumbling from the Ohio Company of Virginia, he asserted that he and his associates did not propose to take lands from anyone who had "legal claim"; and, as one witness observed, Walpole laughed "at the Ohio Company's opposition."[17] Walpole's partners shared the disdain expressed by their leader as clearly seen by their actions in America. Samuel Wharton's brother Thomas, in Philadelphia, employed George Croghan as a company agent and provided him the necessary authorization to begin selling land that had been claimed by the original Ohio Company dating back to 1748. An advertisement soon appeared in the *Pennsylvania Gazette* announcing the availability of land parcels in the Ohio River valley.

News of this sort of activity launched by the Walpole Company served only to heighten alarm among Virginia's Northern Neck planters, who saw their future interests in the tobacco trade quickly dissipating—all of which had the effect of forcing men like Richard Henry Lee to seek out other disgruntled Americans who shared his mounting disgust toward British imperial policies in America. In the months following the *Gaspee* affair, the relationship between Crown and colonies steadily worsened. Richard Henry continued cultivating his ties with Samuel Adams in Massachusetts. He closely followed the events surrounding the infamous "Boston Tea Party" of December 1773 and voiced his concerns to Adams that "something material may happen [to Massachusetts] in consequence of the well deserved fate which befel the tea on your quarter"; then Lee requested a full accounting of the situation in Boston as quickly as possible from his friend in Boston.[18]

The destruction of the tea left Richard Henry in a quandary. Although he sympathized with his Massachusetts compatriots, he never once advocated the destruction of private property as a means of protest. Even in the midst of the Stamp Act crisis and the protests against the Townshend duties, Lee consistently supported boycotts and other economic measures as the most effective means to resist British policy in America. But, Lee recognized that if he were to effectively preserve Virginia's exclusive claim to the Ohio River valley, then he must reach out to other disgruntled colonists. Consequently, he lent his voice in support of the more radical tactics adopted by his Massachusetts brethren while he maintained a tamer approach to the problems in his own area by continuing to advocate policies of nonimportation and nonexportation.[19]

Soon, however, an ugly and potentially dangerous problem reared its head. The longer Virginians sustained their boycotts and embargos, the more difficult it became for small and large planters to pay their debts. Before long, merchants began employing the courts to secure money owed from the financially strapped planters. Lee and his allies began using information gathered through the committees of correspondence as a means to stir public opinion against British policies and as a justification to support an effort to shut down the courthouses, thus preventing their use in debt collections. In April 1774, the House of Burgesses had the responsibility of renewing a 1765 measure known as the Fee Act, which provided funds to the courts to conduct business, including the prosecution of law suits initiated by British merchants. Since the introduction of the Fee Act, burgesses regarded its renewal as a pro forma duty; this time, however, Richard Henry Lee and his friends in the House led an effort to kill the renewal, asserting that the bill "ought not be revived."

The resultant closure of the courts in Virginia served the interests of Lee and the Northern Neckers on several fronts. First, it alleviated the debt crunch on small planters, thereby preventing a potentially riotous situation from developing in the colony of the sort that had punctuated the recent histories of places such as Boston. Second, it allowed the small planters to continue supporting the nonimportation and nonexportation policies, since as long as the courts remained closed, they did not have to worry about debt collections and lawsuits. The chief opposition against the initiative shutting down the courts, of course, came from those Virginians allied with the Walpole Company. Edmund Pendleton drafted a report challenging the authority of the burgesses to shut down the courts in this manner; but Thomas Jefferson rebutted Pendleton, and the two opposing sides settled into a stalemate.

While Richard Henry Lee used his position in the House of Burgesses to resist the potential threat posed by the Walpole Company—by exerting economic pressure on British merchants with the goal of forcing them to recognize Virginia's longstanding claims—George Mason diligently pursued the same goal, asserting the primacy of the original Ohio Company's claims over those made by Walpole and his group. Mason prepared a pamphlet designed to nullify the merger launched by Samuel Wharton and George Mercer a few years earlier by gathering all of Virginia's previous colonial charters that proved that the Crown had given the old Virginia Company exclusive title to western lands stretching to the "South Sea."[20] While Mason sought to abrogate the merger, others in the colony with interests in western lands took more aggressive action—notably, Virginia's governor John Murray, Lord Dunmore.

Lord Dunmore assumed his duties as governor of Virginia in 1771, and he was soon attracted by the potential wealth gained through land speculation. By 1773, as a growing number of Virginians became convinced that the Vandalia colony was going to be realized, they became determined to aggressively stake their claim to western lands. They recalled their frustrated efforts a few years earlier to gain Parliament's recognition of Virginia's claim to Kentucky, and they resolved to pursue that objective by a more direct means. The Shawnee and their Kentucky hunting grounds became the target at the center of the controversy; in April 1774, as Richard Henry Lee helped lead the effort against the Fee Act, a group of frontiersmen attacked Shawnee encampments, beginning what is now known as "Dunmore's War," a short-lived conflagration that came to an end in October 1774.

The governor's motivations for launching his attack on the Shawnee have been suspect. Dunmore's strongest critics have determined that he initiated the war for his own narrowly defined economic interests. More than likely, Dunmore was driven to act by those Virginians desperate to defend their claims to western lands against the Pennsylvanian cohorts of the Walpole Company. Evidence to this effect is found in a resolution adopted by the Virginia Convention in March 1775, extending the following accolade to their beloved governor:

> the most cordial thanks of the people of this colony are a tribute justly due our worthy Governour, Lord Dunmore, for his truly noble, wise, and spirited conduct, on the late expedition against our Indian enemy; a conduct which at once evinces his Excellency's attention to the true interests of this colony, and a zeal in the executive department, which no dangers can divert, or difficulties hinder, from achieving the most important services to the people who have the happiness to live under his administration.[21]

These heartfelt sentiments would soon disappear as the differences between Crown and colony mushroomed into a full-blown war.

VII

As Richard Henry Lee led the effort against the Fee Act and as Dunmore prepared for military action to defend Virginia's claim to western lands, the situation for Lee's friends in Boston steadily worsened. Lee's portent about "something of consequence" happening as a result of the destruction of 342 chests of tea in Boston Harbor came true. Beginning in May 1774, Parliament began implementing punitive measures against Boston for the "Boston Tea Party," collectively known as the Coercive Acts by the British; but from the American perspective, they were regarded as the "Intolerable Acts." Three bills were instituted as a means of asserting Parliament's control over the recalcitrant Bostonians. The first two measures that went into effect were the Administration of Justice Act and the Massachusetts Government Act; and the combined effect extended direct royal control over every aspect of colonial administration. The first prohibited the trying of those accused of committing capital crimes while aiding the government in provincial courts. Instead, they would be tried in another colony or taken back to England. The second, for all practical purposes, annulled the existing colonial charter for Massachusetts. A third measure, which went into effect on June 1, 1774, closed the Port of Boston until restitution had been made for the destroyed tea.

The Bostonians were, of course, outraged by the passage of these measures, and the Boston committee of correspondence drafted a circular letter to be sent to all of the colonies, urging them to come to the aid of Massachusetts. The document made a stinging indictment of the punishment meted out by Parliament and warned that "this attack, though made immediately upon us, is doubtless designed for every other colony who will not surrender their sacred rights and liberties into the hands of an infamous ministry."[22] The Virginia House of Burgesses received its copy of the letter in the midst of the dispute over the Fee Act. The outrage expressed by a large number of the burgesses forced Pendleton and his allies to back off their attempt to reopen the provincial courts. Richard Henry Lee then took the initiative to call for a day of fasting and prayer, demonstrating their sympathy and support for their Massachusetts brethren.

Lord Dunmore, although sympathetic to Virginia's claim to western lands, could not permit this perceived rebuff directed at royal authority in the colonies. Consequently, he dissolved the House of Burgesses and refused to call new elections, moves that effectively shut down the lower assembly. The attempt on the governor's part to defend the integrity of the royal government, however, actually played into the hands of the growing radical element that Lee helped lead. The dissolution of the House brought an immediate end to the session without resolving the dispute over the Fee Act, which meant the courts would remain closed until new elections were called. The burgesses vacated the capitol building in Williamsburg and convened a short distance away inside Raleigh's Tavern. Lee and his compatriots launched a vitriolic attack on Parliament for implementing the "Intolerable Acts" and called for regular communications between the colonies. Later, in a letter to his brother, Richard Henry used somewhat descriptive language to explain the need for committees of correspondence. He wrote that since the "dirty Ministerial stomach is daily ejecting its foul contents upon us," it was necessary for "friendly streams of information . . . to wash away the impurity."[23]

Richard Henry's comments reflected an uncompromising tone that had been developing, since it began to seem that parliamentary leaders were conspiring with Philadelphia merchants to strip away Virginia's 1612 charter claims to western lands. Lee now seemed prepared to advance and pursue a more concrete objective and establish a course of action that disgruntled colonists could promote. He prepared a series of resolutions and was about to submit them to the House of Burgesses when Dunmore dissolved the House. These measures, if adopted, would confirm Virginia's solidarity with their Massachusetts brethren in the wake of the passage of the Coercive Acts, and it would also challenge every parliamentary measure affecting the colonies, dating back to 1763. He urged his colleagues to appoint delegates to meet and "consider and determine on ways most effectual to Stop the exports from North America and . . . such other Methods as shall be most decisive for securing the Constitutional rights of Americans against the Systematic plan formed for their destruction."[24] Lee had his resolutions in hand when Dunmore sent them packing; nonetheless, he confidently believed that they would have passed had he not been "prevented from offering them by a great many of worthy members wishing to have the public business first done."[25] Much to Lee's delight, once the defrocked burgesses gathered in Raleigh's Tavern, they determined to convene an extralegal convention to meet at the beginning of August 1774, which would consist of the colony's most prominent political leaders.

VIII

What angered Richard Henry Lee more so than anything else was the passage of the Quebec Act in May 1774, which adjusted the colonial boundary of Quebec southward to the Ohio River. The measure not only affected Virginia but all colonies that had claims to western lands, including Massachusetts and Connecticut. The Quebec Act, in Lee's mind, set the stage for Virginia to lose its title to the Ohio River valley yet still allowed for the Grand Ohio Company to exploit their interests in the West. Lee no doubt shared the sentiments expressed earlier by George Washington about the Proclamation of 1763 and believed that it was only a temporary measure at best. Now, once Parliament had an opportunity to readjust the borders in North America, rather than restore Virginia's ancient claim, they opted to give the territory to Quebec. News of the Quebec Act had the effect of galvanizing the Virginians and hardening their resolve to take decisive action.

Once the Virginia Convention gathered on August 1, 1774, Richard Henry Lee and the others in attendance all proclaimed their loyalty to King George III; then they moved on to their first order of business. They proceeded to adopt twelve proposals, one of which called for a complete ban on all trade with Great Britain until Parliament had addressed all American grievances. The convention indicated that these complaints would be formalized, "defined and settled at the general congress of delegates for the different colonies" scheduled to meet in Philadelphia.[26] A week later, the convention appointed seven emissaries to represent Virginia in what would become known as the First Continental Congress. The list of delegates included Richard Henry Lee, George Washington, and Patrick Henry. They were joined by several of Lee's old political rivals from the days of the Robinson scandal, including Peyton Randolph, Edmund Pendleton, and Benjamin Harrison.

Lee and his colleagues arrived in Philadelphia at the beginning of September 1774. Richard Henry made a strong impression on several delegates from other colonies. John Adams described Lee as a "masterly man" and was genuinely impressed with how vigorously he opposed Parliament's handling of colonial policy. Adams noted in his diary that "Lee is for the Repeal of every Revenue Law, the Boston Port Bill, the Bill of altering the Massachusetts Constitution . . . and the Removal of all Troops from Boston"; in other words, Lee advocated the repudiation of every law passed by Parliament within the past year.[27]

A few days later, Lee sponsored a motion calling for an end to the importation of all British-made goods as of December 1, 1774.[28] Lee's motion angered many delegates in attendance. Joseph Galloway of Pennsylvania soon emerged as one of Lee's most outspoken critics and functioned in Congress as a spokesman for the Whartons, and others who had ties with the Grand Ohio Company. Galloway rejected the nonimportation agreement as "undutiful and illegal." He elaborated on his views by observing that "if we will not trade with Great Britain, she will not suffer to trade with us at all. Our ports will be blocked up by British men of war, and troops will be sent to reduce us to reason and obedience."[29]

Galloway proposed what he called a "Plan of Union," designed to secure greater autonomy for the colonies in areas relating to trade and taxation while at the same time recognizing the sovereignty of the king and Parliament. He suggested that Parliament should continue regulating colonial trade, but Galloway believed that this sort of arrangement would be impossible to secure if the Congress adopted the extreme measures advocated by Lee and his cohorts. Upon hearing Galloway's proposal, Richard Henry repudiated the system, suggesting that it would "make changes in the Legislatures of the colonies [and] that [he] could not agree to it, without consulting with [his] constituents."[30] Lee simply refused to support any scheme that allowed Parliament and the king to retain the authority implicit in Galloway's plan. Lee and his allies soon prevailed and successfully tabled Galloway's Plan of Union; they then, once again, turned Congress's attention to the matter of nonimportation.

Richard Henry Lee's hard-line stance against Galloway's plan reflected his view that, if Parliament's authority over the colonies remained unchecked, then the Quebec Act would remain unchallenged. He remained a vocal opponent of the Coercive Acts and believed that if this glaring abuse of power stood, then it would serve only to invite the same sort of treatment on the other colonies in the future; but Richard Henry always maintained that the Quebec Act was by far the "worst grievance." Once Galloway's plan was dispensed with, Congress appointed a committee to finalize the details for implementing a commercial boycott of British-made goods. Richard Henry served on this committee, along with Thomas Cushing of Massachusetts, Isaac Low of New York, Thomas Mifflin of Pennsylvania, and Thomas Johnson of Maryland. This committee established the Continental Association—a comprehensive agreement to prevent the sale of all British-made goods in American markets along with plans to ultimately end the exportation of American goods to British ports.[31]

The victory won by the advocates of a nonimportation agreement set the stage for a more uncompromising stance against British rule in America. Richard Henry Lee publicly maintained that he still wished to maintain the imperial connection between Crown and colonies, but only on the condition that Parliament repeal the Coercive Acts and the Quebec Act; in pursuit of that goal, Lee sponsored a series of resolutions that went far beyond the scope of his instructions from the Virginia Convention and thus stunned many of his colleagues. One of the most provocative measures Lee promoted called for the organization of militia forces and for Congress to provide these units with arms and ammunition.[32] Next, he sponsored a motion demanding the removal of all British troops from the city of Boston, and he urged the "free citizens of Boston no longer [to] expose themselves to the dangerous consequences of Military manouvres." Instead, he suggested that they "quit their town and find safe asylum among their hospitable countrymen."[33]

Lee's proposals served only to anger the advocates of reconciliation. Silas Deane of Connecticut noted that Lee's motion calling for militia training was "out of line of our business, and in degree a Declaration of Warr [*sic*]."[34] Consequently, lines in Congress were clearly drawn. Lee's strong defense of Boston in the wake of the Coercive Acts allowed him to work closely with John and Samuel Adams and to begin organizing opposition to any hint of reconciliation. Galloway and his Philadelphia friends fostered ties with Lee's political enemies from Virginia, notably Pendleton and Harrison, and he joined with other sympathetic members, such as John Jay of New York. When Congress began debating a list of grievances to send to King George III, the reconciliationists attempted to strike the Quebec Act from the proposed index. John Jay appealed to Congress, claiming that "if we demand too much we weaken our efforts [and] lose the chance of securing what is reasonable and may get nothing." Richard Henry Lee quickly responded by rejecting Jay's logic and asserting that the Quebec Act was the "worst grievance."[35] In reality, Jay tried to prevent the inclusion of the Quebec Act because he, along with Galloway, tacitly approved of the measure. If the new Canadian border remained at the Ohio River, then Virginia would indisputably lose its exclusive claim to western lands, yet the territory would still remain part of the British Empire. This scenario would give a distinct advantage to the Grand Ohio Company and their well-placed connections in Parliament. The success of the Grand Ohio Company in the fall of 1774, however, now hinged on the successful reconciliation between Crown and colonies.

The dispute over placing the Quebec Act on the list of grievances served only to widen the gap between the growing radical clique, led by Richard Henry Lee and the Adamses, and the reconciliationists. The arguments presented by John Jay heightened Lee's anxiety over the possibility of losing Virginia's claim to western lands, which only intensified Richard Henry's resolve to strike against British rule in America. The string of motions Lee proposed in October 1774 correlated closely with dramatic developments in the struggle for western lands. Not long after the First Continental Congress gathered, news arrived about a memorial sent from Thomas Walpole to King George III. Walpole, reacting to news about the Lord Dunmore's recent war, claimed that if the king did not immediately approve the Grand Ohio Company's grant and strip away Virginia's claims, then he must prepare for an Indian uprising. Reports about Walpole's memorial generated alarm and confusion in America as rumors flew about that the king had approved the grant. With this information in mind, Richard Henry Lee could not ignore the obvious duplicity, as the Crown stripped away the claims to western lands held by Virginia with one hand and then turned around and gave the land to another group of colonists with the other hand. From Lee's perspective, this situation smacked of corruption and conspiracy, and it presented another justification for his uncompromising stance against the king and Parliament. Toward the middle of October, as the atmosphere in Congress grew more tense, delegates began leaving Philadelphia and returning home, after deciding to meet again in May 1775. Those members of Congress who still served on active committees, like Richard Henry Lee, remained behind. Lee drafted a letter for one committee to American colonial agents abroad, informing them of the decisions made by Congress; he continued meeting informally with George Washington and John and Samuel Adams before returning to his wife and family at Chantilly-on-the-Potomac.[36]

IX

In actuality, unbeknownst to Richard Henry Lee and his friends, the Crown vacillated on Walpole's memorial and had not approved the land grant. The author of *American Husbandry*, however, reported that many colonists believed that the Crown had indeed approved the land grant. While representatives of the Grand Ohio Company waited in London for what they hoped would be a favorable response from the king, congressional delegates like Lee in Philadelphia became increasingly agitated. All the while, those in Congress sympathetic to Grand Ohio interests fought a desperate struggle to reconcile the differences between England and America.[37] As Galloway and his coterie prepared their efforts to reconcile the differences between Crown and colonies, Thomas Wharton busily worked behind the scenes to try to prevent the situation in Congress from getting completely out of control.

Even before the First Continental Congress met, the status of the Grand Ohio Company's designs on the Ohio River Valley had started to sour. Benjamin Franklin in London had proven to be a helpful ally toward promoting the Grand Ohio Company's goals concerning colonial expansion. Franklin had lobbied on Thomas and Samuel Wharton's behalf since 1768 while serving as one of Massachusetts's colonial agents. During his tenure in London, Franklin established close ties with several prominent members of Parliament and other notable Englishmen. In 1773, however, his reputation suffered a blow as the result of a scandal involving the private correspondence of Massachusetts's royal governor Thomas Hutchinson. Franklin sent a packet of Hutchinson's letters written in 1768 and 1769 to Thomas Cushing in Boston. As the letters circulated in public, they had the effect of fueling protests in Boston against imperial policies and royal authority.[38]

The revelation of Franklin's duplicity damned him in the eyes of Parliament. Before long, the situation began threatening the interests of the Grand Ohio Company. Consequently, in May 1774, Franklin notified Walpole and Wharton of his plans to resign his shares in the speculative venture. Wharton, however, revealed to Walpole that "when all's finished [Franklin] is to be rein-stated"; he added that he had said enough and that Walpole knew how the matter stood.[39] What motivated Franklin to distribute Hutchinson's private correspondence in this manner remains uncertain. We can only speculate that perhaps Franklin sought to curry favor among the more radical elements of Massachusetts's provincial government, and by vilifying Hutchinson and mak-ing him the principal target, then cooler heads would possibly prevail. In the end, all that remains certain is that the scandal enhanced Franklin's reputation among the disaffected elements in America and allowed him to return to the colonies, where he could assume a more public role as a staunch critic of British rule in America.

Thomas Wharton also understood that Virginia's 1612 charter claims rep-resented the Grand Ohio Company's most significant obstacle to overcome. George Mason's compilation of Virginia charters presented a strong case fa-voring the Old Dominion's exclusive title to western lands. To surmount this hurdle, Wharton realized that he had to find an agent, preferably a Virginian, willing to discredit Mason's argument, and he found one in Patrick Henry. While Galloway prepared his Plan of Union, Wharton secretly met with Henry in Philadelphia. According Wharton, Patrick Henry approached him, inquiring about purchasing some lands from Native Americans, and he indi-cated that he had learned that Wharton was the person to speak to regarding such matters.

While Wharton and Henry discussed the topic, Wharton broached the subject of the king's authority to authorize a land grant; he asked for Henry's opinion on the idea. Wharton asked the Virginian whether or not the Crown had the right to authorize the Grand Ohio Company's grant for the Vandalia colony, or was the territory "within the limits of Virginia"? Henry responded, stating that the "crown had an undoubted right to grant the territory of Van-dalia and that we should have no opposition he believed from Virginia." Whar-ton had found his ace. He wrote to Thomas Walpole in London and related the conversation to his benefactor. As Wharton closed his letter, he indicated "it will be best to keep this gentleman's name private, lest this free communi-cation should injure him."[40]

The actions taken by Thomas Wharton in Philadelphia and his frequent communications with Thomas Walpole in London reveal the sense of urgency these men felt toward the events in America. After being on the verge of com-plete success, they could readily sense how they would lose everything if the differences between Crown and colony could not be resolved. There is little reason to doubt that Wharton was less than pleased with the decisions made by the delegates attending the First Continental Congress, and he understood that, with the failure of Galloway's Plan of Union, they must be better prepared and better organized the next time around. As the colonies prepared for the next intercolonial gathering, Wharton and his merchant–speculator allies busily worked to select Pennsylvania's list of delegates, which included Benjamin Franklin (now back in America), Thomas Willing, John Dickinson, and once again, Joseph Galloway—all of whom were stalwart supporters of the Grand Ohio Company.

X

After Richard Henry Lee returned to Virginia once the Congress had finished its business, he maintained an avid interest in how well the Continental Association worked once it had gone into effect on December 1, 1774. Lee delighted in telling his friend Samuel Adams how "a ship from London . . . [had] been forced to return without being suffered to take on a hogshead of tobacco, because she had a few chests of tea."[41] As Lee monitored these activities, tragedy struck, when his oldest brother Philip died "after a few month's painful illness."[42] During his illness, Philip named Richard Henry as the executor of his estate. Since Philip's heir, Philip Lee II, was only two years old at the time of his father's death, Richard Henry became for all practical purposes master of Stratford Hall. In this capacity, Richard Henry made sure his widowed sister-in-law had all of her financial needs taken care of and that the business operations at Stratford Hall ran smoothly. At the same time, Richard Henry had to maintain the viability of the two full shares of Ohio Company stock that he now controlled as executor of his brother's estate—a situation that mandated his keeping a vigilant eye on the activities of the Grand Ohio Company and its Pennsylvanian backers, as well as his constantly monitoring the political developments within the British Empire.

By the time delegates began arriving in Philadelphia in May 1775, shots had been exchanged between British troops and colonial militiamen at Lexington and Concord in Massachusetts, thus marking the beginning of the War for American Independence. As Richard Henry Lee took his seat in Congress, he vowed "to resist [British policy] by all ways and to every extremity."[43] As business got underway, however, the majority of delegates sided with the Pennsylvanian delegation and favored a more determined effort toward reconciliation. Prior to the exchange of gunfire at Lexington and Concord, the head of Britain's cabinet, Lord North, hoped to close the breach between Crown and colony by sending forth a conciliatory gesture: He proposed that each colony legislate its own taxes and duties, but he added the corollary that any such legislation had to be "approved by his Majesty and the two houses of Parliament."[44]

Needless to say, the reconciliationists in Congress were ecstatic upon hearing the news, but Lee vehemently opposed Lord North's gesture. As each colony received a copy of North's proposal, Richard Henry advised the Virginia Convention to make "proper and spirited observations on the folly, injury, and insidiousness of the proposition" before referring the plan "to the united opinion of N. America in Congress."[45] By the end of May, a committee consisting of Richard Henry Lee, Benjamin Franklin, Thomas Jefferson, and John Adams issued a recommendation calling for the rejection of Lord North's gesture, stating that "we are of the opinion [that] the proposition is altogether unsatisfactory because it imports only a suspension of the mode, not a renunciation of the pretended right to tax us."[46]

The pronouncement, in many respects, strengthened the hand of the growing radical element in Congress. Thomas Jefferson, Patrick Henry, and Benjamin Franklin soon joined the ranks of Richard Henry Lee, and John and Samuel Adams; the American criticism of British rule became even more strident. The shooting war that raged in New England also added fuel to the fire as well. Richard Henry maintained a regular correspondence with George Washington, now serving as the commander in chief of the Continental Army, and he informed him that Congress had approved commissioning an additional 5,000 troops to assist in the fight against Great Britain. Lee assumed a larger role, monitoring the military effort against the British. He served on the Marine Committee, which appointed Silas Deane of Connecticut the task of purchasing a "ship suitable for carrying 20 nine pounders upon one deck" so that America could begin defending her shores.[47]

As Richard Henry Lee assumed a more active role in Congress by attacking British rule in America, he relied heavily on information he received from his brothers William and Arthur, both of whom still resided in England. William served as a sheriff in London and had achieved a high level of support among English political radicals. Arthur accomplished a similar goal, finding himself in the good graces of the radicals after writing a series of essays under the pseudonym "Junius Americanus" between 1769 and 1772.[48] The Lees of Virginia shared the opinion that resonated among English radicals that, if possible, the imperial connection between England and America should be maintained but that the tie between Crown and colony was part of a voluntary compact that could theoretically be dissolved.[49] While William and Arthur maintained a close association with the English radicals, Richard Henry reached across the Atlantic and began corresponding with those in England who shared his opinions. Catherine Macaulay was one notable English radical who drew Lee's attention after she had written a tract opposing the Quebec Act in 1775. After paying his respects for her advocacy of the American effort, he sent an enclosure reporting "how successful the cause of liberty has been in

Canada" and praising the efforts of Generals Richard Montgomery and Benedict Arnold against the British in Quebec.[50]

XI

While Richard Henry Lee fostered closer ties between English and American radicals, the reconciliationists in Congress fought hard to reunite Crown and colonies. As Lee and his group prepared their rejection of Lord North's conciliatory gesture, John Dickinson of Pennsylvania emerged as a leader of the reconciliationists. He understood that the longer the shooting war lasted, the more difficult reconciliation would be. Dickinson and his allies drafted another petition to the king, affirming their loyalty and begging George III to exert his royal authority to "procure us relief from our afflicting fears and jealousies" and allow for a "happy and permanent reconciliation."[51] Unfortunately for Dickinson and his likeminded cohorts, the king ignored the document and instead increased troop strength in the colonies, particularly in Boston. The king also declared that all who opposed British policy were rebels and no longer possessed the constitutional rights of loyal British subjects.

Dickinson and the reconciliationists angered radicals like Richard Henry Lee, so the radicals took delight in the reconciliationists' failure upon learning of the king's response. George III's position became more resolute in October 1775, when he announced to Parliament that "the rebellious war . . . [is] more general and is manifestly carried on for the purpose of establishing an independent empire."[52] These remarks gave Lee and John Adams all the incentive they needed to begin openly discussing a formal declaration of independence. By the end of November 1775, the two delegates began exploring the process of establishing new, individual state governments.

The situation became even more urgent for Lee and his Virginia colleagues. Lord Dunmore issued a proclamation that declared "all indented servants, Negroes, or others (appertaining to the Rebels) free, that are able and willing to bear Arms, they joining his Majesty's forces."[53] Dunmore proceeded to launch attacks on Norfolk and lead attacks against units of the Virginia militia, actions that had the effect of spreading alarm throughout the colony and strengthening the resolve of radicals like Richard Henry Lee. Dunmore's efforts to preserve royal authority in Virginia, as far as Lee was concerned, necessitated a formal declaration of independence. In April 1776, Lee noted that "we cannot be rebels" if we are "excluded from the king's protection and the Magistrates acting under his authority." Adding a sense of urgency to the situation at hand, Lee noted the "indispensable necessity of our taking up government immediately, for the preservation of society."[54] Later, he reinforced his argument in a letter to his friend and colleague Landon Carter, telling him that "it is not choice then, but necessity that calls for Independence, as the only means by which foreign Alliance can be obtained and a proper confederation by which internal peace and union may be secured." As far as Richard Henry was concerned, Britain was responsible for the breach between Crown and colony, effectively forcing the Americans to adopt a stance that was "contrary to our earnest, early and repeated petitions for peace, liberty, and safety."[55]

Soon afterward, a majority in the Continental Congress shifted in favor of the radicals and now agreed with Richard Henry Lee's assessment of the situation. Lee and John Adams secured congressional approval of a measure calling for each colony to establish its own separate government based on new constitutions that did not derive their authority from the Crown; this first crucial step led to a formal declaration of independence on June 7, 1776. On that day, the Virginia Convention instructed their delegates to introduce a measure calling for independence. Lee stood before Congress and presented the following motion:

> That these United Colonies are, and of right, ought to be, free and independent States, that they are absolved from all allegiance to the British crown, and that all political connection between them and the State of Great Britain is, and ought to be, totally dissolved;
> That it is expedient forthwith to take the most effectual measures for forming Alliances;
> That a plan of confederation be prepared and transmitted to the respective Colonies for their consideration.[56]

Congress postponed the debate on this resolution until July 1, 1776; but, in the interim, Congress authorized the formation of a committee—one that included Thomas Jefferson, Benjamin Franklin, and John Adams—to draft an official Declaration of Independence patterned along the lines of the Virginia resolution.

The tentative acceptance of the motion for independence was the result of the uncompromising stance adopted by Lee and his allies in Congress and the unbending resolve on the part of the king and Parliament to force the colonies to submit to the royal prerogative. Although Lord North's conciliatory gesture addressed the issue of taxation, it said nothing about the appropriateness of the Coercive Acts or the Quebec Act—the dual forces that united Richard Henry Lee and the Adamses in the first place. The adoption of the motion calling for independence now repealed all of the Coercive Acts and the Quebec Act in one fell swoop. Finally, Lee could turn his attention back to those issues that concerned him the most—preserving Virginia's exclusive claim to western lands and the formation of a new government in Virginia.

NOTES

1. R. H. Lee to William Lee, May 19, 1769, *Lee Letters*, 1: 35.

2. James Thomas Flexner, *Mohawk Baronet: A Biography of Sir William Johnson* (Syracuse, NY: Syracuse University Press, 1979), 330. See also by Peter Marshall: "Lord Hillsborough, Samuel Wharton, and the Ohio Grant, 1767–1775," *English Historical Review* 80 (October 1965): 717–39; and "Sir William Johnson and the Treaty of Fort Stanwix, 1768," *Journal of American Studies* 1 (July 1967): 149–79.

3. Arthur Lee to R. H. Lee, November 15, 1769, *The Life of Arthur Lee, LL.D.*, 2 vols. (Boston: Wells and Lilly, 1829; reprint, Freeport, NY: Books for Libraries Press, 1969), 1: 198.

4. Holton, *Forced Founders*, 4.

5. *Journals of the House of Burgesses, 1770–1772*, 74; Holton, *Forced Founders*, 5, 13–14 n. 16.

6. Thomas Perkins Abernethy, *Western Lands and the American Revolution* (Charlottesville, VA: University of Virginia Institute for Research, 1937), 116–17.

7. Alfred P. James, *The Ohio Company: Its Inner History* (Pittsburgh: University of Pittsburgh Press, 1959), 146–49.

8. The following narrative is based largely on David Hancock, *Citizens of the World: London Merchants and the Integration of the British Atlantic Community, 1735–1785* (New York: Cambridge University Press, 1995).

9. Hancock, *Citizens of the World*, 81–84.

10. George Mercer to George Mason, August 8, 1771, *Papers of George Mason, 1725–1792*, 3 vols., ed. Robert A. Rutland (Chapel Hill: The University of North Carolina Press, 1970), 1: 135. Hereafter, cited as *Mason Papers*.

11. R. H. Lee to William Lee, September 27, 1773, *Lee Letters*, 1: 97. In the actual text to the letter, Lee referred to the Grand Ohio Company as "Trent's company," a reference to William Trent, who still remained closely associated with Samuel Wharton and the Grand Ohio group in London.

12. R. H. Lee to Samuel Adams, February 4, 1773, *Lee Letters*, 1: 82–83.

13. R. H. Lee to John Dickinson, April 4, 1773, *Lee Letters*, 1: 84.

14. Friedenberg, *Life, Liberty, and the Pursuit of Land*, 121–26.

15. The following narrative is based on Jacob Price, *France and the Chesapeake*, 649–77.

16. Thomas Ludwell Lee to James Mercer, January 13, 1772, *Mercer Papers Relating to the Ohio Company*, 318–19.

17. Thomas Walpole to Osgood Hanbury, February 7, 1770, *Ohio Company Papers*, 311.

18. R. H. Lee to Samuel Adams, April 24, 1774, *Lee Letters*, 1: 107.

19. While residing in London in March 1774, William and Arthur Lee wrote to Richard Henry and others, urging them to withhold their tobacco crops from the English market. Richard Henry embraced this idea, and it became part of a larger program designed to stabilize an increasingly volatile situation in Virginia, as well as protest British policies in America. See Holton, *Forced Founders*, 115.

20. "Extracts from the Virginia Charters (annotated by George Mason)," July 13, 1773, *Mason Papers*, 1: 118ff.

21. Richard O. Curry, "Lord Dunmore and the West" in *The Old Northwest in the American Revolution: An Anthology*, ed. David Curtis Skaggs (Madison, WI: State Historical Society of Wisconsin, 1977), 83.

22. "Circular Letter of the Boston Committee of Correspondence," May 13, 1774, *American Colonial Documents*, 789.

23. R. H. Lee to Arthur Lee, June 26, 1774, *Lee Letters*, 1: 114.

24. R. H. Lee to Arthur Lee, June 26, 1774, *Lee Letters*, 1: 115 n. 1.

25. R. H. Lee to Arthur Lee, June 26, 1774, *Lee Letters*, 1: 116.

26. "The Association of the Virginia Convention," August 1–6, 1774, *American Colonial Documents*, 794–95.

27. *Diary and Autobiography of John Adams*, 2: 120.

28. *Journals of the Continental Congress, 1774–1789*, 34 vols., ed. Worthington Chauncy Ford (Washington D.C.: Library of Congress, 1905), 1: 14, 23. Hereafter, cited as *Journals*.

29. "Joseph Galloway's Statement on his Plan of Union," September 28, 1774, in *Letters of Delegates to Congress, 1774–1789*, 18 vols. (to date), ed. Paul H. Smith (Washington D.C.: Library of Congress, 1976–), 1: 122–23. Hereafter, cited as *Letters of Delegates*.

30. John Adams, "Notes of Debates," September 28, 1774, *Letters of Delegates*, 1: 111.

31. *Journals*, 1: 53.

32. "Richard Henry Lee's Proposed Resolution," October 3, 1774, *Letters of Delegates*, 1: 140.

33. "Richard Henry Lee's Proposed Motion for Quitting the Town of Boston," October 7–8, 1774, *Letters of Delegates*, 1:160–61.

34. "Silas Deane's Diary," October 3, 1774, *Letters of Delegates*, 1: 138.

35. "James Duane's Notes of Debates," October 15–17, 1774, *Letters of Delegates*, 1774.

36. Letter of Congress to Colonial Agents, October 26, 1774, *Lee Letters*, 1: 125–26.

37. *American Husbandry*, 203–4; George E. Lewis, *The Indiana Company, 1763–1798: A Study in Eighteenth Century Frontier Land Speculation and Business Venture* (Glendale, CA: The Arthur H. Clark Company, 1941), 147–49.

38. Andrew S. Walmsley, *Thomas Hutchinson and the Origins of the American Revolution* (New York: New York University Press, 1999), 143–44.

39. Thomas Wharton to Thomas Walpole, May 2, 1774, "Selections from the Letter-Books of Thomas Wharton of Philadelphia, 1773–1783," *Pennsylvania Magazine of History and Biography* 33–34 (1934): 330–31. Hereafter cited as "Wharton Letter-Books."

40. Thomas Wharton to Thomas Walpole, September 23, 1774, "Wharton Letter-Books," 446.

41. R. H. Lee to Samuel Adams, February 4, 1775, *Lee Letters*, 1: 127.

42. R. H. Lee to Arthur Lee, February 24, 1775, *Lee Letters*, 1: 130.

43. R. H. Lee to William Lee, May 10, 1775, *Lee Letters*, 1: 134.

44. "Lord North's motion on reconciliation with the colonies," February 27, 1775, *American Colonial Documents*, 839–40.

45. R. H. Lee to Francis Lightfoot Lee, May 21, 1775, *Lee Letters*, 1: 136.

46. "Rejection of Lord North's motion on reconciliation by the Second Continental Congress," July 31, 1775, *American Colonial Documents*, 841.

47. [The Marine Committee] to Silas Deane, August 1, 1775, *Lee Letters*, 1: 145–46.

48. Louis W. Potts, *Arthur Lee: Virtuous Revolutionary* (Baton Rouge: Louisiana State University Press, 1981), 73–81.

49. Colin Bonwick, *English Radicals and the American Revolution* (Chapel Hill: University of North Carolina Press, 1977), xvii–xviii.

50. R. H. Lee to Mrs. [Catherine] Macaulay, November 29, 1775, *Lee Letters*, 1: 163.

51. "The Second Petition to the King," July 8, 1775, *American Colonial Documents*, 849.

52. "The king's speech to Parliament," October 26, 1775, *American Colonial Documents*, 851.

53. Dunmore's Proclamation, quoted in Selby, *The Revolution in Virginia, 1775–1783* (Williamsburg, VA: The Colonial Williamsburg Foundation, 1988), 66.

54. R. H. Lee to Patrick Henry, April 20, 1776, *Lee Letters*, 1: 177.

55. R. H. Lee to Landon Carter, June 2, 1776, *Lee Letters*, 1: 198.

56. "The Virginia Resolution for Independence," June 7, 1776, *American Colonial Documents*, 867–68.

· 6 ·

Business and Politics

I

$\mathcal{S}$oon after Congress passed Virginia's motion calling for American independence, Richard Henry Lee made preparations to leave Philadelphia and return to Virginia. Lee expressed little interest in helping to draft a formal declaration of independence; that task was left to a committee that included John Adams, Benjamin Franklin, and Thomas Jefferson. Richard Henry's attention was already focused on matters that directly affected Virginia's most immediate problems—specifically, the scheduled appearance before the Virginia Convention of representatives of the Grand Ohio Company, who were seeking to promote their interests in western lands. Lee had received letters from his brother Thomas Ludwell Lee and from George Mason urging him to return to Williamsburg as quickly as possible. At one point, Mason pleaded with his compatriot (and echoed a sentiment that surviving members of Richard Henry's family would later repeat), telling him that "we cannot do without you," adding that Thomas Nelson had been sent to Philadelphia as Lee's replacement.[1] With this information in hand, Richard Henry made arrangements to leave Philadelphia. He informed George Washington of his plans to return to Virginia, noting that, if the general needed any assistance, to direct his queries to him in Williamsburg.[2]

Richard Henry Lee had little time on his hands. Mason informed Lee that the delegation from the Grand Ohio Company was scheduled to appear on June 24 to present their claim to western lands in hopes of securing permission from the Convention to begin selling tracts of land in the Ohio River valley. By the time that day finally arrived, Lee was back in Williamsburg and safely ensconced among his friends. Although the Grand Ohio group had a few allies in the Convention, the majority in attendance feared that if Virginia did not assert its exclusive claim to western lands as defined by the 1612 charter, then they might lose it. Consequently, with this possibility in mind, the Convention refused to recognize the Grand Ohio Company's claim and went further still by negating all direct land purchases from Native Americans. In the aftermath of the decision by the Virginia Convention, many prominent members of the Grand Ohio Company took their losses and withdrew from the organization. In February 1777, Thomas Walpole informed Benjamin Franklin that

> Mr. [Samuel] Wharton having signified to me by letter that in the present unhappy situation of Affairs in America he apprehends he cannot be of further Application to the Government for lands on the River Ohio, he therefore finally closed his Account on the 17th August last against myself & Associates.[3]

There were others who also abandoned the Grand Ohio Company and hastily reorganized another venture under the older name of the Indiana Company. Wharton and others who advocated the goals of the Grand Ohio Company realized that Virginia's decision regarding the status of their claims changed every single aspect of the debate over western lands. The decision for independence forced land speculators to regroup in order to adapt to the changing situation, as the center of power in America swung away from Parliament to the newly forming state governments. These developments reveal that although Richard Henry Lee and his allies had won an important battle, the war for control of western lands was far from over.[4]

II

Once the Virginia Convention had rendered its decision on western lands, members turned their attention toward drafting a new state constitution. Richard Henry Lee endorsed a model of government that he worked on with George Wythe, a plan that was based on a short essay written by John Adams entitled *Thoughts on Government*. As early as November 1775, Lee and Adams met and discussed potential problems relating to state government formation, namely, the concerns expressed by many members of Congress that the effort to establish new state governments would prove to be too disruptive—and these were the same individuals, of course, who remained staunch advocates of reconciliation between Britain and America. These were the concerns that John Adams attempted to address in his brief pamphlet.[5]

Richard Henry Lee shared Adams's sentiments that the most preferable system of government was one based on Virginia's colonial charter with the appropriate deletions in reference to the authority of Parliament and the king of Great Britain. Lee and his allies, then, were not seeking dramatic change; they merely wanted to shift the focus of power away from the Crown and place it in the hands of a locally based governing authority—one that would allow them greater influence over the day-to-day management of affairs concerning Virginia. In April 1776, Lee sent a copy of *Thoughts on Government* to Governor Patrick Henry, telling him that "the business of framing government [is not] so difficult a thing as most people imagine." He urged Henry and others serving as members of the Convention to adopt a plan of government modeled on Adams's essay.[6]

Lee began circulating copies of the proposed state constitution for Virginia, which he began drafting along with Wythe as early as May 10, 1776. The Richmond newspapers printed an article Lee wrote under the title "A Government Scheme." The proposed plan consisted of seven items that established the state legislature as the center of power and authority in the state. This scheme provided for a bicameral legislature. Property holders residing in the state elected members of the lower house, and after the elections, the lower house would then appoint members of the upper house. A combined vote of these two assemblies would determine who would serve as governor for a one-year term, and a separate tally would name those individuals who would serve on the governor's advisory council. Additionally, the state legislature appointed all other executive officers—including judges, the lieutenant governor, and treasurer. The plan allowed for the governor to select the justices of the peace and sheriffs, who would then be confirmed by his advisory council; however, the governor alone designated officers of the state militia and regulated military affairs.[7]

Richard Henry Lee intended for this proposed plan of government to counter the more aristocratic ideas advocated by other prominent members of the Virginia Convention, and for this reason, "A Government Scheme" sparked a controversy. One reader of Lee's article scribbled in the margin of his copy the following remark: "the choice in the people seems the basis of freedom . . . it is at the same time the worm [which] must destroy the happiness [which should] proceed from freedom because nothing [is] so easily corrupted as an ignorant Man."[8] Others serving as members of the Convention shared the views expressed by this individual, and they found a voice in Carter Braxton, one of Lee's old political enemies from the days of the Robinson scandal and an active supporter of the Grand Ohio Company's interests.

At the same time Lee submitted his article to the Richmond papers, Braxton began circulating his own proposed state constitution. It shared some structural similarities with Lee's. For example, Braxton's plan allowed for a representative assembly that, once convened, would elect a governor and an upper house; but that is where the similarities ended. Braxton's plan stipulated that once the lower assembly appointed the governor and the upper house, they should hold their offices for life, so they, according to Braxton, "might possess all the weight, stability, and dignity due to the importance of their office."[9] A full understanding of the competing plans of government advocated by Lee and Braxton cannot be achieved if divorced from the concurrent dispute over western lands. Braxton clearly threw his lot in with the Grand Ohio Company by urging his readers to hear the arguments of the Pennsylvania-based organization "fairly and impartially"; and, in a blatant attempt to promote Grand Ohio Company interests, Braxton submitted copies of a pamphlet written by Samuel Wharton called *A View to the Title of Indiana* as a sort of appendix to his proposed plan of government.[10]

After reading a copy of Braxton's proposal, Richard Henry Lee dismissed it by calling it a "contemptible little tract."[11] However, it was the widespread circulation of Braxton's proposal that explains Lee's rapid departure from Philadelphia after Congress heard Virginia's motion for independence. As the questions over Virginia's new state government were addressed, much to Lee's delight, the Convention adopted a plan similar to the one he advocated. Richard Henry informed one correspondent that Virginia's new plan of government was "very much of the democratic kind."[12] Now, with this battle won, Lee and his allies went about the business of consolidating their power within the perimeters of Virginia's new state constitution.

III

The Virginia Convention's denial of the Grand Ohio Company's petition and its rejection of Carter Braxton's plan of government heightened a growing factional split in Virginia, which would continue to grow and eventually infect the Continental Congress. Proponents of the now defunct Grand Ohio Company had to regroup. After abandoning their old name in favor of the Indiana Company, they found a new champion in Robert Morris. Morris emerged in the early 1760s as the organizational genius behind one of Philadelphia's most prominent trading houses, Willing and Morris. Morris, and his partner Thomas Willing, made their fortunes by shipping a variety of American-made goods across the Atlantic to British ports and by importing British products into the growing American market. The successes of Willing and Morris brought the owners of the firm into close contact with the leaders of Pennsylvania's provincial government as well as with prominent Londoners like Thomas Walpole.

Tobacco still reigned as the most valued commodity in transatlantic commerce at this stage, and Morris steadily increased his enterprises by securing new clients in Virginia and Maryland and by gaining more influence over the American end of the tobacco trade. Willing and Morris would then ship the tobacco to London and work closely with Walpole, who served as France's primary buyer of Chesapeake tobacco. Consequently, Morris established a transatlantic commercial triangle, with Morris based in America, Walpole in Britain, and a wealthy and powerful merchant in France, Jacques-Donatien Leray de Chaumont; in fact, Benjamin Franklin operated as a go-between for these three men. Morris, Walpole, and Chaumont sought ways that would allow them to effectively dominate not only the tobacco trade but also the American fur trade. Consequently, their combined interests led to their active pursuit of western lands in North America.

Morris's involvement with the Grand Ohio Company had its origins with a close business relationship he had with another prominent Philadelphia merchant, John Baynton. When the Grand Ohio Company first formed in 1768, Baynton emerged as one of its principal officers. When Baynton died in 1774, he left his Grand Ohio stock to Robert Morris. As the company façade began breaking down between 1774 and 1776, and following the resignation of Samuel Wharton, Morris emerged as the one with effective charge of the newly reorganized Indiana Company, just as the American colonies proclaimed their independence. Capitalizing on his transatlantic connections with Walpole and Chaumont, Morris set about the task of making the Indiana Company a viable entity once again.[13] Additionally, Morris regarded his close association with the Indiana Company as an opportunity to establish new commercial markets with Spain via New Orleans and the Ohio River valley. Unfortunately for the Philadelphia merchant, Virginia's exclusive claim to western lands remained the primary obstacle obscuring Morris's grand vision.

Benjamin Harrison and Carter Braxton worked as Morris's principal agents in Virginia. Harrison's son worked as an apprentice at Willing and Morris, and a profitable relationship between Morris and the elder Harrison blossomed. Braxton also had a close commercial affiliation with Willing and Morris, both in the areas of trade and land speculation. Under the leadership of Robert Morris, Harrison and Braxton assisted Indiana Company in its pursuit of the same vision of the old Grand Ohio Company, but that goal could not be achieved until Virginia's exclusive claim to western lands had been successfully challenged. Merchants throughout the fledgling nation flocked to Morris's banner, united in the effort to break the Old Dominion's hold on the West and foster commercial ties with their European counterparts.

The dispute that began developing between these two factions centered primarily on the efforts of the original Ohio Company of Virginia's policy of not soliciting new members by selling shares of stock. As a result, Virginians and other Americans desirous of speculative opportunities in the West who were not members of the original company were denied access and, hence, had few options but to try to break the Ohio Company's monopolistic claim to the Ohio River valley. Philadelphia merchant–speculators offered significant enticements to those Virginians, like Harrison and Braxton, in exchange for their cooperation toward opening access to western lands; to that end, they proffered lucrative financial opportunities in a myriad of other commercial ventures launched by the firm of Willing and Morris.

IV

Richard Henry Lee and other Virginia advocates for the Ohio Company interests could readily see that, because of the involvement of the Pennsylvanians and other outsiders, the growing factional dispute would soon extend its reach into Congress. Lee, his two brothers Thomas and Francis Lightfoot, and George Mason led the dominant faction in Virginia's state government, and they worked hard to influence the list of the state's congressional delegation. As the House of Delegates elected members to serve as part of the state's congressional delegation on June 20, 1776, for the 1776–1777 congressional session, Lee and his allies carried the votes, sending both Richard Henry and Francis Lightfoot to Congress along with Thomas Jefferson, Thomas Nelson, and George Wythe—all of whom supported Virginia's exclusive claim to western lands. Harrison and Braxton were conveniently dropped from the list.[14] At the same time, this sort of political maneuvering allowed Thomas Ludwell Lee and George Mason, both allied with Governor Patrick Henry, to dominate affairs in Williamsburg, as Richard Henry left for Philadelphia in charge of his state's congressional deputation.

As Lee resumed his seat in Congress, he found Robert Morris and Benjamin Franklin in their places as leaders of the Pennsylvanian delegation. Once the new session got underway and members turned their attention to the business of the new nation, they began to debate the nature of the new American government now that independence had been declared. During the previous congressional session, John Dickinson of Pennsylvania had submitted a draft proposal of a new national constitution called the Articles of Confederation and Perpetual Union. Dickinson's draft was completed and transcribed in the official *Journals of the Continental Congress* on July 12, 1776. Dickinson clearly sought to establish a strong, centralized government that would eclipse the localized authority of the new state constitutions. Richard Henry Lee, immediately after taking his seat, lodged his objections to Dickinson's proposed plan, especially a provision found in Article 13 that gave Congress the authority to set the boundaries of those states "which by Charter or Proclamation, or under any pretence, are said to extend to the South Sea."[15] Lee and his allies recognized the statement for what it was, an attempt to dispossess Virginia of its charter claim to the Ohio River valley. In an effort to combat Dickinson's proposal, Lee and the like-minded members of the Virginia delegation forged an even stronger link with the New England radicals led by John and Samuel Adams and found that they had enough influence to effectively dominate the agenda before Congress, much to the chagrin of Robert Morris and his allies.

V

Proponents of the Indiana Company's interests quickly realized that they would lose as long as Richard Henry Lee and New England allies dominated Congress. What alarmed Robert Morris even more was that the growing influence of the Lee family in particular posed a direct challenge to a variety of his business ventures stretching across the Atlantic into Britain and France; and as business and politics became more entwined, Morris and Richard Henry Lee were soon on a collision course that would allow for only one victor. At the same time, however, both men understood that they had to work together toward preserving American interests while dealing with the military confrontation between British and American forces. Yet, one simply did not trust the other, a situation that made seemingly routine congressional duties matters of intense controversy. Many of these conflicts revolved around tasks fulfilled by the Committee of Secret Correspondence, which handled sensitive communications between Congress and American diplomats and commercial agents stationed abroad. Tensions between Lee and Morris mounted as Congress sent agents overseas, some of whom were allied with the Virginian, and others with Morris and his group.

Silas Deane from Connecticut soon emerged at the center of controversy that would eventually reduce Congress to a squabbling rabble. In February 1776, Congress appointed Deane as a commercial agent representing American interests in Paris. Congress charged Deane with the authority to borrow money from French sources and purchase supplies that could no longer be reliably secured from the British. At the same time that Deane served Congress in this capacity, he was also employed as a proxy for Willing and Morris. Robert Morris hoped that Deane's efforts in Paris might not only secure needed supplies for America but would also provide new business opportunities for his trading firm. Additionally, since Morris already had contacts in France and an infrastructure in place to facilitate the shipment of those supplies, any potential conflict of interest was easily overlooked.

Benjamin Franklin joined Deane in Paris the following September as the American commissioner to France. Congress promoted Deane to the rank of commissioner as well and, in December 1776, sent Thomas Morris (Robert's half brother) to France to replace the vacant position of commercial agent. Consequently, by the end of 1776, Robert Morris had several close allies placed in prominent positions, which not only allowed for a secure supply line of needed materials but also allowed Morris to directly profit from the activity. Thomas Morris shifted the American commercial base of operations from Paris to Nantes, a northwestern French coastal town, where he could work more closely with Jacques-Donatien Leray de Chaumont. In February 1777, Franklin's nephew Jonathan Williams arrived in Nantes to begin serving as another trade representative for the United States in France.

The placement of Franklin, Deane, Thomas Morris, and Williams represents the emergence of an American diplomatic corps that was strongly influenced by Robert Morris, a situation that is easily understood due to the Philadelphian's prominence as a merchant.[16] Once the shooting war with Great Britain began and after Congress declared American independence, the influential role played by the Lees of Virginia could not be overlooked or easily denied. Additionally, William and Arthur Lee's residing in London at the time of these events made it advantageous for Congress to assign them important diplomatic roles as well. Congress sent Arthur Lee to Paris, where he took his place as a third American commissioner alongside Franklin and Deane. Soon afterward, William Lee received his appointment as a commercial agent and moved to Nantes to take his place with Thomas Morris and Jonathan Williams. Unfortunately for the new nation, the collective impact of these appointments was to allow the factional splits in Congress to be transferred across the ocean to Paris and Nantes.

Chaumont exacerbated the situation when he invited Franklin and Deane to take up residence in his chateau, Passy, near Paris. The French merchant's home provided more than adequate facilities, which allowed the Americans to conduct business and entertain distinguished guests as they sought to build support for the American effort in France. Unfortunately, Chaumont's invitation to Arthur Lee could be described as lukewarm at best, so the Virginian declined and took a room in a Paris hotel instead. As the Americans established their respective residences, the close ties between Franklin, Deane, and Chaumont became stronger, as did their mutually shared disdain for Arthur Lee.[17]

The appointment of William Lee, however, proved to be the most immediate cause of concern for Robert Morris and his associates. Morris informed Deane of William's pending arrival and informed him that another mutual friend, John Ross, would soon arrive in Nantes. Ross's task was to survey all of the documents in Thomas Morris's possession concerning the activities of Willing and Morris. The Philadelphia merchant told Deane that if Ross should find "my Brother to have been faulty . . . get from him all letters & papers that regard the Public or my own business together with a Power of [attorney] from my Brother to Act in his name and behalf."[18] The only logical reason for this sort of request on the part of Robert Morris would be to prevent these documents from falling into the hands of William Lee, who would no doubt turn them over to his older brother in Congress, Richard Henry Lee. Morris, however, also understood that this sort of cat-and-mouse game could not continue indefinitely, and as long as both Morris and Lee worked together on the Committee for Secret Correspondence, the risk of discovery could not be ignored.

VI

As far as Robert Morris was concerned, his primary problem was Richard Henry Lee's continued presence in the Continental Congress. If Lee lost his seat, then the Lee–Adams junto would likewise be broken, and the balance of power in Congress would tilt in favor of Morris and his group. As the winter of 1777 drew to a close, Morris and his associates sought ways that would prevent the Virginia House of Delegates from reappointing Lee when his term expired. To this end, Morris relied heavily on his Virginia allies Benjamin Harrison and Carter Braxton to target Lee. Additionally, Morris worked with John Hancock of Massachusetts, who then served as president of Congress, but as a wealthy merchant, he readily cast his lot in with Robert Morris.

As early as February 1777, rumors soon began circulating that Richard Henry Lee along with Samuel and John Adams were weakening America's military efforts against the British by calling for the removal of General George Washington as the Continental army's commander in chief. In April, Patrick Henry alerted Richard Henry to the situation, telling Lee "you are again traduced by a certain set . . . who say that you are engaged in a scheme to discard Genl. Washington." Shortly thereafter, Samuel Adams commented on a story circulating in Massachusetts that involved him in a similar conspiracy against Washington. Adams dismissed the rumors, accurately characterizing them as scurrilous reports spread by John Hancock and Robert Morris.[19]

These rumors were designed to serve a political purpose, not to abrogate a reported plot against Washington. Morris and his allies hoped to capitalize on New England's growing disdain toward Washington's rather dismal performance on the battlefield while casting aspersions on Lee's loyalty toward his fellow Virginian. In this manner, the goal of circulating such stories was to divide Richard Henry Lee and his New England allies by trying to force Lee to rise and defend his friend George Washington and thus alienate and distance him from the general's New England detractors. Other rumors that were prevalent at the time reinforce this agenda, as Lee soon found himself on the defensive, accused by unnamed persons of favoring "New England to the injury of Virginia." Lee described such stories as "contemptibly wicked" words spoken by the "poisonous tongue of Slander." Yet, despite these protestations, the stories had an impact, as a haggard Richard Henry Lee dared his political enemies to "produce a single instance" that would prove their assertions.[20]

Richard Henry Lee's opponents, however, did not stop at merely accusing him of trying to force Washington out as commander in chief; they went further by accusing Lee of deliberately trying to undermine the value of Virginia's wartime currency and possibly cause an economic crisis by refusing to accept paper money as payment for rent from his tenants. As with the most persistent rumors, there was an element of truth behind this particular charge, but it was in no way as insidious as Lee's enemies made the situation seem. One of the most serious problems that renters had to face at this time was the limited flow of cash in local economies. As rent collectors employed by Lee reported, they visited the homes of his tenants only to discover they could not pay their rents because they could not sell their crops. In an attempt to address this problem, Lee provided his tenants with a new rental agreement that allowed them to substitute tobacco or wheat in lieu of the £5 rent payment. Lee believed that these terms favored all parties concerned and would "prevent the multiplicity of law suits, which would be exceedingly disagreeable to me, and very hurtful to the Tenants."[21] Since Lee, however, maintained such a prominent role within Virginia's political and social system, his critics charged that others might follow his example and adopt similar practices, thereby further weakening the local economy.[22]

Once again, Richard Henry found himself on the defensive. He reiterated that his only motivation for revising his tenant contract was simply that his tenants could not pay their rents "because they could not sell their produce." Lee believed that he followed a suitable course because he was in a better position to get his tenants' crops to markets; therefore, his collectors could collect tobacco or wheat instead of cash, and all accounts would be settled. As the scandal intensified, Lee sent a plea to Governor Henry, stressing that his desired goal was to "prevent my total ruin, and at the same time be not injurious to" his tenants. He added that he sent a Mr. Parker, one of his rent collectors, to reveal the changes in the contract with his tenants, and there did not seem to be any controversy as a result of the changes. Lee emphasized, once again that "it was evidently better for me to get something than nothing."[23]

The new agreement between landlord and tenant did not provoke any problems in January 1776, when they took effect, but a year later his political opponents interfered with the collections and fomented a rent strike. In January 1777 Joseph Blackwell, another rent collector employed by Lee, reported that "a great impediment in collecting your debts has been owing to a sett of Vile men who have undertaken to Asperce your Charictor and telling your Tenants and others that you Indevour . . . to deprecate the Vallue of paper currency."[24] Unfortunately, Blackwell did not identify the "vile men," but more than likely they were the same "certain set" that Patrick Henry warned Lee about a few months later in April 1777, when they spread rumors that Lee sought to replace Washington as commander in chief.

Much to Richard Henry Lee's dismay, the stories had an impact, and as the House of Delegates held congressional elections for the 1777–1778 session, Lee's name was dropped from the list. As news of this reached Philadelphia, Richard Henry arranged for his immediate departure to return to Virginia and defend his name and reputation in person. Lee's enemies in Congress could barely contain their glee upon hearing the news. William Duer of New York, one of Morris's allies, wrote that "the Chaste Colo. Lee will I am credibly informed be left out of the new Delegation for Virginia which is now in agitation. The mere contemplation of this Event gives me Pleasure."[25] As far as Lee's political opponents were concerned, the situation continued to improve. In reaction to the news that Richard Henry had lost his seat, Francis Lightfoot tendered his resignation as well. Now, no Lees were left in Congress to assist the New England radicals or interfere with Robert Morris's commercial activities in France.

Once he returned to Chantilly-on-the-Potomac, residents of Westmoreland County promptly elected Lee to the legislative assembly, where he demanded an immediate investigation of the charges lodged against him. Witnesses to these events observed that Lee provided an eloquent defense on his behalf and was justly exonerated. Some of his political opponents had to give Richard Henry credit. John Bannister indicated that, although "he was not fond" of Lee, he nonetheless considered the charges made against Lee a "flagrant act of injustice, and a precedent dangerous in its nature."[26] George Wythe, who then served as the Speaker of the House of Delegates, issued a formal apology to Richard Henry Lee and sponsored the following motion:

> Resolved, That the thanks of this House be given by the Speaker, to Richard Henry Lee, Esq., for the faithful service he rendered to his country, in discharge of his duty, as one of the delegates from this State in general Congress.[27]

Richard Henry heard this resolution and stood to thank the House of Delegates for their "candor and justice," adding that he considered the "approbation of my country . . . the highest reward for faithful services, and it shall by my constant care to merit that approbation by a diligent attention to public duty."[28] After this exchange of words, the House held another election, and Lee was restored to his seat in Congress, along with his younger brother Francis Lightfoot. As the Lees found cause to celebrate, William Duer sourly wrote to friends that he was sorry to inform them "that Colo. R.H. Lee is returning to Congress Crowned with Laurels. . . . I suppose he will return here more riveted than ever to his Eastern Friends."[29]

Comments such as the ones made by Duer reveal several important facts. First, he had an informant watching these events in Virginia and reporting back to him in Philadelphia, most likely Benjamin Harrison, who was elected to Congress again in October 1776 and served while Lee defended his name in Virginia. Second, Duer's reference to Lee's "eastern friends" was no doubt a reference to John and Samuel Adams, and the tone of Duer's comment lends credence to the suggestion that Lee's enemies intended to quash the Lee–Adams junto by forcing Lee to lose his seat in Congress one way or another. The efforts failed, and they now had to bide their time until another opportunity presented itself that they could exploit.

VII

Richard Henry Lee resumed his seat in Congress in August 1777, and he immediately launched a full-scale assault on his political opponents, especially those that he thought threatened the success of military effort against the British. Silas Deane was the first to feel the brunt of Lee's efforts. Richard Henry and his allies secured a motion recalling Deane from his station in Paris. The immediate basis for Deane's recall was his proclivity toward awarding full commissions to French officers who were willing to serve in the Continental army; other charges stemmed from questionable guarantees Deane made to secure foreign loans for the fledgling country.

Naturally, Deane thought that the charges lodged by Lee in Congress were unjustified and that Congress was responsible for the misunderstandings that now existed between France and the United States. The man from Connecticut rested his defense on the observation that, when he first arrived in Paris, Congress had failed to clearly identify his mission. This crucial lack of direction left the New Englander in a situation out of his depth and in a quandary. At one point, he wrote to Congress begging for directions, telling his correspondents that "without further intelligence and instructions," he could not "proceed in my negotiation[s] either with safety or honor."[30] Unfortunately, the failure of Congress to instruct Deane left him to his own devices, and that is where difficulties began to arise.

As Deane searched for direction from congressional leaders in Philadelphia, he informed his superiors "a number of good gentlemen of rank and fortune, who have seen service and have good characters, are desirous of serving in the United Colonies, and have applied." He quickly added: "Pray let me have orders on this subject. If it be politic to interest this kingdom in the present contest, what way so [effectual] as to get into their debt for supplies, and employ persons of good family and connections in it in our services?"[31] Delays in receiving the advice and guidance he sought led the agent to act independently, and consequently, he began issuing commissions to French officers without prior approval from Congress.

As more French officers arrived in America demanding the commissions promised by Deane in Paris, General Washington's staff officers began issuing stiff protests in response. The appointments granted by Deane left Congress in a bind. On the one hand, Congress did not have the funds to honor the commissions, but members were afraid to turn the French officers away, out of concern that this might cost the United States French support for the war against Britain. As Washington's officers stepped up their protests, the general implored Congress to do something to stem the flood of Frenchmen coming into Continental officer ranks. Washington wrote to his friend Richard Henry Lee, asking "what Congress expect[s] I am to do with the many foreigners [Congress has] at different times promoted to the rank of field-officers?"[32] Washington could not afford to ignore the situation any longer. Valued members of his staff, like Nathaniel Greene and Henry Knox, threatened to resign if the influx of French officers did not immediately stop.

Richard Henry Lee attempted to mollify the commander in chief, telling him that his complaints deserved the "greatest attention" but that Congress could not yet take action; Lee's loss of his congressional seat coincided with Washington's query, complicating matters still further. Richard Henry tried to explain that the controversy involved three categories of foreign officers. The first group consisted of those who came voluntarily and did not seek a commission. The second included those sent on recommendations from important allies in the French government—and they could not be easily discarded. Lee noted that the general's problem related to a third group: "those who came from France generally under agreement with our Commissioners, or one of them at least." The best that Lee could offer Washington was to tell the general that unfortunately "the strongest obligations rest upon us (tho' the inconvenience is great) to make good the engagements."[33] In other words, Washington was forced to deal with the difficulties because of the political nature of the appointments.

Richard Henry Lee's most immediate concern was to regain his seat in Congress so that he could resume his supportive efforts waging war against the

British; but he also understood that Congress could not afford antagonizing the French government at this juncture. At the time this controversy flared up, Washington and his army had not scored a significant victory over the British since the battles of Princeton and Trenton during the previous winter; also, the American commissioners were involved in the delicate negotiations of trying to get France to declare war on Britain. Due to these matters, Lee tried to pacify Washington as best he could and only hint at trying to address the problem again at a later date.

Lee lived up to the promise upon his triumphant return to Congress in August 1777. He crafted a carefully worded reprimand denouncing Silas Deane's conduct without insulting the French. The admonishment made it quite clear that the only French officers affected were those who "proceeded upon the encouragement and conventions made and signed at Paris by Silas Deane." The document made it crystal clear that Congress would not honor those commissions since "Mr. Deane had no authority to make such offers." Consequently, the reprimand stated that Congress was not "bound to ratify or fulfill them."[34] These strong comments set the stage for Deane's formal recall as an American commissioner in Paris.

VIII

Silas Deane's motivations for commissioning so many French officers has been a topic of historical controversy since the time the events first transpired. Sympathetic portraits of Deane emphasize the lack of guidance he received from Congress, despite his urgent requests for instructions and the genuine need for French support in the aftermath of the formal declaration of independence in July 1776. One point, however, that cannot be overlooked is that Deane's lack of direction from Congress never prevented him from faithfully promoting the interests of Robert Morris and his allies in Congress. As a result, when Deane's conduct is viewed through the rubric of the Indiana Company's pursuit of western lands, his motivations can be interpreted as part of larger effort to break Virginia's hold on the Ohio River valley.

As early as October 1776, Deane was obviously sensitive to the point that Congress could not afford to pay for all of the commissions he was authorizing, and he proposed a solution to the dilemma. Deane suggested that Congress "apportion a certain tract of western lands, to be divided at the close of the war among officers and soldiers serving" in the Continental army. Deane surmised that "this would have a good effect since the poorest soldiers would then be fighting literally for a freehold; in Europe it would operate beyond any pecuniary offers."[35] In other words, Congress could afford to pay for the

French commissions, but Congress would first have to deny Virginia's exclusive title to western lands and open the area to the French officers who served and to the Continental regulars who were retiring.

Deane continued to pursue this argument by suggesting that Congress use the territory to pay the expenses of America's war against the British as well as the commissions he was doling out to eager Frenchmen. He observed that "a grant be made of a tract of land at the mouth of the Ohio, between that and the Mississippi, equal to two hundred miles square." Once Congress approved this grant, Deane said Congress could establish a land company composed of Europeans and Americans to dispose of large tracts through sales, thereby "defraying or discharging the public debt or expenses."[36] Clearly, Deane did not see any problem with such propositions as, according to John Dickinson's draft of the Articles of Confederation and Perpetual Union, Congress had full authority to set the boundaries of those states, like Virginia, whose borders extended to the South Sea.

Deane never seemed to get the message that Richard Henry Lee and others tried to communicate to him. A month after his reprimand, Deane persisted in his effort to get Congress to use western land as collateral to secure foreign loans. In October 1777, Deane negotiated a £2 million loan anchored by a land grant. Delegates in Congress immediately denounced the "mode of raising [collateral] by appropriation of vacant lands." The Committee for Foreign Affairs (formerly the Secret Committee) then drafted a strongly worded letter clarifying, once and for all, the status of the western lands. The letter stated, "it remains doubtful whether there is any vacant land [that is] not included within some one of the thirteen states." The document further noted that

> it is an undetermined question of great magnitude whether such land is to be considered as common stock or the exclusive property of the state within whose charter bounds it may be found. Until this business shall be determined in Congress and approved by the states, you will readily discover the difficulty of doing any thing in the way of raising money by appropriation of vacant lands.[37]

The point of contention alluded to by the authors of this letter was the status of Dickinson's draft of the Articles of Confederation. If Congress approved the document with the provision allowing Congress to set the borders of the states with large land claims, then Deane's efforts could be easily realized. If, on the other hand, Congress rejected the Dickinson draft, then Virginia's charter claims remained inviolate. The lines were drawn and now the battle began.

Just over a week later, Congress conclusively determined the status of western lands and confirmed Virginia's long-standing exclusive title to the Ohio River valley. Congress settled the issue through debates over two critical amendments for John Dickinson's draft of the Articles of Confederation on October 15, 1777. The first proposition stipulated that it was "essential that the limits of each respective territorial jurisdiction should be ascertained by the articles of confederation"; therefore, "every State [was to] lay before Congress a description of their territorial lands . . . and a summary of the grants, treaties, and proofs upon which they are claimed or established."[38] Richard Henry Lee voted against this amendment while Robert Morris supported the proposal, and both men recognized the provision for what it was—an attempt to once and for all strip away Virginia's exclusive claim to western lands.

The amendment's emphasis on "grants and treaties" represented an overt challenge to Virginia's 1612 charter claim because the terminology attached greater significance to documents such as the 1768 Treaty of Fort Stanwix and individual arrangements made between merchant–traders and different Indian tribes—both of which would give Pennsylvania an advantage over Virginia in the quest for western lands. More important, by forcing Virginia to assert its claim based on the permission of the English Crown, against whom the Americans were now rebelling, men like Lee were put in an increasingly awkward position, as they would have to defend the authority of the king with one hand while challenging his authority with the other. The opposition to the amendment, however, carried the day, and state governments retained control over their territorial claims.

Later that same day, another amendment concerning western lands was presented to Congress for debate that stipulated that Congress should "have the sole and exclusive right and power to ascertain and fix the western boundary of such states as claim to the South Sea, and to dispose of all land beyond that boundary . . . for the benefit of the United States."[39] When this measure came to a vote, both Lee and Morris agreed and cast their vote in opposition to the amendment; but they came to their decision for different reasons. Lee's rationale remained consistent with his opposition to any motion that challenged Virginia's exclusive claim to western lands. Morris, however, had a more complicated problem to confront. Morris opposed congressional control at this juncture because Lee and the Adams still effectively controlled Congress. Consequently, since the first amendment failed, the passage of the later provision would work against the interests of both Robert Morris and Pennsylvania.

As far as Morris was concerned, and as long as he still had friends serving in Virginia's House of Delegates, he still had a venue to promote his commercial interests through that state's assembly.[40] When Congress tallied the final vote on the second proposed amendment to the Articles of Confederation, the opposition prevailed once again. Those states that had long-standing claims to western lands would remain unaltered, while those states identified as "landless states" were still denied access to the territory. Two weeks later, Lee hammered a final nail in the coffin of the dispute over western lands by sponsoring a measure that stipulated how "no State shall be deprived of territory for the benefit of the United States."[41]

The October 15 debates over the status of western lands under the Articles of Confederation set the stage for Congress to approve a final draft on November 15, 1777, and send it forward to the states for their approval. Robert Morris and his friends came out on the losing end of the debate, as by all accounts Richard Henry Lee and his allies triumphed across the board. With the debate over western lands and the Articles of Confederation behind him, Lee now turned his attention back to the matter of Silas Deane in Paris. Within a week of signing off on the Articles of Confederation, Lee set forward a motion formally recalling Silas Deane as an American commissioner and named John Adams as Deane's replacement.

IX

The recall of Silas Deane galvanized Robert Morris and his allies in Congress and forced them to take action. It was difficult enough for them to have to deal with Richard Henry Lee and Samuel Adams in effective control of Congress, but now, if they allowed for John Adams to go to Paris and join Arthur and William Lee, then the Lee–Adams junto would also have effective control over the commercial and diplomatic affairs relating to the war against Britain. Richard Henry Lee once again emerged as a target as Morris and his colleagues launched another effort to remove Lee from the Continental Congress. Rumors involving Lee in another plot to remove George Washington as commander in chief started circulating again. On December 18, 1777, Benjamin Harrison sent a letter to Robert Morris in Congress, informing him that

> We have a story circulating here that there has been a motion made in Congress to divide the command of the army and that R.H.L. was at the bottom of it. It makes much noise, and if true, will effectually do his business, we are also informed that Genl. Washington's character has been attacked publicly by S & J Adams, and that the Genl. has been so informed.[42]

As such stories floated about in the winter of 1777–1778, they became linked with a controversial chain of events known as the "Conway Cabal." These were the same stories spread in February 1777 with the intent to tarnish Lee's friendship with the general and divide the Lee–Adams junto. When the rumors first began circulating, they could easily be dismissed because of Washington's recent victories at Trenton and Princeton. Unfortunately for the general, he had a dismal spring and summer campaign in 1777, and this made it more difficult for him to ignore this sort of challenge.

According to the rumors, those implicated in the plot sought to remove Washington from command in favor of Horatio Gates, the so-called hero of Saratoga. Several congressmen attributed the October 1777 victory over General John Burgoyne to the perceived skill and leadership of Gates, and they began openly discussing the possibility of supplanting Washington with Gates. These rumors coincided with a similar effort promoted by loyalist forces in America. In December 1777, a Boston newspaper printed a collection of letters attributed to Washington. The publisher noted that recently "he was favored with a letter from a friend, now serving in the loyal corps under Brigadier-General [Oliver] De Lancey of New York," which included a packet allegedly found among the "prisoners at Fort Lee," containing letters from Washington to friends and family supposedly written in June 1776. These letters depicted Washington as depressed and saddened by the revolt against the British, particularly about his reputed disloyalty to King George III. At one point in the letters, the general described his situation as "truly irksome," and he resented "being perpetually obliged to act a part foreign to [his] true feelings."[43]

There is little reason to doubt that these letters were forgeries, written and distributed by loyalists as part of a larger attempt to discredit Washington in the eyes of Congress and perhaps even his officers. Another purpose for the letters was also to perpetuate rumors hinting toward a deep-seated resentment between Richard Henry Lee and Washington, which suggests a possible connection between the true authors and Lee's enemies in Congress. In one missive, Washington allegedly wrote that "very few countries have to boast of more men of respectable understanding; I know of none that can produce a family, all of them distinguished and clever men, like our Lees." The initially complimentary tone is replaced with harsh criticism as the author added that, "it is obvious that this is no longer the case; and the reason must be that they are no longer worthy of it." The writer commented on how the "people at length have found this out; or, no doubt, R.H. Lee would now have been governor, the grand object of all his aims."[44]

Passages such as the one quoted above reveal several important factors worthy of consideration. First, rumors circulated claiming how Richard Henry was seeking to displace Washington with Gates while a series of specious letters suddenly appeared in print where the general castigates Lee and disparages his motives as nothing more than an effort to seek personal aggrandizement. Additionally, it is important to note that the letters appeared simultaneously in the Philadelphia papers, the city where British general Sir William Howe had set up his winter camp. The Boston paper printed a total of seven letters, and the editor later distributed them in pamphlet form. Although the documents relating to Washington's disdain toward Lee never posed a serious threat to Lee's position in Congress, they lent credibility to the rumors that Richard Henry disliked Washington and sought to replace him as commander in chief.

A month after the letters appeared in print, Lee addressed the contents of the pamphlet in a letter to the general. Richard Henry wrote that

> The arts of the enemies of America are endless, but all wicked as they are various. Among other tricks, they have forged a pamphlet of letters entitled 'Letters from Gen. Washington to several of his Friends in 1776.' The design of the forger is evident, and no doubt it gained him a good Beef Steak from his Masters.[45]

Upon receiving this letter from Richard Henry, Washington expressed his interest in reading the pamphlet. He informed his friend in Congress that he had

> seen a letter published in a handbill at New York, and extracts republished in a Philadelphia paper, said to be from me to Mrs. Washington, not one word of which I ever did write. Those contained in the pamphlet you speak of are, I presume, equally genuine, and perhaps written by the same author. I should be glad, however to see and examine the texture of them if a favorable opportunity to send them should present.[46]

The candor with which Lee and Washington discuss these forgeries negates any serious consideration that Lee participated in a plot against the general. The existence of the pamphlet does, however, provide strong evidence of a methodical attempt to separate Washington from his core support in Congress, which thereby would have made his removal from command that much easier should an opportunity have arisen.

These circumstances lend further credibility to suggestions that, although Richard Henry Lee did not participate in some sort of conspiracy against Washington, a plot of some sort did exist—the Conway Cabal. There are simply too many coincidences to ignore: just as the letters depicting Washington as lukewarm in his support for the patriot cause appeared, Americans are reveling in reports of Horatio Gates's victory in the Saratoga campaigns. Contemporary evidence does exist that reveals some Americans anticipated Washington's dismissal as early as October 1777. Robert Morton of Philadelphia kept a journal during the British occupation of the city and implied that there was a concerted effort on the part of some distinguished citizens to negotiate an end to the war.[47] Such talk dissipated, however, as news arrived about Gates's victory in New York on October 22, 1777. Robert Morris noted that "Genl. Howe is now in a bad way, for if the News from the Northward be all true We may sweep New York & and in the End serve him as Gates Served Burgoyne."[48] Morris's tone however, indicates that America could best capitalize on the Saratoga victory if Gates held the top spot rather than Washington. The Conway Cabal had the unintended effect of actually strengthening Washington's position as commander in chief as well as allowing Lee and his friends to remain firmly in control of Congress. Consequently, Richard Henry's political enemies had to seek other ways to achieve their desired goals.

X

As Richard Henry Lee battled the rumors challenging his loyalty to George Washington, he also had to face a personal family crisis. Lee took a short leave of absence from Congress and returned to Virginia. On his way back to Chantilly-on-the-Potomac, he stopped at Thomas Ludwell's home, Bellview, in Stafford County. Richard Henry's older brother was ill and resting at his plantation. Not long after his visit, Lee recorded in his journal that "my very dear brother Thomas Ludwell Lee expired a few minutes before 2 o'clock in the day, after a severe and long illness of 6 weeks and 3 days."[49] Now Richard Henry assumed partial responsibility as an executor of his brother's estate and made sure that the needs of Thomas's widow, Mary, and her two children, George, age ten, and Lucinda, age seven, were met. Richard Henry now managed three plantations, Chantilly, Stratford, and Bellview, while at the same time he became a second father of sorts to his nephew and niece. Lee maintained a close relationship with George and Lucinda. When George turned fifteen, Richard Henry sent him to Massachusetts with a letter of introduction to Samuel Adams, asking his old colleague to secure an apprenticeship for his nephew. Lee described George as "very diligent in his studies, and of a fine disposition," adding that "his mother would breed him to commerce."[50] Additionally, Lucinda in many respects became another daughter to Richard Henry. She spent a lot of her time at Chantilly with his other children, and Lucinda developed a very close and fond relationship with her uncle.

Yet, during these personally trying times, Richard Henry was still hounded by his political enemies in Virginia and in Congress. As he worked to settle his deceased brother's estate, he began receiving correspondence from his two brothers in Europe, revealing their suspicions about Silas Deane's activities in France.[51] As early as November 1777, William Lee warned his older brother to anticipate a "cabal" against their family. Richard Henry, however, did not receive the letter until early 1778, which certainly in Lee's mind explained the recent attempts to label him as one of Washington's enemies in Congress.[52]

These letters from Arthur and William Lee arrived in America at the same time that Deane returned in compliance with his recall ordered by Congress in November 1777. Immediately upon his arrival, Deane insisted that Congress grant him an audience so that he could defend his name and reputation. In the process, he launched a volley of attacks against the Lees of Virginia. Richard Henry, of course, responded in kind by accusing the former commissioner of violating the public trust while serving as an American agent in France. These exchanges were traded back and forth for over a year and triggered a political crisis that not only brought Congress to a standstill but also threatened vital areas of concern relating to the diplomatic efforts of the Americans in Paris.

At the outset, Richard Henry optimistically predicted that the "safe arrival of Mr. Adams & the recall of Deane [would] benefit the public business."[53] Unfortunately, Lee made a miscalculation, and 1778 soon proved to be the most acrimonious year on record for the Continental Congress. Factional divisions and personal rivalries became open sores as delegates made charges against their political opponents. As these events reached a fever pitch, the rancorous debates soon became inextricably linked to the French alliance and to new challenges regarding Virginia's exclusive claim to western lands.

XI

Prior to Silas Deane's departure from Paris, the American commissioners and their French counterparts signed the Treaty of Amity and Commerce, which set the stage for direct military support for the American cause from the French government. When John Adams arrived, clearing the way for Deane's departure, French officials expressed little interest in speaking with the new commissioner. They openly proclaimed their sentiments by publicly favoring Deane with certificates of commendation and a diamond-studded portrait of the French king Louis XVI. As the prospects of a French–American alliance loomed forward, British diplomats hastily attempted to negotiate a peace settlement with the Americans. Richard Henry Lee sat on the committee established to prepare a response to the British overture, and he along with his fellow committeemen urged Congress to reject the offer because it did not explicitly recognize American independence. Lee observed that, "when the king of G.B. shall be seriously disposed to peace, Congress will readily attend to such terms as may [be] consistent with the honor of Independent nations."[54] Lee freely expressed his opinions regarding the British proposal, of course, knowing full well that French aid was on its way. In July 1778, Admiral Comte d'Estaing and his fleet sailed into New York Harbor with Silas Deane and Conrad A. Gerard, sent by the French foreign minister Vergennes to solidify the alliance between France and the United States. Events soon revealed that Gerard's sympathies rested with Deane and the Morris faction in Congress, a situation that threatened to tear apart the new diplomatic alliance.

Richard Henry Lee initially welcomed the arrival of the French diplomat, but as he found himself having to defend his family's name in the wake of several charges made by Deane, the cozy relationship that existed between Gerard and Deane became a major cause of irritation for Lee. Before long, Richard Henry became convinced that Gerard was intimately involved with the attacks made by Deane. As Lee's criticism of Gerard's involvement in these matters became more open, Richard Henry and Samuel Adams soon were inaccurately labeled as leaders of an anti-French (or anti-Gallican) party in Congress. In spite of the dubious nature of the label, it resonated with Lee's political enemies, and the ensuing controversy became the dominant affair in the Continental Congress.

The conflict that mushroomed in 1778, of course, had a long history and bore a close relation to congressional battles dating back to the decision favoring American independence, the raucous debates over the Articles of Confederation, and Virginia's exclusive claim to western lands. Additionally, it is important to note that Silas Deane and Conrad Gerard also had a long history together. When Deane first arrived in Paris in 1776, Vergennes appointed Gerard as Deane's translator while the American began establishing commercial ties with Jacques-Donetien Leray de Chaumont. The association that soon developed between these three men also revolved around Deane's connections to the firm of Willing and Morris in Philadelphia. As Chaumont developed a closer relationship with Deane, Chaumont revealed sincere interest in acquiring land in North America. By the end of the 1770s, the French merchant had acquired more than 100,000 acres in upstate New York and sought an additional 80,000 acres in the Ohio River valley—which was naturally claimed by Virginia and not for sale.[55] After Benjamin Franklin arrived to take the lead of the American commission, Chaumont arranged for the Americans to use his estate, Passy, as their headquarters. When the commissioners inquired about the cost of renting the home, Chaumont dismissed such inquiries and made it clear that he did not want a rent payment—he wanted land in North America.[56]

After Deane returned to America and sought an audience before Congress to defend his actions in France, Richard Henry successfully stalled his opponent's efforts; he attempted to sort out the intricate details and learn the full story of Deane's activities in Paris, which depended on his receiving more information from his two brothers still residing in France. Eventually, Deane abandoned the notion that he would ever receive a full hearing before Congress. As these events transpired, Congress divided into pro-Lee and pro-Deane factions. Lee received the support of Henry Laurens of South Carolina, then president of Congress, along with Samuel Adams and James Lovell of Massachusetts. Robert Morris, John Jay, and Oliver Ellsworth of Connecticut emerged as Deane's most outspoken advocates. By September 1778, the vitriolic rhetoric from the pro-Deane camp reached new heights, as Ellsworth characterized Lee and Samuel Adams as the leaders of an "ass-ridden" junto.[57]

While Deane's friends championed his cause in Congress, the former commissioner took his case to the American press. In December 1778, Deane published an editorial casting suspicion on Arthur Lee's conduct as a commissioner in Paris and accused Richard Henry of betraying the American cause to a known British spy, Dr. John Berkenhout. Lee once again found himself on the defensive and responded by publishing his own editorial response. He acknowledged meeting with Berkenhout, but he rejected the insinuation that he knew this man was a spy, as Deane had charged.[58] Berkenhout, who recorded the encounter in his personal journal, confirms Lee's account of the events. The English spy noted that after he arrived in Philadelphia, Lee paid him a visit; afterward, he introduced him to Samuel Adams and "several other members of Congress." Berkenhout indicated that the only topics of conversation were the Declaration of Independence, the alliance with France, and the reasons why the British ought to make immediate peace with the Americans. During these discussions, Berkenhout played the role as one sympathetic to the American cause and introduced himself as a friend of Arthur Lee, looking to settle in America. The spy then suggested that he might return to Britain in order to present the American point of view to the British government.[59]

For obvious reasons, Lee bitterly resented Deane's specious innuendos and responded by leveling several charges of his own. Richard Henry had received letters from his brothers in France by this time and now accused Deane of stealing "large sums of the public's money."[60] Later, Lee accused Deane of duplicitous behavior bordering on treason. He traced Deane's career in public service for his audience and placed particular emphasis on his opponent's close association with the firm of Willing and Morris. Richard Henry reminded his readers of how Deane, without congressional permission, entered into "written Contracts with a host of [French] officers, from the ensign to the Major General," and then not only passed on "the expenses, the pay, the commands, and the pensions of these gentlemen" to Congress, but also "enraged the army" as well. Lee stressed that it was for these reasons that Congress demanded "your return [to America] and not the injurious motives" Deane ascribed to his political opponents.[61]

The public exchange between Silas Deane and Richard Henry Lee revealed just how blurred the lines between public service and private interest were during the American Revolution. As Lee received more information from his brothers about Deane's conduct in France, the cumulative data strongly suggested that Deane did release sensitive American intelligence to British officials through his private secretary, Edward Bancroft.[62] Arthur Lee also indicated that Franklin was involved with similar activity, since he maintained close contacts with his British friends Thomas Walpole, Charles Pratt, Lord Camden, both of whom were then serving as members of Parliament. As the dispute heated up, Deane accused Lee of wanting to sacrifice the French alliance and negotiate separately with the British.[63] Lee vigorously denied such claims, but the problem for the Virginian was that he was becoming increasingly suspicious of French motives—not because he desired a separate peace with the British but because he was skeptical of the close association between Deane and Gerard.

By this time, the Deane–Lee imbroglio had taken its toll on Congress. Henry Laurens resigned his seat in disgust, and John Jay of New York took over the duties as president of Congress. Lauren's resignation, John Adams's Paris appointment, and Jay's elevation tipped the balance of power in Congress in favor of the Morris faction. In January 1779, Gerard confirmed many of Lee's worst fears when the French minister began talking openly about the boundaries of the new nation. Gerard indicated his belief that the Proclamation of 1763 and the Quebec Act of 1774 had already determined the boundaries of the United States. The collusion between Deane, Gerard, and the Morris faction in Congress convinced Lee that this was merely another attempt to strip away Virginia's exclusive claim to western lands—a motive that had obvious appeal to the French as well as to Robert Morris and his cohorts. Lee and his friend Samuel Adams began insisting that the Mississippi River was the western boundary of the United States, and they demanded that America be granted free navigation of the river. Consequently, they both were quickly identified as being opposed to the French alliance.

Robert Morris, Gouverneur Morris (no relation to Robert), and President John Jay, all of whom defended Deane in Congress, accepted Gerard's assessment of America's boundaries. Jay and Gouverneur Morris both expressed concerns over unfettered American access to the Mississippi River. They dreaded the possibility of American farmers' shipping their produce down the Mississippi to New Orleans and thus depriving New York City of much needed commercial business. Richard Henry Lee, however, feared that without guarantees of free navigation of the river, the value of western lands would decline and the future viability of Virginia's tobacco economy would dissipate. While Congress began finalizing the details in the Treaty of Amity and Commerce, Lee's group proved victorious, as they won recognition of the Mississippi River as America's western boundary; however, questions pertaining to the free navigation of the river would remain unresolved for several more years.

XII

The Deane–Lee imbroglio had taken its toll on Richard Henry Lee. As the spring of 1779 rolled around, an emotionally bruised and battered Richard Henry Lee found that he had successfully defended Virginia's exclusive claim to western lands while at the same time allowing for the establishment of the French alliance; yet, he found little reason to celebrate these accomplishments.

He spoke disparagingly of public service. He wrote to Virginia's governor, Thomas Jefferson, and said that although "nothing but the certain prospect of doing essential service to my country can compensate for the injuries I receive," he would nonetheless tender his resignation on May 31, 1779. In a more private moment, as he mulled over the events of the past year, Lee wrote a bitter assessment in his journal of the absurd charges made against him and his family:

> The improbability of a malicious story serves but to help forward the currency of it—because it increases the scandal—so that in such instances the world like the Romish priests, are industrious to propagate a belief in things they have not the faith themselves, or like the pious [St. Augustine?] who said he believed some things because he knew they were absurd and improbable.[64]

As May 31 rolled around, Lee and his brother Francis formally resigned their seats in Congress. On that same day, Arthur Lee sent a letter to Congress announcing his resignation as an American commissioner as well.

Although Richard Henry no longer played an active role in Congress, he maintained a vigilant watch on his political opponents and worked to strengthen Virginia's claim to western lands. Toward that end, after Congress secured the French alliance, Lee's friend George Mason introduced a motion in Virginia's House of Delegates to establish a land office so that Virginia could begin selling tracts of land to finance the state's war effort against the British. Mason's proposal invalidated all claims that had not been surveyed before April 1775, which left only Virginia-based land companies with recognized claims. Advocates for the Indiana Company immediately lodged protests with the Continental Congress, which promptly ordered Virginia to postpone the establishment of the proposed land office. Mason coolly responded that since the Articles of Confederation had not yet been ratified, Virginia was still an independent commonwealth and was not bound by congressional authority on such matters.[65]

Congress and Virginia had reached an impasse. The ratification of the Articles of Confederation had stalled since New Jersey, Delaware, and Maryland refused to sign the document until Virginia abandoned its claim to western lands. The controversy threatened America's ability to effectively deal with the more immediate military threat posed by the British. Lee could take satisfaction in thwarting his political opponents' designs on Virginia's claim to western lands, but just as he submitted his resignation to Congress, the British launched an invasion of Chesapeake Bay. Consequently, Richard Henry's respite was short-lived, as he now had to confront a much greater threat—the British imperial fleet bearing down on his beloved Potomac home.

NOTES

1. George Mason to R. H. Lee, May 18, 1776, *Mason Papers*, 1: 271.
2. R. H. Lee to General George Washington, June 13, 1776, *Lee Letters*, 1: 201.
3. Thomas Walpole to Benjamin Franklin, February 10, 1777, *George Mercer Papers*, 673–74.
4. Abernethy, *Western Lands*, vii, 149–62.
5. John Selby, "Richard Henry Lee, John Adams, and the Virginia Constitution of 1776," *Virginia Magazine of History and Biography* 84 (October 1976): 391.
6. R. H. Lee to Patrick Henry, April 20, 1776, *Lee Letters*, 1: 179.
7. R. H. Lee, "A Government Scheme," *Revolutionary Virginia: The Road to Independence, a Documentary Record*, 7 vols., ed. William J. Van Schreeven and Robert L. Scribner (Charlottesville, VA: University Press of Virginia, 1975–1983), 6: 367–68. Hereafter, cited as *Revolutionary Virginia*.
8. Selby, "Richard Henry Lee, John Adams, and the Virginia Constitution of 1776," 390 n. 9.
9. [Carter Braxton], "An Address to the Convention of the Colony and Ancient Dominion of Virginia; on the Subject of Government in General, and Recommending a Particular Form to their Consideration. By a Native of that Colony," May 4, 1776, *Revolutionary Virginia*, 6: 523–26.
10. [Braxton], "An Address to the Convention," 523–26.
11. R. H. Lee to Edmund Pendleton, May 12, 1776, *Lee Letters*, 1: 190.
12. R. H. Lee to General Charles Lee, June 29, 1776, *Lee Letters*, 1: 203.
13. John E. Selby, *The Revolution in Virginia, 1775–1783* (Williamsburg, VA: The Colonial Williamsburg Foundation, 1988), 142; George E. Lewis, *The Indiana Company, 1763–1798: A Study in Eighteenth Century Frontier Land Speculation and Business Venture* (Glendale, CA: The Arthur H. Clark Company, 1941), 158, 172.
14. "List of Delegates to Congress," *Letters of Delegates*, 4: xxi.
15. "Dickinson's Draft of the Articles of Confederation," in *The Articles of Confederation: An Interpretation of the Social-Constitutional History of the American Revolution, 1774–1781*, by Merrill Jensen (Madison: The University of Wisconsin Press, 1940), 258.
16. Potts, *Arthur Lee*, 180–81; Thomas J. Schaeper, *France and America in the Revolutionary Era: The Life of Jacques-Donatien Leray de Chaumont, 1725–1803* (Oxford: Berghahn Books, 1995), 161–67.
17. Arthur Lee to R. H. Lee, September 5, 1777, Lee Family Papers, 8 reels. Edited by Paul Hoffman, reel 3; Abernethy, *Western Lands*, 183; Potts, *Arthur Lee*, 179; and Schaeper, *France and America*, 133–34.
18. Robert Morris to Silas Deane, January 31, 1777, *Letters of Delegates*, 6: 176.
19. Abernethy, *Western Lands*, 186.
20. R. H. Lee to Patrick Henry, May 26, 1777, *Lee Letters*, 1: 301.
21. R. H. Lee, "A Tenant Contract," January 1776, Virginia Historical Society, Richmond, VA.
22. Sloan, *Principle and Interest*, 34–36.

23. R. H. Lee to Patrick Henry, May 26, 1776, *Lee Letters*, 1: 298–99.

24. Joseph Blackwell to R. H. Lee, January 16, 1777, quoted in Mary Elizabeth Virginia, "Richard Henry Lee of Virginia: A Biography" (Ph.D. diss., State University of New York, Buffalo, 1992), 244.

25. William Duer to John Jay, May 28, 1777, *Letters of Delegates*, 7: 139.

26. John Bannister to Theodoric Bland [n.d.], *Lee of Virginia*, 182.

27. John Bannister to Theodoric Bland [n.d.], *Lee of Virginia*, 182.

28. John Bannister to Theodoric Bland [n.d.], *Lee of Virginia*, 182.

29. William Duer to Robert R. Livingston, July 9, 1777, *Letters of Delegates*, 7: 327–28.

30. Silas Deane to the Secret Committee, August 18, 1776, *The Revolutionary Diplomatic Correspondence of the United States*, 6 vols., ed. Francis Wharton (Washington D.C.: Government Printing Office, 1889), 2: 120–22. Hereafter, cited as *Diplomatic Correspondence*.

31. Deane to the Secret Committee, *Diplomatic Correspondence*, 120–22.

32. George Washington to R. H. Lee, May 17, 1777, *The Writings of George Washington: Being His Correspondence, Addresses, Messages, and Other Papers, Official and Private*, 12 vols., ed. Jared Sparks (Boston, MA: Ferdinand Andrews, Publisher, 1839–1840), 8: 74.

33. R. H. Lee to George Washington, May 22, 1777, *Lee Letters*, 1: 293.

34. "Journal of Congress," September 8, 1777, *Diplomatic Correspondence*, 2: 388.

35. Deane to the Secret Committee, October 1, 1776, *Diplomatic Correspondence*, 2: 157.

36. Deane to the Secret Committee, December 1, 1776, *Diplomatic Correspondence*, 2: 204.

37. The Committee for Foreign Affairs to the Commissioners at Paris, October 6, 1777, *Letters of Delegates*, 8: 64.

38. *Journals of the Continental Congress*, 9: 806.

39. *Journals of the Continental Congress*, 9: 807.

40. This interpretation calls into question what might be an overly simplistic breakdown of political factions in Congress offered by H. James Henderson in *Party Politics in the Continental Congress* (New York: McGraw-Hill, 1974), 147–48. On these two particular amendments, Henderson presented a dichotomy along "centrist" and "states' rightist" lines. Henderson's breakdown and analysis of the vote suggest that Morris was a "centrist" in the morning of October 15, since he voted in favor of the first amendment; that afternoon, however, Morris became a "states' rightist" because he voted against the second amendment. Such a ideological switch seems unlikely, and consequently, another explanation is needed to explain the motivations behind the votes on these two particular amendments.

41. *Journals of the Continental Congress*, 9: 840.

42. Benjamin Harrison to Robert Morris, December 18, 1777, quoted in Chitwood, *Richard Henry Lee: Statesman of the Revolution*, 215.

43. "Letters of General Washington to Several of his Friends in the Year 1776" (Philadelphia: The Federal Press, 1795). The complete printing history of these letters remains elusive. They first appeared in a Boston newspaper in December 1777. The only copy currently available is a reprint version published in 1795.

44. "Letters of General Washington," 30.

45. R. H. Lee to George Washington, January 2, 1778, *Lee Letters*, 1: 371.

46. George Washington to R. H. Lee, February 15, 1778, *Writings of Washington*, ed. Fitzpatrick, 10: 465.

47. Robert Morton, "The Diary of Robert Morton," *Pennsylvania Magazine of History and Biography* 1 (1877): 11–13.

48. Robert Morris to James Wilson, October 22, 1777, *Letters of Delegates*, 8: 698.

49. R. H. Lee, "Journal Entry," April 13, 1778.

50. R. H. Lee to Samuel Adams, April 6, 1783, *Lee Letters*, 2: 280–81.

51. William Lee to R. H. Lee, November 30, 1777, *The Letters of William Lee*, 3 vols., ed. Worthington C. Ford (Brooklyn, NY: 1891; reprint, New York: Burt Franklin, 1968), 1: 279–81; and Arthur Lee to R. H. Lee, *The Life of Arthur Lee*, 2: 114–18.

52. Alonzo T. Dill, *Francis Lightfoot Lee: The Incomparable Signer* (Williamsburg, VA: Virginia Independence Bicentennial Commission, 1977), 47.

53. R. H. Lee to Arthur Lee, May 27, 1778, *Lee Letters*, 1: 410.

54. "Draft of an Answer to the First Peace Commission," June 6, 1778, *Lee Letters*, 1: 411.

55. It is interesting to note that there is still today a community in New York called Leraysville. A mansion still stands that was once occupied by Leray's children, who fled to the United States once the French Revolution began in 1789.

56. Abernethy, *Western Lands*, 183; Roger Kennedy, *Orders from France: The Americans and the French in a Revolutionary World, 1780–1820* (New York: Alfred A. Knopf, 1989), 21–26.

57. Oliver Ellsworth, "Communication to the Public by a Friend to Truth and Fair Play," September 7, 1778, *Letters of Members of the Continental Congress*, 8 vols., ed. Edmund C. Burnett (Washington D.C.: Government Printing Office, 1921–1936), 4: 409.

58. R. H. Lee to the Printer of the *Pennsylvania General Advertiser*, December 16, 1778, *Lee Letters*, 1: 458–59.

59. Carl Van Doren, *The Secret History of the American Revolution* (New York: The Viking Press, 1941), 107.

60. R. H. Lee to the Printer of the *Pennsylvania General Advertiser*, December 16, 1778, *Lee Letters*, 1: 457.

61. R. H. Lee to Silas Deane, January 22, 1779, *Lee Letters*, 2: 13–14.

62. R. H. Lee to Silas Deane, January 22, 1779, *Lee Letters*, 2: 26.

63. Ironically, just as Deane raised questions concerning Lee's commitment to the French alliance, the British captured a ship owned by Carter Braxton. On board the ship, the captors found a letter from Braxton to John Ross, Robert Morris's agent in Nantes. In the letter, Braxton questioned the wisdom of the French alliance and proposed that Ross join him in a scheme to smuggle British-made goods into America. Selby, *The Revolution in Virginia*, 228–29.

64. R. H. Lee, "Journal Entry," n.d.

65. George Mason to R. H. Lee, June 19, 1779, *Mason Papers*, 2: 522–25.

· 7 ·

Defending the Potomac

I

$\mathcal{A}$s Richard Henry Lee contemplated his resignation from Congress, he began receiving disturbing reports from the war front, which had recently shifted to Virginia. Lee heard that the British had "burned Portsmouth, and Suffolk, and every house they came to." More troubling, however, were the stories describing "murders in cold blood and rapes without end." Lee noted that such conduct rivaled "every outrage and every ravage" and would even "disgrace the worst Savages." These accounts undoubtedly hastened his departure from Congress so that he could, if needed, defend his own home and hearth from the British marauders.[1] From the outset of the War for American Independence, Lee carefully monitored British activity in the rivers surrounding the Northern Neck. His active interest in naval matters began early as July 1776, as soon as he learned Lord Dunmore had established a base of operations at Gwyn's Island, near the mouth of the Rappahannock River. What concerned him the most about Dunmore's new base was that it placed the governor in an advantageous position to disrupt the commercial traffic in Chesapeake Bay, and it also provided convenient access to the Potomac River, thus allowing him opportunities to ravage the great plantation homes along the river with impunity.

The threat posed by Virginia's renegade governor prompted George Mason to join with another colleague, John Dalton, and organize the Potomac Navy, and while Lee remained preoccupied with political matters, Mason and Dalton kept him informed of their efforts—particularly those designed to defend Alexandria, the most important port servicing the plantations of the Northern Neck.[2] By the end of July, British captain Andrew

Snape Hammond, commander of the British frigate *Roebuck*, joined Dunmore. At that time, they shifted their base from Gwyn's Island to St. George's Island at the mouth of the Potomac. Panic swept through the Northern Neck as residents anxiously awaited Dunmore's next move.

Chantilly-on-the-Potomac afforded Richard Henry many opportunities to view ship movements in the river from his second floor window. On July 20, four British warships appeared within sight of Chantilly at sunset. He gathered together a small militia force because he expected he might have to fend off a British landing party. The invasion never materialized, and after the small flotilla moved further to the northwest, Lee speculated that the ships were looking to secure fresh water or burn Alexandria.[3] Richard Henry hoped that the Potomac Navy could capitalize on Dunmore's "great want of both water and provisions" during their forays up the river, but these hopes soon dissipated when Lee learned that one of Virginia's most prominent planter–shippers— John Goodrich Sr. and his sons—had allied themselves with Dunmore. Since late 1775, Virginians had been voicing their suspicions regarding the Goodrich family's loyalties, but it was not until mid-1776 that the Virginia Convention finally confirmed that Goodrich and his sons were now openly serving the British.

Such news proved to be a startling development to planters like Richard Henry Lee, since the Goodriches operated their own private fleet, consisting of twelve ships. Portsmouth, Virginia, was their base of operations, and Lord Dunmore understood that their loyalty to the Crown was a recognized asset. In a letter to George Germain, Dunmore noted that the Goodriches were "perfectly well acquainted with every River, Creek, or Branch within . . . [Chesapeake] Bay."[4] As long as the Goodriches remained on the loose, Lee understood that not a single plantation or tobacco warehouse in Virginia would be safe. Consequently, when he returned to Congress in August 1776, he vigilantly sought information on the Goodriches. The next February he expressed his frustration that the Goodriches continued darting in and out of Virginia's waterways, using the many islands as bases and working with other "Tories on the Eastern shore of Maryland."[5] Later in November 1778, Lee voiced his concern that the Goodriches' fleet seemed to be growing larger. He informed one correspondent about "[Goodrich's] pirates," which now infested the American "Coast . . . from New York to Cape Fear," and he strenuously urged some type of organized military action to stop their depredations because "they not only injure our Commerce greatly in these middle States, but they prevent in great measure our water communication between us and our Eastern friends."[6] With the Goodriches wreaking havoc in Virginia, Lee's thoughts were never far from Virginia, no matter what the situation he had to confront in Congress.

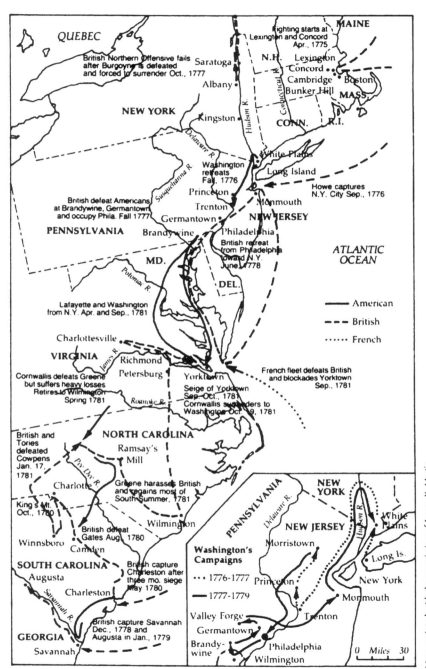

Figure 7.1.　The War for American Independence.

II

Throughout his tenure in Congress during the crucial years from 1776 through his resignation in 1779, Lee had to constantly maintain a careful watch on Virginia's interests in Congress and the harassments unleashed by the Goodriches along his state's coastal reaches. After the disastrous defeat of General John Burgoyne at Saratoga in the fall of 1777, the British high command shifted toward a southern strategy, targeting American commerce and soliciting Loyalist support in the region. In May 1778, Sir Henry Clinton replaced William Howe as commander in chief of British forces in America; in 1779, Clinton dispatched one of his senior naval officers, George Collier, with the assignment of orchestrating a series of strikes in Chesapeake Bay. Clinton's plans did not involve large-scale land operations but, rather, small raids designed to destroy tobacco warehouses and disrupt trade along the waterways feeding into Chesapeake Bay.

In the first few weeks of May 1779, Collier's ships descended on Portsmouth and moved inland to capture a supply depot located in Suffolk, Virginia. During this raid, the British burned at least 100 ships and more than 30,000 hogshead of tobacco, and William Goodrich played a leading role in this attack. Although this raid occurred along the James River, the situation forced Richard Henry Lee to begin preparing for a similar assault within days after returning to Chantilly. He immediately sent off letters to prominent Virginians with the intent of marshaling together a united effort to stop the British incursions, and he offered a systematic plan with that objective in mind. The first order of business was to remove all types of supply depots that would tempt them to attack, especially in those areas "where troops may be landed from vessels protected by ships of war." Next, Lee called for the expansion of the navy and suggested combining the fleets from Virginia and Maryland. He believed that a flotilla consisting of "eight gallies on our part and six on that of Maryland, well-manned and . . . carrying thirty-two and twenty-four pounders" could successfully "baffle" the British. Finally, he implored his fellow Virginians to abandon the practice of building defensive forts along the major waterways—a tradition dating back to the state's early history and reminiscent of his own father's defensive strategy. Lee believed that they must instead adopt a defense based on "movable batteries" because "forts, under the idea of strength, delude men to make collections which they otherwise would not, and which tempt an enemy to come for plunder where they would not otherwise visit."[7]

After sending his advice forward to the Virginia House of Delegates, Richard Henry reactivated his commission as a colonel in Westmoreland County's militia. He then turned his attention to organizing soldiers under his command in the event of a British landing, but much to his dismay, he found the militia was "weak and defenceless" with very little ammunition and a dearth of essential supplies. Lee immediately began scrounging for weapons that he could use to arm his men so they could adequately defend the forty miles of exposed Potomac shoreline that was under his watch.[8] He arranged for detachments from his militia to guard unprotected tobacco warehouses and would not hesitate to lead his men into neighboring counties if needed. As Lee reported on a friend in Congress, "a [recent] landing of the enemy in [King George County] obliged me to lead the Militia to prevent them from burning our Warehouses" and "between two and three hundred hogshead of tobacco."[9]

Richard Henry Lee submitted detailed reports of his efforts to defend the Potomac to members of the Continental Congress as well as Virginia's House of Delegates. It was a task he considered essential so that state officials could coordinate their efforts with national forces and so that all people concerned could more easily map out the movements of British ships and troops. In one instance, Lee described how a small British party landed in Northumberland County, adjacent to his own Westmoreland County, with a support group consisting of ten vessels. Although he characterized them as small ships, he noted that at least two of them had thirty cannons on board. Sixty British soldiers came ashore and burned tobacco warehouses and three private homes while "carrying off several negroes with them." They fled the scene as they heard the Northumberland militia approaching; nonetheless, such actions served only to confirm in Lee's mind that the British planned to burn "every Warehouse on [the] Potomac River."[10] With this gloomy prospect in mind, Lee recognized that dark days would follow.

III

Richard Henry hoped the situation would soon turn in favor of the American effort—a hope enlivened as members from his own militia group, while on patrol, found an American prisoner of war who had fled from his captors while they were preoccupied with the destruction of another tobacco warehouse. Lee described him as an "Eastern man . . . captured some time ago and detained" by the British. The former prisoner provided vital information about the British fleet that had recently entered the Potomac River. The man listed the names of six vessels, each with several cannons, four of which belonged to Goodrich's fleet. Richard Henry's newfound informant also divulged that a British marine force consisting of eight men accompanied Goodrich and that they had already "plundered and burned five private homes."[11] What was unknown to the escapee, however, was that another five British men-of-war, including George

Collier's flagship, the *Raisonable*, were still out in force patrolling the Chesapeake Bay. An additional twenty-eight supply ships sailed alongside the warships, and there were an estimated 2,000 British troops on board these vessels.

When Richard Henry Lee learned of this sizable fleet, he could not conceal his despondent tone as he informed one correspondent that "our militia cannot be every where, and where they are not, these plunderers land and destroy." Lee clearly recognized that the British outmatched the state's militia in every imaginable way, yet that realization did not deter his efforts to prepare a full-scale defense of the Northern Neck's Potomac shore. He hoped to organize the assistance of neighboring states, recalling how a group of Philadelphia merchants had once agreed to help Virginia "clear the [Chesapeake] of obstructions to their commerce." With their help, Lee optimistically believed that the "enemy may be removed without much difficulty."[12] Unfortunately, the plan never materialized.

United state action against the British failed because the effort occurred in the shadow of the looming Deane–Lee imbroglio in Congress. Lee found himself in June and July 1779 fending off the British while at the same time defending his family's name against the erroneous charges made by Deane and his advocates in Congress—all of whom were heavily tied to the merchant activity of the Philadelphia-based firm of Willing and Morris. The struggle between these two competing factions did not end with Lee's resignation, because the central issue that caused the conflict—Virginia's exclusive claim to western lands—remained unresolved. In many respects, the situation became even more bitter and acrimonious after Lee's departure from Congress. The two sides traded barbs with one another, always accusing the other of possessing British sympathies and willing to sacrifice the American cause for their own personal gain.

As Deane and his friends kept the story of Richard Henry's supposedly treasonous dealings with Dr. John Berkenhout alive in the press, Arthur Lee sent evidence from Paris that Deane had forwarded a copy of the Treaty of Amity and Commerce between France and America to Samuel Wharton in London "some days before its conclusion." Arthur Lee expressed his alarm about this episode, since Wharton was not a member of the diplomatic corps but rather a private businessman allied with prominent British parliamentarians. Once Richard Henry Lee received this intelligence from his younger brother, he was convinced that this sort of evidence revealed the "enormity" of Deane's collusion with the enemies of America.[13] Lee also began to publicly criticize the behavior of Jonathan Sargeant of Pennsylvania, as well as Charles Thomson, also of Pennsylvania, who had served as secretary of Congress since its inception. Lee accused both men of launching a cover-up, since they were both "long acquainted" with the evidence but failed to bring it to the attention of Congress. Richard Henry bitterly denounced Thomson's conduct in particular as behavior "rendering him unfit to be the Secretary of Congress, as any other Whore in Philadelphia." He angrily observed that "it is impossible that justice can be done, either to the community, or to individuals, unless [Deane was] properly understood."[14]

To Lee's defense, the significance of Deane's communication with Wharton cannot be discounted. The correspondence provided proof of collusion between these two men, and it is doubtful that Deane would have taken such a step without getting the nod from Benjamin Franklin. When Wharton received a copy of the treaty, there is little doubt that Wharton let Thomas Walpole, his business associate in Parliament, know about the developments occurring across the English Channel. As a result, the evidence suggests that the combined effects of Deane's recall and this information's coming to light posed a direct threat to the established transatlantic commercial interests of Willing and Morris; and the situation only worsened for Deane's friends with the arrival of John Adams as Deane's replacement. After Adams arrived, Arthur Lee successfully forced the removal of Jonathan Williams from America's commercial agency in Nantes and replaced Franklin's nephew with John Daniel Schwieghauser and Richard Henry's oldest son, Thomas. Consequently, Adams's arrival resulted in wholesale changes in Nantes, as Morris's network was eclipsed by Lee and Adams.

As the Deane–Lee imbroglio intensified in the summer of 1779, Richard Henry Lee recounted how, from the moment Schweighauser assumed his position, there emerged a "wicked attempt to destroy the reputation of Mr. Schweighauser . . . by Chaumont and his friends at Nantes."[15] Lee's accusations later appeared in print in August 1779. Richard Henry also accused Robert Morris of assisting Deane's efforts to discredit the Lee family name, which began circulating in the winter of 1778–1779. Lee referred to correspondence between Morris and Deane that came into his possession where they proclaimed "their triumph, the disgrace of their opponents, and the honorable and lucrative return of [Deane] to Europe."[16] Richard Henry later elaborated on his suspicions that French minister Gerard had "powerfully supported the [Deane] faction, [and] that his support has given life, vigor, and effect to their plans." Lee went as far as suggesting that Deane would not have had the nerve to publish his December 5, 1778, letter against the Lees "had he not been sure of M. Gerard's countenance."[17]

Richard Henry Lee, much to his chagrin, had to divide his time between defending his family's name and reputation from the charges lodged by Deane and his advocates while trying to monitor British movements in Chesapeake Bay and the Potomac River.[18] The situation finally reached a resolution in January 1780, when Lee joyously reported that "S. Deane has avoided the consequences of a suit [brought] against him in Philadelphia by [Arthur] Lee and has fled to France"; but, unfortunately, the damage had already been done.[19] The level of acrimony between prominent men serving in the Continental Congress and elsewhere did irreparable damage. For Richard Henry, it convinced him not to rely on specious hopes of military assistance from his neighboring states. Consequently, as the British invasion began to intensify in the months following Silas Deane's final departure, Lee understood that Virginia had to take care of itself and not count on outside support.

IV

Personal family matters made the presence of British warships even more troubling for Richard Henry Lee in the late summer of 1779. His wife, Anne, was pregnant with his eighth child, and in addition to his own brood, he also had to keep close tabs on the widows and children of his deceased brothers, Philip and Thomas. In August, Anne gave birth to Richard Henry's third son, whom they named Cassius. Shortly thereafter, Lee wrote to a friend commenting on his infant son's temperament that by the age of only five months Cassius seemed "as if he would be no Lover of Tyrants."[20]

Richard Henry Lee lamented the failure to implement a uniform policy to defend Virginia's shores from the British. Not long after Lee resigned his seat in Congress, he characterized his state as one that possessed two frontiers, "one bordered by wilderness, the other by Sea . . . and into the latter the most savage." Reports of the successful expedition of George Rogers Clark in the West pleased him, but he quickly noted that "the eastern frontier has not yet been so successful."[21]

Lee regarded Virginia's primary problem as the existence of more than 1,000 miles of navigable rivers, and he urged Governor Thomas Jefferson and the House of Delegates to address this problem. He offered his services, noting that his congressional tenure afforded him an opportunity to serve as the chair of the Marine Committee, where he gained valuable knowledge in the areas of coastal defense. Richard Henry then proffered a twofold plan to provide a comprehensive defense of Virginia's eastern frontier. He emphasized, however, that before any such plan would work, the need to first address an urgent problem: providing not only adequate pay for sailors to man ships but also provisions for punishing officers who refused to engage the enemy.[22]

Richard Henry's suggestion found a receptive audience, and he let his family know about his pending return to public service. He also notified friends in Congress, like Samuel Adams, by sardonically commenting that "after a relaxation of 11 months," he planned to return to public business.[23] He made preparations to take a seat in the spring 1780 session of the House of Delegates in the state's new capital, Richmond, Virginia—a location that afforded a more defensive position from British vessels in the area. As soon as the delegates met, Lee's colleagues named him chair of the committee to craft a defense of the eastern frontier, a plan they hoped could be implemented by the fall of 1780.

Lee's participation on this committee came during one of the bleakest periods of the War for American Independence. That same spring, General Benjamin Lincoln surrendered his army along with Charleston, South Carolina, to the British. Other defeats soon followed. After Lincoln's debacle in Charleston, Congress set the stage for another failure by appointing the "hero" of Saratoga, General Horatio Gates, as commander of the American forces in the South. Gates launched a disorganized assault on British troops at Camden, South Carolina, in August. The ensuing battle was an unmitigated disaster, and Gates fled the field of battle. Seventy-two hours later, Gates emerged in Hillsborough, North Carolina, unscathed while his army remained behind in shambles. Not long after Gates's humiliation at Camden, Americans learned of Benedict Arnold's defection; since he was one of Washington's most talented generals, his betrayal served only to demoralize American forces still further.

As reports of the difficulties further south filtered northward, Virginia obtained crucial intelligence regarding British strategy. Richard Henry Lee confirmed that a packet of letters from Major General Alexander Leslie to Lord Cornwallis, who had just recently replaced Clinton as the British commander in chief, had been intercepted and was in the possession of the House of Delegates.[24] The letters revealed Leslie's intention of establishing a base at Portsmouth, where he would await further instructions from Cornwallis. Leslie's comments signaled the beginning of another assault on Virginia, one that would pave the way for Cornwallis to invade at a later date. The correspondence also revealed what, at least for Richard Henry, proved to be an even more alarming situation. British vice admiral Mariot Arbuthnot had already made preparations for what he described as a "secret expedition . . . for the annoyance of the Rebels in Virginia" and indicated that Benedict Arnold would lead the campaign.[25] Lee and his colleagues could readily sense that Britain's southern strategy was rapidly coming to a head and that Virginia would represent the last battlefield.

V

As Virginia braced for the impending assault, the committee Richard Henry Lee chaired finalized the details of a defensive strategy for the eastern frontier and presented it to the House of Delegates for their consideration. The plan focused primarily on building up the state's navy, and it urged his colleagues to authorize funding for six additional vessels with cannons for "suppressing the enemy's cruisers in the bay of Chesapeake and its dependencies." To address manpower shortages, it called for new laws sanctioning the impressments of sailors and raising the pay scales for both officers and enlisted men. As a means of encouraging enlisted men to join, Lee and his colleagues added provisions for the distribution of captured enemy cargo "among the officers and men." Additionally, they advocated an impost, or trade duty, on various products shipped into Virginia, as well as revisions in current law to allow for orphans thirteen and older to be placed under the command of "the most prudent captains that can be found to take them."[26]

The House of Delegates quickly endorsed all of the recommendations made by Lee's committee, and a few days later, Richard Henry left Richmond, returning to Chantilly so that he could monitor the implementation of the defensive plan. Once he was back home, he sent letters to General Washington, providing him with accounts of Arnold's activity along the James River. Lee passed along reports that Arnold had "Six ships, 7 or 8 brigs & 10 other vessels," with between "1500 and 2000 troops at Jamestown." In all likelihood, Lee believed that Arnold would continue moving up the James River with "the Design . . . to plunder & interrupt our Attention to the Southern War."[27]

As Lee continued receiving intelligence about Arnold's activities, he also monitored the movements of a small British fleet that had entered into the Potomac River under the command of Captain Thomas Graves toward the end of May 1781. Much to Richard Henry's alarm, within a week of entering the river, Graves established a beachhead on Blackstone's Island, a location within sight of both Stratford Landing and Chantilly-on-the-Potomac. Richard Henry and his son Ludwell, who had recently returned from France with his uncle Arthur Lee, watched the British from the upper floors of Chantilly and were ready to sound the alarm if Graves dispatched a landing party from the island.[28]

Fortunately for Richard Henry and his immediate family, Chantilly Landing could not be seen from the island and could not be approached unless the invaders possessed intimate knowledge of the intricate creeks and streams in the vicinity. Stratford Landing, however, did not have the benefit of natural cover. Certainly, it was the target of Graves's foray, because the British flotilla could easily have seen the extensive dockyard stretching out into the river, along with the warehouses and mill, making it an obvious target for the British to strike. Two days after he arrived at Blackstone's Island, Graves made his move, as British troops launched an attack on Stratford Landing. Richard Henry, leading the Westmoreland County militia, led a successful effort to turn the invaders back. Afterward, Lee sent detailed accounts of the brief altercation, dubbed the Battle of Stratford Landing, to friends and colleagues. He wrote to one correspondent that

I am at present lamed by my horse falling on me in a late engagement with the enemy who landed under cover of heavy cannonades from three vessels of war upon a small body of our militia well posted—After a small engagement we had the pleasure to see the enemy, tho superior in number, run to their boats and precipitately reembark having sustained a small loss of killed and wounded.[29]

Lee owed his good fortune to a decision by Graves to only burn homes and destroy tobacco warehouses. He did not have the resources to fight sustained battles with local militia or anyone else. Consequently, when his men met resistance, they beat a hasty retreat back toward Blackstone's Island. Nonetheless, the victory invigorated Richard Henry and the militias in the area. The short battle, however, also highlighted the need for additional support, if the British planned to remain in the Potomac River. He wrote to members of Congress urgently requesting additional support for Virginia, more ammunition, and that some of the French forces stationed in the north be sent south. Lee explained that "hostile Vessels [are] plundering along our extensive shores," and the "Militia is constantly on foot." Without some sort of immediate relief, Richard Henry feared the worst would happen.[30]

VI

After receiving initial reports about Benedict Arnold's movements along the James River, General Washington dispatched the Marquis de Lafayette to Virginia; but as far as Richard Henry Lee was concerned, that was not enough. His calls went unheeded, and as a result, all he could do was stand by and watch the British continue sailing up the Potomac River. Graves's fleet moved past Chantilly and traveled as far north as Washington's plantation Mount Vernon, before turning back toward Chesapeake Bay.[31] The lack of support from neighboring states during this time of crisis annoyed Lee. His only course of action was to do his best toward maintaining the best coastal defense possible with his limited resources. As the enemy remained in the vicinity, however, Lee became increasingly concerned after realizing he had misplaced his commission as a colonel in the state militia. He quickly sent a letter forward to Governor Jefferson informing him that the "frequent moving of my Papers to get out of the way of the Enemy" has resulted in the loss of the document. As long as Graves remained in the area, Richard Henry had to be prepared, in the event of his capture. Should such events transpire, Lee reiterated that "a Commission may be necessary in case of falling into the enemies hands," and he asked Jefferson to address the situation as soon as possible.[32] Three days later, however,

Lee determined he could no longer wait; he took his family and abandoned Chantilly so that he could move to safer quarters further inland.

"You may observe by the place from whence I write," Richard Henry informed his brother, "that Chantilly is no longer our place of residence."[33] He established a temporary home at a plantation once occupied by George Washington's mother, Mary Ball Washington, called Epping Forest. Lee and his family remained there a month before venturing back to Chantilly. Once he was back in his home, he continued monitoring enemy movements in the area, as well as the progress of the American southern campaigns against the British. Lee's initial abandonment of Chantilly coincided with Lord Cornwallis's entry into Virginia with his army. The British commander's forces soon joined those commanded by Benedict Arnold at Petersburg, about forty miles south of Richmond. The two commanders then crossed the James River in pursuit of Lafayette's army.

Cornwallis's presence in Virginia caused Richard Henry the most consternation. Lee was well aware of the weakened defenses of the Northern Neck. He took count and determined that, all told, the four largest counties in the Neck could muster only about 420 militiamen, a woefully small force, should Cornwallis turn his army in that direction. His worst fear was that the British army would continue marching northward toward the Potomac. His concerns were temporarily calmed when he learned that Cornwallis had turned his army toward Charlottesville instead of the Potomac, but panic set in when Lee received word that 1,700 British troops had landed in Gloucester County. He could no longer countenance the ineptitude in Richmond that characterized, in Lee's mind, Jefferson's handling of the crisis, and he urged Congress to give Washington dictatorial powers.[34] He bitterly criticized other states as well, noting that Virginia had received "no assistance from our Sister States or from our Ally, whilst our veteran regulars have been all sacrificed in the common cause."[35] Virginia had done her part, and Lee deeply resented the lack of support from others, a sentiment that would remain with him for a long time after the war with Britain had ended.

VII

The presence of Cornwallis's army made Richard Henry fear another possible grave consequence: slave rebellions. He noted to one correspondent that "2 or 3000 negroes" were marching with the British, that many planters in the area had "lost every slave they had in the world," and that "this [had] been the case of all who were near the enemy." As Lee recounted the various personal losses sustained by many of his friends, either at the hands of Cornwallis's army or in the wake of Graves's fleet, he concluded that the British "appear to carry on the war more upon the views of private plunder & enriching individuals, than upon any plan of national advantage."[36]

As the summer of 1781 approached, British troop movements in Virginia sparked the concern in Lee's mind that, should the enemy occupy the central portion of the state between the York River and Rappahannock River, then the Northern Neck would be cut off and barred from receiving needed support. He was well aware that Cornwallis's men had removed "every kind of Stock" they could find, and what "they cannot remove they destroy." He voiced his frustration over what he regarded as a chaotic situation and his inability to assist, even when called. "Half our militia [has been] . . . drafted for the Marquis," Lee noted, "but how to get at him I know not, as the enemy is between us and them."[37] As far as Richard Henry was concerned, Virginia seemed to be on an endless downward spiral, and he blamed much of the problem on Thomas Jefferson, who vacated his office as governor soon after the British invasion began. Lee regarded this behavior as the kind that placed Virginia in "the moment of its greatest danger." As the summer drew to an end, Richard Henry understood that he was helpless in terms of Jefferson's abandonment of his office, so he did what he could to prepare for another British assault on the Northern Neck. Lee requested additional supplies from Richmond, but his concerns soon tapered off as he received reports that Cornwallis began concentrating his forces at Yorktown, leading Lee to the conclusion that the next major military activities would occur in that part of the state, not the Northern Neck.[38]

Richard Henry's hopes began to rise about the American cause in September as he received news that General Washington and the French commander Comte de Rochambeau had arrived in Virginia leading a combined force of 12,000 soldiers. Soon after their arrival, they joined together with Lafayette's army. Lee dispatched 200 men from the Westmoreland County militia, including his son Ludwell, so that they could do their part in assisting Washington.[39] Lee indicated that he would be unable to accompany his son because he labored "under a severe fit of the gout"; but the colonel was delighted to learn that after his son arrived, General Washington appointed him to serve as one of Lafayette's staff officers, a post Ludwell Lee held until the end of the war with Great Britain.[40]

Although Lee's health problems kept him confined at Chantilly, he devoted a considerable amount of time and energy addressing the problem of feeding the army that Washington and Rochambeau commanded. He gathered provisions, calling upon his neighbors to turn over all the available flour and wheat in the Northern Neck so that it could be transported to Washington's army as it encamped in the area around Yorktown. He wrote to the general, urging him, under military necessity, to empower either justices of the peace, first militia officers, or members of the House of Delegates to "take one half of the bacon and salt beef in possession of every family, and dispatch the supplies in pressed wagons and carts, or Vessels immediately to the army." Lee believed such an extension of authority was necessary because "victory must not be prevented by the want of victuals, and these must be obtained at any rate."[41] Richard Henry continued his efforts to requisition supplies from various sources throughout the Northern Neck. He received the sanction of Jefferson's replacement, Governor Thomas Nelson, who directed Lee to gather corn and wheat from residents along the Potomac and Rappahannock Rivers. Before long, Richard Henry reported that he had secured more than 1,000 barrels of corn and more than 100,000 bushels of wheat. He added sixty bushels of oats and 30,000 pounds of hay for the army's livestock, which he also acquired from residents of the Northern Neck.[42]

While Lee garnered food and supplies for Washington's army, the American forces laid siege to Yorktown. Americans and French troops hemmed Cornwallis in on all sides. When the British commander learned that Admiral Comte de Grasse and the French fleet had arrived in the Chesapeake Capes, cutting off British reinforcements from New York, he assessed his bleak situation, and on October 16, 1781, he ordered a desperate move to abandon Yorktown by attempting a risky night crossing of the York River to Gloucester. The effort failed, and early the next day, he requested terms for surrender from General Washington. When Richard Henry Lee learned of Cornwallis's surrender, he wondered if the American success at Yorktown would secure "an independent peace in the spring?"[43] Little did he realize it would take another two years before Britain and America would finally sign the treaty that would officially end the War for American Independence.

VIII

Although the diplomatic wrangling between Britain and the United States was far from over, Richard Henry Lee began contemplating the postwar situation for America the moment Washington and Rochambeau arrived in Virginia. He identified what he regarded as two major areas of concern. First, Lee said Virginia must pay off its war debt as soon as possible. Second, he advocated the establishment of a permanent defense plan for Chesapeake Bay to avoid similar problems the state faced against the British in the event of another war. Additionally, Lee called for all tobacco planters in Virginia to load all available ships with tobacco and dispatch them immediately to Holland. He believed the revenue from these shipments would raise enough capital to fund Virginia's debt.

Richard Henry also thought speed was essential so that planters "may avail [themselves] of the present [market price] before individual Traders under a free navigation can fill the foreign markets."[44] Richard Henry Lee hoped Virginians would take immediate advantage of the presence of the French fleet because of the continued threat posed by pirates in the area. He suggested that Virginia secure the purchase of captured British warships from Admiral de Grasse because he was certain that "piratical practices . . . will undoubtedly commence again . . . [as] soon as the French fleet goes away." Lee believed he acted on good authority, noting that he was "well informed that several companies [of pirates] are forming on the eastern Shores of the State & Maryland & on the Tangiers to carry on this infamous and distressing plan of plunder."[45]

Lee's concern over Virginia's postwar situation resulted in large part from the lack of support his state received from its neighbors and from Congress during the British invasion. Congress's inability, in particular, led Richard Henry to advocate an independent course for Virginia to address the immediate needs of the state. Of course, Lee understood that to a large extent, Congress's hands were tied because Maryland had refused to ratify the Articles of Confederation until March 1781; but this realization did little toward ameliorating Lee's concerns, because the Maryland delegation had refused to ratify until Virginia abandoned its exclusive claim to the Ohio River valley. All this meant to Lee was that Maryland would not hesitate to sacrifice its sister state in an attempt to preserve the interests of a group of politically well-connected land speculators.

Richard Henry Lee was certainly familiar with the dispute over Virginia's western lands and its effect on the ratification of the Articles of Confederation. He recognized this potential obstacle as early as November 1778. At that juncture, Delaware, Maryland, and New Jersey refused to endorse the proposed plan of government. By the spring of 1779, after the British army had ravaged both New Jersey and Pennsylvania, Delaware and New Jersey reluctantly signed the Articles, leaving Maryland as the last holdout. Still, the two hesitant signatories maintained that elements of the document remained "unequal and disadvantageous" to their state's interests.[46] Lee rejected the stance taken by these three states. He laid the blame squarely on the "secret machinations" of the "most heated Opponents of [Virginia's] claim," yet Lee was not insensitive to their concerns. He proposed that Virginia would voluntarily fix its boundary at the Ohio River and "that the Country beyond [be] settled for [the] common good." He asked only that Virginia receive adequate compensation for expenses the state incurred as a result of George Rogers Clark's expedition against the British in the West. Richard Henry genuinely believed that this "would be [Virginia's] wisest course."[47] Lee also believed, since this proposition essentially dissolved the Ohio Company of Virginia, that Congress should nullify the purchases made by other land companies in the ceded territory.

As the British invasion of Virginia began to intensify in the fall of 1780, the state reiterated its willingness to cede all of its western lands to Congress—that is, if that body agreed to sell the land at a fair price, apply the money collected toward paying off the national debt, and compensate Virginia for the expense "actually incurred in wresting that country from the British possession by her arms alone."[48] Richard Henry communicated these sentiments to his old friend in Congress, Samuel Adams. He believed that when these terms were agreed to, then Maryland would be denied a "just objection to signing the Confederation." If Maryland still resisted after the Virginia cession, Lee said that the twelve states that had already signed on should "take care of themselves by confederating without that refractory sister."[49] Maryland remained recalcitrant. In January 1781, Virginia paved the way for Maryland to join the union by ceding all of its claims to western lands in the interest of national unity in the face of the British invasion. Maryland relented and finally signed the Articles of Confederation; however, representatives of the state set the stage for future conflicts by insisting that "by acceding to the said confederation, this state doth not relinquish . . . any right or interest she hath with the United or Confederated States to the back country."[50]

The reason for Maryland's protestations, in spite of the overtures and concessions made by Virginia, was due to the corollary that Congress, upon receiving the ceded territory, would nullify all land company purchases made in the territory once claimed by Virginia—a sharp rebuke to land speculators who controlled the Indiana Company of Pennsylvania and the Illinois-Wabash Company based in Maryland. As a result of this additional provision, prominent members of Congress, such as Robert Morris, resisted the Virginia cession. Maryland's ratification was a matter of expediency. As a consequence, after Cornwallis surrendered at Yorktown, Morris and his allies in Congress sought ways to backtrack and retain Virginia's cession without abrogating the speculative purchases of the Indiana and Illinois-Wabash companies.

This sort of maneuvering in Congress demonstrated that Robert Morris remained a formidable leader in the Continental Congress. As Maryland prepared to sign the Articles, Congress was in the process of abolishing the old committee system in favor of a series of executive offices. In February 1781, Congress elected Morris as superintendent of finance, a post he accepted the following May. The new superintendent immediately set upon the task of restructuring the American trade and monetary systems with the goal of promoting a stronger, more centralized national government. By November, as the military crisis eased and as Morris initiated these changes, his allies in Congress took a bold step and rejected Virginia's cession of its western lands. The final report on this matter asserted that the land claimed by Virginia north of the Ohio River, in actuality, belonged to the Six Nations of the Iroquois and was in fact part of New York—not Virginia. Congress's argument rested on the dubious argument first offered by Conrad Gerard in 1779: that Virginia's boundaries had long since been determined first by the Proclamation of 1763, and later by the Quebec Act of 1774. Congress now asserted that private individuals had purchased the territory outside these boundaries before the war with Great Britain began; therefore, their purchases remained intact. Consequently, the only territory to which Virginia had legal claim was the area north of the Carolinas, south of Maryland, and east of the Appalachian Mountains.

This sort of incredulous revision of Virginia's territorial boundaries found justification in a pamphlet titled *Plain Facts*, written and distributed by Richard Henry Lee's old adversary, Samuel Wharton, who no longer resided in London but now served as part of the Pennsylvanian delegation in the Continental Congress. Wharton presented an account of events surrounding the 1768 negotiations at Fort Stanwix that represented the foundation of the Indiana Company (formerly known as the Grand Ohio Company). He demanded that Virginia prove its claim to western lands, confident that no such proof existed. Consequently, Wharton concluded that, in the absence of such evidence, Virginia's 1781 cession was invalid because "no man can give what he does not own."[51] Such comments astounded Lee and other members of Virginia's delegation who were suspicious of Morris and Wharton. They had expected that Congress would willingly accept the cession without question. Lee told one correspondent that Wharton and his supporters once complained of how the "avarice and ambition of Virginia" had prevented confederation. "Now when Virginia had yielded . . . more than half her Charter claim," Lee noted, "the argument will be applied to the terms as improper." Richard Henry placed the blame squarely on the shoulders of "land jobbers who have long had in contemplation immense possessions in this ceded country, under the pretence of Indian purchases."[52]

The blatant refutation of Virginia's long-standing claims presented by Wharton in *Plain Facts* startled the members of the Old Dominion's congressional delegation, including James Madison, who supported much of Morris's agenda in Congress. Madison disputed the suggestion that the position adopted by Congress on Virginia's boundaries represented a final decision, and he went as far as suggesting that such language threatened the existence of the union. In response to Congress's action, the Virginia House of Delegates asked Thomas Jefferson and George Mason to write a legal brief defending the state's charter claims; thus, the stage was set, once again, for another battle over western lands.

IX

The specious claims made by Congress regarding Virginia's cession, for obvious reasons, sparked outrage in the Old Dominion and galvanized Richard Henry Lee and his friends to take immediate action against this abuse of power in Congress. Robert Morris and his agenda in Congress now became the target. In his attempt to strengthen the national government, Morris proposed, as early as February 1781, that Congress collect an impost, or trade duty, amounting to a 5 percent tariff on various products shipped into the United States. Morris believed that Congress needed some sort of independent income to conduct day-to-day business and retire the national debt. Before such a law could be enacted, the Articles of Confederation would have to be amended, which meant that before the impost could be put into effect, the unanimous consent of all thirteen states had to be secured. Morris regarded this as a temporary setback and remained confident that the military threat posed by the British army in 1781 would marshal the states and Congress behind his cause. Events seemed to prove Morris correct. That summer Virginia became one of the first states to endorse the plan, and by February 1782, all states had signed on, with the exception of Rhode Island; however, that state's delegation had already expressed their support for the measure. They only had to wait for final instructions from their state legislature before officially signing the impost plan. Morris was confident that his plan could not fail.

Events suddenly changed, however, when Rhode Island abruptly recalled all of its representatives and sent a new slate of delegates, led by David Howell, who openly opposed the impost plan. Howell challenged Morris to explain why Congress needed an independent source of income. He reminded his colleagues that in January 1781 Virginia ceded its claims to western lands so that Congress could have a means of raising revenue. He questioned the decision to rescind the cession in November 1781 while allowing the territory to remain in the hands of private speculators. Howell also noted that Rhode Island depended heavily on the collection of trade duties as a means of retiring its own state debt, and he indicated his state's reluctance to give that revenue to Congress, when the sale of western lands could easily fill the national coffers.

Howell's argument set the stage for Rhode Island to withdraw its support of Morris's impost plan, and since it required unanimous consent, the bill effectively died. The Rhode Islander had effectively tied the impost plan to the ongoing dispute over western lands and forced Morris and his cohorts into an awkward position. They now had to find some way to simultaneously win passage of the impost plan and disallow Virginia's 1781 cession. Morris devoted much of his time in 1782 trying to salvage his impost plan, but his efforts failed; and in November of that year, Rhode Island made its rejection official. Congress quickly dispatched a special delegation to try to change the small state's mind, but Morris's hopes diminished further when he suddenly received word that Virginia had repealed its earlier approval of the impost plan.

The news of the Old Dominion's repeal caused Morris and his nationalist supporters to panic. One of Morris's Virginia allies, James Madison, wrote to Benjamin Harrison, who then served as the state governor, asking who was responsible for the repeal. In January 1783, Harrison sent word back to Madison that it was none other than Richard Henry Lee who sponsored the measure rescinding the impost; using his core support in the legislature, Lee successfully passed his measure through the House of Delegates. Virginia's repeal of the impost represented a clear response to Congress's rejection of Virginia's 1781 cession, and once again, Richard Henry thwarted Morris's agenda. Even Lee's enemies in Congress had to acknowledge that the Virginian had outmaneuvered them. Samuel Wharton commented on Lee's "extraordinary" conduct and "unexampled Perverseness" in regard to his state's "futile Claim to the immense Western region."[53]

Reports of Richard Henry Lee's role in the repeal of the impost sparked a new round of acrimonious personal attacks on his character and reputation. Rumors flew about that opponents of the impost were actually British sympathizers. Samuel Griffith and John Francis Mercer introduced a motion in Virginia's House of Delegates claiming that Richard Henry and Arthur Lee were leaders of a "British Party" in Virginia. Mercer revived the old stories of Richard Henry's encounter with Dr. John Berkenhout and also circulated a letter from French foreign minister Vergennes that cast doubt on Arthur Lee's commitment to the French alliance. As the scandal made its way to Congress, Samuel Adams and Henry Laurens were also identified, along with the Lees, as ringleaders of this treasonous group.

Mercer quoted from a 1778 letter from Vergennes to Conrad Gerard indicating that he refused to communicate with the American commissioners because he "could not distinguish between them and he suspected Dr. Lee and all about him."[54] Simultaneously, similar rumors spread through the halls of Congress. Samuel Osgood of Massachusetts told one correspondent that "a British interest is strongly suspected even among those who are zealous for the Independence of these States."[55] Although Osgood did not mention any names, Richard Henry and Arthur Lee's names were soon attached to the controversy as leaders of the so-called British Party threatening the security of the United States.

Virginia's House of Delegates tried to dispense with these erroneous stories by passing a unanimous resolution exonerating Richard Henry Lee, stating that his "public conduct entitles him to the fullest confidence and warmest approbation of his country."[56] Yet, in spite of this show of support, Lee could not contain his disgust toward his political enemies. He wrote to his brother-in-law Dr. William Shippen Jr., in Philadelphia, that he "was going to write a word or two about politics—but Mum for that—Some penetrating eye may see it, or curious ear may hear what I have written; and with lengthened face, shrug'd shoulders, and important air, whisper 'an enemy to the French Alliance.'"[57] In the end, these transparent rumors did nothing to alter Virginia's decision to repeal the impost plan, nor did the stories lessen the high regard many of Lee's colleagues bestowed upon him.

X

Robert Morris and the advocates of the impost now had no other option than to concede defeat. In April 1783, they withdrew their initial plan and submitted a modified plan. The 1781 impost plan called for a levy "upon all goods" imported into the United States; the revised version listed specifically which items would be subject to the duty, thereby clearly demarcating which revenue would be collected by the state governments and which would go into the national coffers.[58]

In spite of the modification, Richard Henry Lee made it clear that he opposed the collection of any type of impost. He simply no longer trusted anything even remotely associated with Robert Morris. Lee challenged the notion that the impost would help fund the national debt and countered that its existence, even in its modified form, threatened the solvency of Virginia. As Richard Henry told one correspondent, "besides the danger to liberty that it threatens," he feared the impost would "strangle our infant commerce in its birth, make us pay more than our proportion, and sacrifice this country to its northern brethren."[59] He added that if Congress acquired the power to levy taxes, then it would only be a matter of time before the individual states would be "gradually sapped [of that] all important power of the purse."[60] Richard Henry solicited the opinions of others but found very few Virginians in his social circle that shared his opinion regarding the government's overall taxing authority; however, Lee did find support to defeat the modified plan when the matter came to a vote in the House of Delegates.[61] In the eyes of nationalist-oriented leaders like Robert Morris, Virginia's repeal of the 1781 impost and subsequent rejection of the modified plan highlighted the central weaknesses of the Articles of Confederation—that essentially one faction could stop national policy dead in its tracks. As Lee sought to defend the Potomac from British depredations during the darkest days of the War for American Independence, he had to constantly fend off attacks of a personal nature from his political enemies. Richard Henry regarded his struggle against the British and his fight with Morris and his cohorts in the same light—as part of his determined effort to preserve Virginia's most vital interests and its position as a leading force within the American union. Although he emerged from these battles wounded in mind, body, and spirit, he persevered and soon found himself again in Richmond, where he resumed his place among his peers.

NOTES

1. R. H. Lee to Arthur Lee, May 23, 1779, quoted in Robert Fallow and Marion West Stoar, "The Old Dominion under Fire: The Chesapeake Invasions," in *The Chesapeake Bay in the American Revolution,* ed. Ernest McNeill Eller (Centreville, MD: Tidewater Publications, 1981), 447–48.

2. Dean C. Allard, "The Potomac Navy of 1776, " *Virginia Magazine of History and Biography* 24 (October 1976): 411–12.

3. R. H. Lee to Landon Carter, July 21, 1776, *Lee Letters*, 1: 209.

4. Lord Dunmore to George Germain, March 30, 1776, quoted in George M. Curtis III, "The Goodrich Family and the Revolution in Virginia, 1774–1776," *Virginia Magazine of History and Biography* 84 (January 1976): 52.

5. R. H. Lee to Robert Morris, February 3, 1777, *Lee Letters*, 1: 253. Lee used various spellings of the Goodrich name, none of them, however, utilizing the correct spelling. Throughout Lee's correspondence, readers will see references to Guthridge, Guntridge, and Gutride. The situations detailed in the letters, however, leave no doubt that he is in fact referring to the Goodrich family.

6. R. H. Lee to General William Whipple, November 29, 1778, *Lee Letters*, 1: 455.

7. R. H. Lee to George Mason, June 9, 1779, *Lee Letters*, 2: 67–68.

8. R. H. Lee to [Colonel William Davies?], October 7, 1781, *Lee Letters*, 2: 259; R. H. Lee to Thomas Nelson, October 28, 1781, *Lee Letters*, 2: 263–64. Although these letters were written after the fact, both contain summaries of Lee's efforts to organize the Westmoreland County militia in the summer of 1779.

9. R. H. Lee to Henry Laurens, June 18, 1779, *Lee Letters*, 2: 72.

10. R. H. Lee to Samuel Adams, June 18, 1779, *Lee Letters*, 2: 72.

11. R. H. Lee to Samuel Adams, June 19, 1779, *Lee Letters*, 2: 75.

12. R. H. Lee to Samuel Adams, June 19, 1779, *Lee Letters*, 2: 75.

13. R. H. Lee to Henry Laurens, May 27, 1779, *Lee Letters*, 2: 58.

14. R. H. Lee to Henry Laurens, May 27, 1779, *Lee Letters*, 2: 58.

15. R. H. Lee to Henry Laurens, June 6, 1779, *Lee Letters*, 2: 64.

16. R. H. Lee to Henry Laurens, August 1, 1779, *Lee Letters*, 2: 99.

17. R. H. Lee to Henry Laurens, August 13, 1779, *Lee Letters*, 2: 120; R. H. Lee to Arthur Lee, August 14, 1779, *Lee Letters*, 2: 124.

18. R. H. Lee to the Editor of the *Pennsylvania Packet*, August 17, 1779, *Lee Letters*, 2: 125–30; R. H. Lee to the Editor of the *Pennsylvania Packet*, August 24, 1779, *Lee Letters*, 2: 132–38; and R. H. Lee to the Editor of the *Pennsylvania Packet*, August 31, 1779, *Lee Letters*, 2: 138–42.

19. R. H. Lee to Samuel Adams, January 18, 1780, *Lee Letters*, 2: 169.

20. R. H. Lee to Samuel Adams, January 18, 1780, *Lee Letters*, 2: 169.

21. R. H. Lee to Thomas Jefferson, July 8, 1779, *Lee Letters*, 2: 83.

22. R. H. Lee to Thomas Jefferson, July 8, 1779, *Lee Letters*, 2: 83–84.

23. R. H. Lee to Samuel Adams, January 18, 1780, *Lee Letters*, 2: 170.

24. R. H. Lee to Samuel Adams, November 10, 1780, *Lee Letters*, 2: 211.

25. Admiral Arbuthnot to Captain Symonds, December 4, 1780, in "The Old Dominion Under Fire," 458.

26. "Plan for the Defense of the Eastern Frontier," December 1780, *Journal of the House of Delegates*, 12 vols. (Richmond, VA: 1828), 7: 43–44. Hereafter cited as *Journal of the House of Delegates*.

27. R. H. Lee to General George Washington, January 7, 1781, *Lee Letters*, 2: 212.

28. "Burnt All Their Houses: The Log of HMS *Savage* during a Raid up the Potomac River, Spring 1781," ed. Fritz Hirschfeld, *Virginia Magazine of History and Biography* (October 1991): 522.

29. R. H. Lee to Samuel Adams, April 1, 1781, *Lee Letters*, 2: 218–19.

30. R. H. Lee to Samuel Adams, April 1, 1781, *Lee Letters*, 2: 218–19.

31. "Burnt All Their Houses," 524.

32. R. H. Lee to Thomas Jefferson, May 10, 1781, *Lee Letters*, 2: 223.

33. R. H. Lee to Arthur Lee, May 13, 1781, *Lee Letters*, 2: 224.

34. R. H. Lee to James Lovell, June 12, 1781, 2: 237.

35. R. H. Lee to Arthur Lee, June 4, 1781, *Lee Letters*, 2: 230.

36. R. H. Lee to William Lee, July 15, 1781, *Lee Letters*, 2: 242.

37. R. H. Lee to Arthur Lee, June 4, 1781, *Lee Letters*, 2: 230–31.

38. R. H. Lee to [Colonel William Davies?], August 22, 1781, *Lee Letters*, 2: 245.

39. R. H. Lee to William Davies, September 5, 1781, *Lee Letters*, 2: 250–53.

40. R. H. Lee to General George Washington, September 17, 1781, *Lee Letters*, 2: 253.

41. R. H. Lee to William Davies, September 5, 1781, *Lee Letters*, 2: 253; R. H. Lee to General George Washington, September 17, 1781, *Lee Letters*, 2: 255.

42. R. H. Lee to Thomas Nelson, October 28, 1781, *Lee Letters*, 2: 262–63.

43. R. H. Lee to Thomas McKean, November 22, 1781, *Lee Letters*, 2: 266.

44. R. H. Lee to William Davies, September 3, 1781, *Lee Letters*, 2: 249–50.

45. R. H. Lee to William Davies, September 5, 1781, *Lee Letters*, 2: 251.

46. "Eight States Sign the Articles of Confederation," July 9, 1779, *The Documentary History of the Ratification of the Constitution*, 18 vols., ed. Merrill Jensen et al. (Madison: State Historical Society of Wisconsin, 1976–), 1: 124–37. Hereafter, cited as *DHRC*.

47. R. H. Lee to Samuel Adams, September 10, 1780, *Lee Letters*, 2: 201.

48. R. H. Lee to Samuel Adams, September 10, 1780, *Lee Letters*, 2: 201.

49. R. H. Lee to Samuel Adams, September 10, 1780, *Lee Letters*, 2: 201.

50. "Maryland Signs [the Articles of Confederation]," March 1, 1781, *DHRC*, 1: 136.

51. Samuel Wharton, *Plain Facts* (Philadelphia: 1781), 4–5, 148.

52. R. H. Lee to Samuel Adams, February 5, 1781, *Lee Letters*, 2: 214–15.

53. Samuel Wharton to John Cook, January 6, 1783, *Letters of Delegates*, 19: 550.

54. *Journals of the Virginia House of Delegates*, December 12, 1782.

55. Samuel Osgood to John Lowell, January 6, 1783, *Letters of Delegates*, 19: 638.

56. *Journals of the Virginia House of Delegates*, December 12, 1782.

57. R. H. Lee to William Shippen Jr., January 7, 1783, *Lee Letters*, 2: 277–78.

58. "Grant of Power to Collect Import Duties," February 3, 1781, *DHRC*, 1: 140–41; "Grant of Temporary Power to Collect Import Duties and Request for Supplementary Funds," April 18, 1783, *DHRC*, 1: 146.

59. R. H. Lee to R. Wormley Carter, June 3, 1783, *Lee Letters*, 2: 282.

60. R. H. Lee to William Whipple, July 1, 1783, *Lee Letters*, 2: 283.

61. R. H. Lee to William Whipple, July 1, 1783, *Lee Letters*, 2: 284; see also Richard H. Lee, *The Life of Richard Henry Lee and His Correspondence*, 2: 113.

• 8 •

"Mr. President"

I

$\mathcal{A}$lthough Richard Henry had not held a seat in Congress since the spring of 1779, he clearly demonstrated that he wielded a lot of influence within his home state and could thereby shape national policy. After his departure from Congress in the midst of the Deane–Lee imbroglio, he devoted much of his time rebuilding his reputation, an endeavor he met with success. He became more influential within Virginia's state government. In 1780, he served a brief stint as Speaker of the House of Delegates, but he spent most of his time monitoring defensive efforts in the Northern Neck. After Cornwallis's surrender at Yorktown, Richard Henry Lee's colleagues placed his name in nomination for state governor; however, he placed a disappointing third place, behind John Page and Benjamin Harrison. Yet, despite this setback, Virginia's attorney general, Edmund Randolph, observed that in 1783, when it came to politics in the Old Dominion, three personalities were dominant—Richard Henry Lee, Patrick Henry, and John Tyler.

Patrick Henry rarely attended meetings of the House of Delegates and consequently relied heavily on Tyler to act as his surrogate. Tyler served as Speaker of the House during the 1781, 1782, and 1783 sessions. After this last meeting drew to a close, Richard Henry attempted to challenge what he regarded as Henry's de facto control of the House of Delegates by running again for the office of Speaker. Lee lost to Tyler, which served to illustrate the degree of power wielded by Henry in the state. The main areas of departure between Lee and Henry fell within the realm of tax collection. Richard Henry actively promoted efforts calling for Virginia's compliance with its monetary requisitions to Congress, believing that this would negate the need for a national impost.

Lee's defeat in the race for Speaker resulted from a coalition that consisted of Henry's base and a pro-Morris group in Virginia that was determined to lessen Lee's influence in state politics.

Richard Henry's opposition to the modified impost remained strong only because Congress had not clarified its position on Virginia's 1781 cession of western lands. In June 1783, Congress appointed a commission to review the matter and subsequently announced the following March that Congress found Virginia's original terms acceptable. This action dramatically extended the national domain and paved the way for Lee and his friends in Virginia to support the modified impost of 1783. The progression of Virginia's land cession and the eventual passage of the modified impost strongly indicated that some sort of trade-off occurred. Each side had determined to protect its own set of vested interests, and in the end, they reached a compromise. The resolution of the conflict signaled a shift in the political balance of power in Congress. Once the Articles of Confederation were ratified in 1781, the nationalists under the direction of Robert Morris reigned supreme. The Articles, however, imposed term limits stipulating that no one person could serve in Congress for more than three out of six years. As a result, by the spring of 1784, several prominent nationalists were rotated out of office. Morris then resigned in disgust as superintendent of finance, thus setting the stage for Richard Henry Lee's return to Congress. In June 1784, Virginia's House of Delegates appointed him to the Continental Congress, and Lee, once again, started making preparations to leave his beloved Chantilly-on-the-Potomac.

II

The period between the British surrender at Yorktown and Richard Henry Lee's reappointment to Congress was a trying time for the Virginian. He defended his home and state against British depredations and "stock jobbering" land speculators, and his family continued to grow. Anne Lee gave birth to another child, a son they named Francis. Although Richard Henry and Anne now celebrated the birth of their fourth son and the third birthday of Cassius, Richard Henry suffered another personal loss as well. About this same time, Richard Henry learned of the death of his dear sister, Hannah. Lee had maintained close ties with his older sister.

For most of Richard Henry's adult life, Hannah remained a widow, the Mistress of Pecketone. She married Gawain Corbin in 1747, but in 1760, her husband suffered a horse-riding accident and died of his injuries. Hannah Lee Corbin inherited an impressive estate that included several tracts of land in the counties of Westmoreland, King George, and Fauquier; 500 acres in Lancaster county; two-thirds of a 3,000-acre plantation in Caroline County; and numerous slaves.[1] As he convalesced during his final days, Gawain Corbin displayed a particularly vindictive spirit. He revised his last will and testament, mandating she would have to surrender half the inheritance to their daughter, Martha, and that, should Hannah ever remarry or move from Westmoreland County, she would have to surrender the bulk her inherited property to their daughter. To make matters worse, Corbin named Richard Henry as the chief executor of the estate, legally binding him to enforce this injustice inflicted upon his sister.[2]

Hannah Lee Corbin remained undeterred. She threw herself into the management of her properties, and since all of her brothers played such prominent political roles, she kept abreast of matters of state as well. Later, when she met and fell in love with Richard Hall, she arranged for him to move in with her at Pecketone, where they lived together as lovers without securing the marriage sacrament. Since she never married Hall, Hannah never technically violated the terms imposed on her by her deceased husband. When she gave birth to a child, she gave the infant the Corbin surname even though Hall was the father. Although her relationship with Hall raised eyebrows in the community, her brothers remained steadfastly by her side; young Arthur, the exception, said on learning about the illicit union that "sooner in me might every faculty be changed than I would cease to love her. Even now compassion steals upon me and melts me into tears for her perversion."[3]

Richard Henry Lee respected and cherished his older sister. They would frequently engage in political debates with each other. In one set of letters, Hannah wrote her brother complaining about how Virginia's laws expected widows to pay taxes on their property yet did not allow them to vote. Richard Henry responded by agreeing with his sister about the unfortunate circumstance she described. He advocated the extension of suffrage to women who never married and widowed landowners. Richard Henry noted that "the doctrine of representation is a large subject, and it is certain that it ought to be extended as far as wisdom and policy can allow," adding that he saw no reason why either "wisdom" or "policy" should "forbid widows having property from voting."[4]

Unfortunately, this brief dialogue represents the only extant letter between Richard Henry and Hannah; nonetheless, the exchange reveals a deep sense of mutual respect and admiration, and the loss of his sister in 1782 was certainly an emotional setback for Richard Henry. Once again, he took on the sad task as executor of another sibling's estate. He was now the oldest surviving child of Thomas Lee. During America's struggle for independence, Richard Henry suffered the loss of Philip in 1775, Thomas Ludwell three years later in 1778, and now Hannah in her fifty-fifth year. In 1782, as Richard Henry turned fifty-two,

Figure 8.1. State claims to western lands, early 1780s.

he no doubt had a greater sense of his own mortality—after all, both of his older brothers were forty-eight years old at the time of their deaths. With such gloomy thoughts, Lee made arrangements to leave Anne and his two young boys, Cassius and Francis, and travel northward to Trenton, New Jersey, so he could again turn his attention to the public's business.

III

Richard Henry Lee arrived in Trenton ready to take his seat and get to work in November 1784. The intense political battles he waged in Congress between 1776 and 1779, with Congress's ineffectiveness in dealing with the British invasion of Virginia in 1781, had to a degree shaken his confidence in Congress's viability. Rather than seeking an extension of congressional authority, as Robert Morris and his supporters sought, Lee's experience confirmed his belief that more power should be concentrated at the state level. What he witnessed immediately after his arrival only served to strengthen his conviction that a Congress with limited powers would best serve the overall needs of the new nation. He was disturbed by what he described as the "strange insensibility" toward public service that he detected soon after his arrival. A week after the session was scheduled to begin, only a few members had bothered to even show up and take their seats—there was not even a quorum of delegates. Much to Lee's amazement, this situation remained unchanged for two more weeks.[5] The complete lack of enthusiasm and effort among the congressmen present made his stance on elevating state government over national authority more resolute.

By the end of November, a quorum had been achieved, so elections for executive offices could thus be held. After what delegates described as a contentious meeting, Congress accorded Richard Henry Lee with the honor of sitting in the president's chair—but it took a dozen ballots before the matter was finally settled.[6] Lee regarded his duties as president as perfunctory. His role was to help organize Congress's agenda, to keep the states informed, to notify American agents abroad about new policies instituted by Congress, and to receive and entertain foreign dignitaries. One of the first matters that Congress addressed concerned the location of the nation's capital. Trenton was regarded as temporary seat, and there was little interest expressed in staying there. Although Lee hoped that Congress would move further south, bringing him closer to Virginia and his family at Chantilly, the vote favoring New York City carried the day. Lee then immediately set to the task of notifying state executives of the decision and arranging Congress's agenda so it could resume business after the relocation.[7]

The most pressing matters, as far as Lee was concerned, related to unre-
solved foreign policy issues. There were two points of obvious concern for Lee.
The first involved the continued presence of British soldiers on American soil.
Article 7 of the 1783 Treaty of Paris, establishing a peace settlement between
Great Britain and United States, stipulated that British soldiers would be evac-
uated with "all convenient speed"; yet, more than a year later, the soldiers remained in place, and there was no sign indicating their impending departure.
The second issue concerned the eighth article of the peace settlement, guar-
anteeing the United States free navigation of the Mississippi River "from its
source to the ocean." The problem with the latter article was that the great
river fell within Spain's territorial dominions; consequently, the matter remained unresolved. Both of these issues struck at the heart of the United
States' national integrity and economic viability; thus, it remained high on
Lee's agenda during his presidency.

The items on Lee's agenda that concerned him the most were consistent with his long-standing interests in promoting westward expansion. After Congress finally acknowledged Virginia's 1781 cession and the Ohio
River valley was no longer within his state's territorial limits, Lee still believed that Virginia's future rested with America's firm control of its western
lands. As long as British soldiers occupied this region and as long as access to
the Mississippi River remained unsettled, the western reaches of the new nation could possibly be wrenched away by America's more powerful European
neighbors. Additionally, Richard Henry remained committed to the use of
money raised through the sale of public lands as the surest means of paying
down the debts the United States owed to France and Holland, and other nations as well.[8]

In most respects, the agenda set forth by Lee mirrored the itinerary he
had promoted since the 1760s, which encouraged the development of a
western empire to foster economic and political stability. When Britain
thwarted that goal with the Proclamation of 1763 and the Quebec Act of
1774, Lee helped lead the struggle for independence. When unscrupulous
land speculators threatened his desired objective, he aggressively defended
Virginia's claim to western lands to the exclusion of all others because he did
not trust their motives. When Congress agreed to the terms Lee and other
prominent Virginians stipulated, he then heartily backed the cession of the
Old Dominion's territorial claim, thereby helping to establish a national domain for the United States. Before this agenda could be secured, however,
four objectives had to be met. First, treaties between the United States and
Native American tribes inhabiting the region had to be negotiated; second,
British soldiers would have to evacuate American territory; third, a coherent
national policy providing for the orderly sale and settlement of the national
domain had to be established; and fourth, the future commercial interests of

the United States had to be guaranteed by securing the free navigation of the Mississippi River.

IV

Soon after his presidential term began, Richard Henry Lee confirmed that agents representing the United States had signed treaties with the Six Nations of the Iroquois and several other western tribes. He anticipated that, in the spring of 1785, other treaties would be signed with the remaining tribes inhabiting the northwestern sections of the Ohio River valley. Lee was hopeful that the United States could foster relationships with most of the tribes and maintain peaceful coexistence in the American west. His optimism soon diminished, however, as he received reports that the Shawnee, who inhabited territory in what is now the state of Kentucky, had refused to sign treaties with the United States. Adding to Lee's consternation were further reports that the reluctance expressed by the Shawnee was the result of "some active British emissary"—a situation that, in Richard Henry's mind, graphically highlighted the potential problems posed by tolerating the continued presence of British soldiers on American soil.

Lee feared that the British soldiers remained "sullen after defeat" and were merely waiting for "just provocation to renew . . . combat" with the United States. As far as he was concerned, if the rumors were true regarding British interference with American–Shawnee negotiations, then this represented a grave "transgression" against the 1783 peace settlement. He also accused British soldiers of stealing slaves from New York and spiriting them away to Canada, posing another potential challenge to American sovereignty. Lee fumed and expressed his frustration whenever he received this sort of information, but in the end, he acknowledged that the British could justifiably defend such actions because of the refusal on the part of many Americans to pay their outstanding debts to British merchants.[9]

In spite of such interference, Richard Henry believed that the United States must stay the course and establish amicable alliances with the Native Americans inhabiting the valleys of the Mississippi and Ohio Rivers. He understood that if America was going to consolidate its hold over its western reaches, an Indian war must be avoided. Consequently, in pursuit of this desired goal, Lee became increasingly preoccupied with the orderly settlement of the national domain. As more Americans flooded into the trans-Appalachian region, Richard Henry feared that hotheaded Americans might trigger the war he sought to avoid. With these concerns in mind, Lee began to devote more of his time and attention to a comprehensive national policy regarding the sale and settlement of western lands.

V

Congress had been considering a land policy long before Richard Henry Lee assumed his place as president. In the days immediately following Congress's acceptance of Virginia's cession in March 1784, Congress appointed a committee led by Thomas Jefferson and David Howell of Rhode Island to establish a procedure for selling the national domain and funding debt payments. By the end of April, Jefferson submitted the Land Ordinance of 1784 to Congress and the states, for their consideration. Resistance to the plan surfaced immediately, as land speculators in various states insisted that the land be parceled out in large tracts, rather than the small plots recommended by the proposed ordinance. The dispute persisted to the end of the 1784 legislative session, and Congress finally tabled the ordinance for consideration at some future date.[10]

When Richard Henry took the helm as president of Congress, he urged members to resume their deliberations on the ordinance. He relayed dire warnings from George Washington, who warned of a pending Indian war along the frontier if matters regarding western settlement were not finally resolved. Lee said that Congress must either provide for the orderly sale of the land or risk losing it all—along with its collateral benefits—because of squatters, an Indian war, or perhaps a renewed conflict with Great Britain.[11] Congress finally heeded Lee's call, and nearly a year after tabling Jefferson's ordinance, Congress renewed its consideration of the matter.[12]

Now Richard Henry Lee had the opportunity to confront the same problems Superintendent of Finance Robert Morris faced when he tried to pass the impost in 1781 and 1783. Lee had to await unanimous consent from all the states before the proposed ordinance could go into effect. A month after the debate began, only nine states had consented to the ordinance; but Lee remained confident the others would follow suit. Interestingly enough, as Richard Henry reported on the progress of the ordinance to George Washington, he indicated that only "one Man . . . keeps the Ordinance from passing"; unfortunately, Lee never mentioned the name of that particular individual.[13]

Richard Henry renewed his optimism a few days later as William Grayson, one of Lee's friends in Congress from Virginia, indicated that final approval of the ordinance was at hand. Grayson served on the Grand Committee assigned the task of finalizing the details of the ordinance. The two Virginians communicated quietly with each other during the deliberations, thus allowing Lee to follow the debates while maintaining a respectable distance from the day-to-day deliberations. Lee passed on the information he received to Washington and no doubt encouraged Grayson to do the same. Grayson informed Washington that "the President was kind enough to furnish me with an extract of your letter to him on the subject of the back country," providing confirmation of the collusion between this trio from Virginia.[14] Finally, on May 20, 1785, President Richard Henry Lee announced the passage of what became the Land Ordinance of 1785. Congress could now begin the orderly disposal of the national domain, and Lee estimated that Congress had approximately ten million acres at its immediate disposal. The passage of the ordinance gave Congress controlling authority to regulate the settlement of the region, which Lee hoped would facilitate the signing of peace treaties with the recalcitrant Shawnee and other tribes, which would secure an additional twenty million acres for the United States.[15] Finally, President Lee could turn his attention to the matter of securing the free navigation of the Mississippi River for the United States.

VI

Richard Henry Lee was well aware of America's tenuous relationship with Spain. He noted that Spain was "extremely jealous of our approximation to her South American territory" and fearful that the United States might pose a threat to Spain's American empire. Yet with these concerns in mind, Lee made preparations to receive the Spanish foreign minister Don Diego de Gardoqui and then await the final resolution of the issue regarding American access to the Mississippi River. Just as Congress passed the Land Ordinance of 1785, Lee received word that the Spanish minister had arrived in Philadelphia and that the dignitary would arrive in New York City a few days later to pay his respects to Congress. Lee, however, was concerned about the pending negotiations, because although the delegates had elected him president, they had also named John Jay of New York as the American secretary for foreign affairs, which meant that Jay would head the negotiations. Lee shared his view of the dismal prospects for free navigation with correspondents. He told them that Gardoqui would offer lucrative commercial benefits in exchange for the United States' abandoning its demands for full access to the river—an accurate prognostication, as events soon demonstrated.[16]

Richard Henry's tenor toward the negotiations with Spain owed, in large part, to the position Jay adopted in 1779 when he was willing to abandon the Mississippi River valley during the congressional debates over the Treaty of Amity and Commerce with France. Lee was confident that, if America persisted in its demands for access and free navigation of the river, Spain would eventually acquiesce. He simply did not have confidence in Jay's commitment toward pressing the issue. Gardoqui met with President Lee in late July 1785, and the negotiations began soon thereafter. As late as October, Richard Henry, with an exasperated tone, commented on how the talks "proceed slowly," and he expressed his certainty that they "will not hastily be concluded."[17]

Questions surrounding American access to the Mississippi represented a matter of immediate concern to the southern states, especially those living in the areas that would soon become the states of Kentucky and Tennessee. Consequently, Congress divided along sectional lines, as those committed to westward expansion vied with those seeking to preserve eastern domination over American commercial activity. In anticipation of possibly losing access to the river, Lee and George Washington joined several other prominent Virginians in calling for Kentucky's admission to the union. They hoped that action along these lines would foster closer ties with the settlers in that region and the eastern seaboard. In pursuit of that goal, both Lee and Washington also promoted the construction of a canal system linking the Ohio River to the Potomac, thereby establishing an all-water route from Kentucky to Chesapeake Bay without relying on the Mississippi River.

Interested parties in Virginia soon formed the Potomac River Company and the James River Company, the latter aspiring to link the James and the Potomac via a canal system to allow for even more commercial development of the region. All who were concerned with these endeavors understood that these plans required a tremendous outlay of capital as well as extensive preparations. Members of Virginia's House of Delegates and Congress began openly discussing these projects as early as May 1785.[18] Lee, along with many others, bought shares of stock in the Potomac Company to help finance its plans. He was pleased to relate the widespread interest in the enterprise, noting that by June 1785, £40,000 in shares had been sold to private individuals.

Such activity, with Lee's involvement, sparked controversy, as delegates from Maryland and Pennsylvania criticized what may be regarded as preferential treatment for Virginia. These two states were concerned about the long-term effects that the Potomac Company would have on their local economies if the effort should prove successful. They were concerned that the Potomac Company's ambitious plans might divert western commerce that flowed down the Susquehanna River to Baltimore, to the Potomac and Alexandria instead. Delegates from these states then proposed their own canal projects linking the Delaware River to Chesapeake Bay, thus garnering more immediate benefits for Delaware, Maryland, and Pennsylvania. This sort of wrangling no doubt kept the Jay–Gardoqui negotiations in abeyance as well. In the end, more than likely, it was the speculative fever behind the competing canal interests that spelled defeat for American access to the Mississippi River.

Gardoqui was confident he could sway American interests away from the Mississippi River for three reasons. First, he understood that the United States was in the midst of an economic depression, and by making commercial concessions to the United States (as Lee predicted), he thought America would forgo its demand for access to the river. Second, he knew that many prominent Americans opposed westward expansion, and he hoped he could play the sectional jealousies off one another and thereby preserve Spanish interests. Third, he intended to win support by offering Spanish recognition of America's territorial boundaries and offer his country's assistance in forcing British troops to evacuate American soil. The sectional jealousies, however, flared up to such a degree that the Jay–Gardoqui negotiations continued well into 1786 and never reached a satisfactory conclusion in terms of American access to the Mississippi; it would take another decade before issues found resolution.[19] The failure of Jay's negotiations and the contentious struggle between the competing canal companies set the stage for more general discussions calling for internal improvements and congressional reform in general.

VII

John Jay's inability to secure American interests in the West and the failure on the part of Congress to establish stable commercial ties with other European nations contributed to an atmosphere of anxiety and concern as reflected in the correspondence of several delegates in Congress.[20] For many Americans, however, issues involving canals and internal commerce paled in comparison to the inability to establish commercial ties with other nations. Getting products to the eastern seaboard simply did not matter if they could not be profitably sold abroad in foreign markets. This realization led many Americans to start looking for ways to extend congressional authority over trade policy, and it renewed efforts for Congress to secure a source of income separate from the states.

James Madison, who in the early 1780s was often allied with Robert Morris, emerged as one of the earliest proponents of what he characterized as a "common treasury," derived from a tax levied by Congress; but he found little support from his fellow Virginians.[21] He supported Morris's impost plan, and when that measure failed, he sought ways to amend the Articles of Confederation. Madison's inability to secure a source of independent revenue for Congress made it mandatory for Congress to do more to gain access to foreign markets in order to bolster America's infant economy. "We have lost by the Revolution our trade with the West Indies," an exasperated Madison wrote to his colleague Richard Henry Lee. His concern was that America lost one commercial venue "without having gained new channels to compensate" for the loss.[22] Lee recognized the problem to which Madison referred, but he nonetheless defended the Articles of Confederation; resisted calls for extending congressional control over trade policy; and blamed Europe, not the United States, for the failure to negotiate treaties.

Richard Henry pointed out that "Congress [has] a clear right to make whatever Treaties of Commerce they shall judge proper." The only limitations that were in place allowed individual states to impose trade duties on products entering their states, as a measure to protect domestic industries. Lee felt these were justifiable parameters because they ensured the survival of state economies, and he regarded any argument to the contrary as disingenuous at best. The provisions under scrutiny by some members of Congress, Lee believed, simply allowed individual states to make slight changes in trade policy to suit their individually unique commercial circumstances.[23]

Lee reserved the bulk of his criticism for the Europeans for essentially refusing to open their markets to American goods, and he targeted Great Britain in particular. He regarded strong commercial ties to that nation as unlikely because the British "appetite for Commerce has ever been ravenous, and its wishes always for Monopoly."[24] Lee's commentary reflected the views first expressed in his denunciation of the Townshend Duties imposed by Parliament in 1767. As far as he was concerned, little had changed since then in relation to the economic policies championed by the king and Parliament.

The views set forth by Richard Henry made it clear that he thought any effort to open British markets to American goods was fanciful at best. He also raised concerns that, if Congress gained control over trade policy, it would hurt the southern economy. "Giving Congress a power to Legislate over the Trade of the Union would be dangerous in the extreme to the 5 Southern or Staple states," Richard Henry told Madison.[25] The lack of ships and trained sailors in the South would allow the northern states to impose "a most pernicious and destructive Monopoly." He also thought that the relationship between the North and South could only deteriorate and inevitably become, for the South at least, no different than what the American colonies suffered under British rule. Additionally, Lee did not seem able to shake his memories of his experiences with Robert Morris and his friends, as Richard Henry noted that "the Spirit of Commerce throughout the world is a spirit of Avarice and could not fail to act as above stated." In the final analysis during his presidency, Richard Henry Lee was not oblivious to the commercial dilemmas confronting the new nation, but he did think extending the power of the national government was the wrong course of action. He warned that, if his colleagues pursued that course of action, "the remedy [could] be worse than the disease."[26] As November 1785 approached and as Lee's term as president drew to a close, the issue remained hotly debated without a resolution in sight.

VIII

Another unresolved issue that vexed Richard Henry Lee early in his presidency was the loss of American ships to the North African Barbary kingdoms dotting the Mediterranean coast. During Lee's tenure as president, Barbary corsairs seized two American ships, the *Maria* and the *Dauphin*. One of the victims, James Leander Cathcart, later recounted how the pirates swarmed onto the *Maria*, stripped the crew to their underwear, and seized everything of value on board the vessel. They were next forced belowdecks of another Algerian ship, housed with an additional thirty-six prisoners, and taken to Algiers. Three days later they arrived at their destination and were paraded through the streets, jeered at by mobs, then auctioned off at the local slave market.[27] As news about the events reached the United States, American diplomats stationed in Europe, John Adams and Thomas Jefferson, worked to get the Americans released; but their efforts were of no avail. As attempts continued to reach a solution, Dey Mahomet of Algiers let an American envoy, John Lamb, know that he would return the Americans in exchange for a ransom amounting to $3,000 per man for a total of $63,000—an outrageous sum for the new nation to pay.

The early negotiations for this growing crisis fell onto Richard Henry Lee's desk in New York City. "Curse & doubly curse the Algerines," he told one correspondent, because he feared, "these Pirates . . . have . . . made war on our Commerce."[28] Lee was genuinely at a loss as to how he could address this problem. He understood that paying an exorbitant ransom was simply out of the question, so he searched for an explanation for why the Algerians had targeted American ships. He speculated that perhaps Britain sponsored the attacks "in revenge for our separation," adding that he thought "all things are possible with the corrupt Politicians of this day." Although his suspicions on the British proved false, Richard Henry astutely noted that "if we cannot purchase a peace from these Barbarians before they taste the sweets of plundering our Commerce, it may be long before we can quiet them."[29]

Richard Henry Lee's term as president officially ended on November 4, 1785. Contrary to his belief in a limited role for the national Congress, his contemporaries regarded Lee as one of the most active and energetic individuals to occupy the president's chair since the establishment of the office in 1774. His declining health forced him to resign his seat as soon as his term ended. The pain caused by his "gouty feet" necessitated a one month's leave of absence in August 1785, and when he returned to his duties, he eagerly counted the days for his presidency to end. Although he had little patience for such things, he found that he still had to battle his political opponents who willingly cast aspersions on his character. About midway through his presidency, Benjamin Franklin submitted his resignation as an American commissioner, a request that Congress readily approved. Immediately afterward, rumors flew that Lee had forced Franklin to resign because of the long-standing animus between the two men.

Richard Henry Lee and Franklin had little use for one another. Bad feelings between them certainly developed during the Deane–Lee imbroglio of 1778–1779, as made abundantly clear as Lee began substituting Franklin's name with the euphemism "wicked old man." At the height of the Deane scandal,

Richard Henry pondered, "how . . . long must the dignity and honor of these United States be sacrificed to the bad passions of that old man under the idea of his being a philosopher?" He added that if Franklin were to remain a part of America's diplomatic corps "with all the imperfections on his head," then he should be sent to Russia, where he can do no harm.[30] Although Lee had no love for Franklin, he vigorously defended Franklin's name and reputation, and that of his office; and when rumors circulated, he forced Franklin to resign his commission. Lee wrote that the moment he received Franklin's request, he forwarded it to John Jay's desk, indicating that he should handle the entire matter. He emphasized that this occurrence "did not enter at all into [his] business," and he appealed "to all those acquainted with [his] political progress, for a full testimonial that neither indolence, inattention, nor neglect have marked [his] proceedings" while serving in the office of president.[31]

Such attacks only made Richard Henry Lee relish the prospect of returning to Chantilly that much more. When his term ended, he gathered all the papers relating to the post and turned them over to Nathaniel Gorham of Massachusetts, who would serve as interim president until Congress elected a new one. Lee was back home by the beginning of December 1785. He dispatched a letter to Gardoqui, indicating that should the Spanish minister have any questions, he could contact Lee at Chantilly through his cousin Henry Lee, who still served in Congress.[32] The House of Delegates appointed Richard Henry to another term, but he refused the request, citing the "precarious state of his health." Lee noted that "attacks of gout had gotten so bad he could no longer write letters, and he had to hire a personal secretary to complete his correspondence."[33] Although his presidency in many respects provided the crowning jewel to his long and distinguished political career that was behind him, Lee took renewed delight in returning to Chantilly-on-the-Potomac and being with his family.

NOTES

1. Elizabeth Dabney Coleman, "Two Lees, Revolutionary Suffragists," *Virginia Cavalcade* (Autumn 1953): 19.

2. Nagel, *The Lees of Virginia*, 55.

3. Arthur Lee, quoted in Nagel, *The Lees of Virginia*, 56.

4. R. H. Lee to Hannah Corbin, March 17, 1778, *Lee Letters*, 1: 392.

5. R. H. Lee to Thomas Lee Shippen, November 10, 1784, *Lee Letters*, 2: 292; R. H. Lee to James Madison, November 26, 1784, *Lee Letters*, 2: 306.

6. *Journals*, 27: 648; Richard Dobbs Spaight to Edward Hand, December 28, 1784, *Letters of Delegates*, 22: 94.

7. R. H. Lee to the States, December 24, 1784, *Letters of Delegates*, 22: 85.

8. R. H. Lee to Patrick Henry, February 14, 1785, *Lee Letters*, 2: 332.

9. R. H. Lee to Patrick Henry, February 14, 1785, *Lee Letters*, 2: 332–33.

10. "Ordinance for the Sale of Western Lands," May 20, 1785, *DHRC*, 1: 156–57.

11. R. H. Lee to George Washington, April 18, 1785, *Lee Letters*, 2: 349.

12. R. H. Lee to the Governor of New Jersey, April 30, 1785, *Lee Letters*, 2: 351.

13. R. H. Lee to George Washington, May 7, 1785, *Lee Letters*, 2: 354–55.

14. William Grayson to George Washington, April 15, 1785, *Letters of Delegates*, 22: 338–41.

15. R. H. Lee to William Short, June 13, 1785, *Lee Letters*, 2: 373.

16. R. H. Lee to George Washington, July 23, 1785, *Lee Letters*, 2: 377; R. H. Lee to James Madison, August 11, 1785, *Lee Letters*, 2: 382.

17. R. H. Lee to George Washington, October 11, 1785, *Lee Letters*, 2: 391.

18. R. H. Lee to Thomas Jefferson, May 16, 1785, *Lee Letters*, 3: 358.

19. Arthur Whitaker, *The Spanish-American Frontier: 1783–1785* (Lincoln: University of Nebraska Press, 1927), 74–76; Frederick W. Marks III, *Independence on Trial: Foreign Affairs and the Making of the Constitution* (Baton Rouge: Louisiana State University Press, 1973), 25–32.

20. Charles Pinckney to Benjamin Guerard, January 2, 1785, *Letters of Delegates*, 22: 98–103; Rufus King to Elbridge Gerry, June 5, 1785, *Letters of Delegates*, 22: 433.

21. James Madison, "A Bill Authorizing an Amendment in the Articles of Confederation," June 21, 1784, *The Papers of James Madison*, 23 vols., ed. Robert A. Rutland et al. (Chicago: University of Chicago Press, 1973), 8: 83–84. Hereafter, cited as *Madison Papers*. For more on Madison's evolving nationalism and his affiliation with Robert Morris, see Lance Banning, "James Madison and the Nationalists, 1780–1783," *The William and Mary Quarterly*, 40 (1983): 227–255.

22. James Madison to R. H. Lee, July 7, 1785, *Madison Papers*, 8: 315.

23. R. H. Lee to John Adams, August 1, 1785, *Lee Letters*, 2: 379–80.

24. R. H. Lee to James Madison, August 11, 1785, *Lee Letters*, 2: 382–83.

25. R. H. Lee to James Madison, August 11, 1785, *Lee Letters*, 2: 382–83.

26. R. H. Lee to James Madison, August 11, 1785, *Lee Letters*, 2: 382–83.

27. A. B. C. Whipple, *To the Shores of Tripoli: The Birth of the U.S. Navy and Marines* (New York: William Morrow and Company, 1991), 25–26.

28. R. H. Lee to Thomas Lee Shippen, October 14, 1785, *Lee Letters*, 2: 392.

29. R. H. Lee to Samuel Adams, October 17, 1785, *Lee Letters*, 2: 396–97.

30. R. H. Lee to Samuel Adams, September 10, 1780, *Lee Letters*, 2: 202–3.

31. R. H. Lee to Thomas Lee Shippen, June 13, 1785, *Lee Letters*, 2: 371.

32. R. H. Lee to the Spanish Minister to the United States, December 3, 1785, *Lee Letters*, 2: 406.

33. R. H. Lee to John Adams, December 12, 1785, *Lee Letters*, 2: 408.

· 9 ·

Killing Ourselves for Fear of Dying:
Debating the Federal Constitution

I

$\mathcal{A}$fter Richard Henry Lee returned to Chantilly in December 1785, he devoted his time to the management of affairs on his plantation, settling accounts with friends and associates, but mostly he enjoyed spending time with his wife and children.[1] As he approached his fifty-fourth birthday, Lee surprisingly still found his home full of children. All told, he had nine children; only his two oldest sons, Thomas and Ludwell, had moved on and established homes of their own. His five daughters, Nancy, Hannah, Henrietta, Ann, and Sarah, and his two sons Cassius and Francis, Richard Henry soon discovered, were now the true mistresses and masters of Chantilly.[2] After Francis turned three, Lee realized that his youngest son now could move out of the nursery and into one of the upstairs bedrooms. Lee now had the opportunity to transform the downstairs nursery into a library. After all these years, he finally had a permanent home for his vast collection of books, a place where he could retreat into a private world and enjoy reading the various histories and novels he had gathered over the years—an experience he had not enjoyed since his youthful days at Stratford Hall more than thirty years earlier.

Now, as a private citizen, Lee reveled in his role as master of Chantilly, but he did not completely ignore public matters. Public education was one local issue of great concern for Richard Henry Lee. Beginning in 1783, he served as a school trustee for an institution in Fredericksburg, where, along with eleven other trustees, he helped hire teachers and raise funds for the school. These activities reflected an avid interest in educational matters that Lee had always maintained. Additionally, with such a large family of his own and with the burden of paying for each child's schooling, his experience led him to the

187

conclusion that publicly funded schools were a necessity. Richard Henry believed that a popularly elected government could not flourish "without virtue in the people" and that, since "knowledge is a principle source of virtue," public schools were a "fundamental concern in all free communities."[3] Lee's opinions were shared by many of his contemporaries, all of whom recognized that ignorance was a republic's greatest, most deadly enemy. This shared realization hastened the establishment of a public school system in Virginia.

Richard Henry also continued monitoring the progress of the Jay–Gardoqui negotiations relating to the free navigation of the Mississippi River. As Congress wrangled with the idea of suspending American access to the river for a period of twenty-five to thirty years, Lee thought the United States should simply put the matter to rest and concentrate on internal improvements that would lessen its dependence on the great river. Richard Henry regarded the most invective denunciations of Jay's proposals as "generally weak and indecent." To insist on full access to the Mississippi at this stage, Lee thought, would do nothing more than risk war between Spain and the United States; and Spain could prove a valuable ally, considering that the dey of Algiers had formally declared war on the United States.[4] Lee simply saw no point in delaying the inevitable. He changed his earlier assessment and now believed that "Spain will not agree to the Navigation within her limits," so "why risk, for an unattainable Object, the loss of valuable objects, and the incurring pernicious consequences?"[5] The Potomac and James River companies represented the best course of action for Virginia and the United States to follow.

The lingering controversy about the most viable canal path involving Virginia, Maryland, Pennsylvania, and Delaware now forced a measure of interstate concern. Efforts to address these concerns began in fits and starts. In the summer of 1785, while Richard Henry Lee served as president of the Continental Congress, delegates from Virginia and Maryland met at Mount Vernon and agreed to share the task of regulating commerce along the Potomac River.[6] The agreement reached at the Mount Vernon proved controversial and provided ammunition for those who resisted the calls for commercial reform. Over the course of several months of wrangling, several states agreed on the need to call a convention to discuss economic matters, which would meet on the first Monday in September 1786 at Annapolis, Maryland. The Annapolis Convention failed to address the issues at hand, however, because delegates from only five states showed up. Consequently, those who were there simply agreed to call for another convention, at which all states would be represented and then disbanded.[7]

Richard Henry Lee was not too upset by the failure of the Annapolis Convention, because, as more states joined in, the more skeptical he became. As he heard talk of revising the Articles, he was that much more inclined to

balk. What soon triggered concern and then alarm was news from Massachusetts that a band of 400 or 500 farmers, led by Daniel Shays, began terrorizing
the western reaches of that New England state. The rebellion became in object of grave concern for the majority of American political leaders. Secretary
of War Henry Knox warned George Washington that if the Shaysites joined
with farmers in similar situations in Rhode Island, Connecticut, and New
Hampshire, their numbers could increase to "a body of twelve or fifteen thou-
sand desperate and unprincipled men."[8] Although Washington noted that the
situation in Virginia was calm, he told Richard Henry Lee's cousin that "the
reins of government" had to "be braced and held by a steady hand"; otherwise,
such an occurrence could easily develop in the Old Dominion as well.[9] As the
potential for this sort of crisis loomed, Richard Henry once again received calls
to return to public service, and as winter set in, Lee made preparations to leave
Chantilly and resume a seat in the Continental Congress.

II

The panic created by Shays' Rebellion caused Richard Henry Lee to receive
two calls to public service during the winter of 1786–1787. The House of Delegates appointed Lee to Congress in January 1787. About that same time, Congress called for the states to send representatives to Philadelphia to attend a
general convention authorized to "amend and revise" the Articles of Confederation; Congress slated the meeting to begin in May 1787. A few weeks after
his reappointment to Congress, Virginia's governor, Edmund Randolph, asked
Lee to attend the upcoming Philadelphia Convention. Richard Henry declined the governor's request, indicating that "the circumstances of my health,
sir, will not permit me to think of going northward sooner than the middle of
June."[10] He took comfort as he learned that George Washington and George
Mason had received similar calls and had accepted their appointments. This
news prompted Lee to note that there were "so many gentlemen of good
hearts and sound heads appointed to the Convention at Philadelphia" that he
felt a "disposition to repose with confidence in their determinations."[11]

Although he did not plan to attend the convention, Richard Henry was
never short on advice to those who were planning to go. He submitted a list
of proposals to George Mason in May 1787, just as the delegates began arriving in Philadelphia. Lee believed that Congress should secure the exclusive
power to print paper money; he also wanted to ensure Congress's ability to assert its authority over state legislatures, urging the convention to adopt language to clarify "that any state act of legislation that shall contravene, or oppose, the authorized acts of Congress, or interfere with the expressed rights of

that body, shall be *ipso facto* void and of no force whatsoever."[12] These suggestions represent a dramatic departure from many of his views expressed while he sat in the president's chair. Congress's inability to effectively deal with foreign affairs, recalcitrant state governments, and startling events such as Shays's Rebellion more than justified Lee's change in tone. His comments to Mason also suggest that Lee understood that substantial changes in the Articles of Confederation would occur as a result of the Philadelphia Convention. Overall, Richard Henry anticipated the changes favorably, and he acknowledged that "alterations" in the Articles of Confederation could prove beneficial. He did not advocate these changes, however, because he thought the Articles had failed: Lee attributed the nation's problems to the "vicious manners" from certain states and individuals, rather than to "mistakes in [the] form of government already in place." He supported significant changes because he believed it would simply be easier to revise the existing constitution than change the hearts and minds of those refusing to abide by laws and procedures already in place.[13] In this frame of mind, Lee continued making recommendations to his friend, requesting that Congress receive the authority to enforce requisitions from states refusing to comply. Richard Henry commented on how the "states have been unpardonably remiss in furnishing their federal quotas." His expressed views represent a centrist position. On the one hand, he defended the Articles of Confederation, blaming the nation's problems on recalcitrant individuals; on the other hand, he eagerly anticipated substantial changes and indicated his approval.

True to his letter to the governor, Lee left Virginia to attend Congress in June 1787, and along the way, he stopped in Philadelphia to visit his sister Alice and her husband, William Shippen Jr. He wrote to his brother and indicated that he found "the Convention ... very busy & very secret." He knew that those in attendance were planning to make substantial revisions in the Articles of Confederation. Apparently, in spite of the convention delegates' efforts to maintain secrecy, Richard Henry obviously found a line into the inner workings of the gathering. After he left Philadelphia, he frequently referred to the "new system" that he expected to emerge from the deliberations. In the aftermath of Shays's Rebellion, Lee had warmed to the idea of substantial revisions, as did many of his friends and colleagues. Before leaving Philadelphia and completing his journey to New York City, Richard Henry summarized his expectations that would result from the convention. He anticipated "a Government not unlike the [British] Constitution" that consisted of a bicameral legislature and a separate executive branch. "This departure from Simple Democracy," Lee noted, "seems indispensably necessary, if any government is at all going to exist in N. America." The "new system" he described would be much stronger than the one, "which at present attempts to rule the Confederation."[14]

III

Richard Henry Lee resumed his seat in Congress in August 1787. While he waited for the Philadelphia Convention to conclude its business and send a draft of its proposals to Congress, Lee participated in other debates before Congress. Once again, one area of significant concern for Lee pertained to western lands. The Northwest Ordinance of 1787 was under consideration before Congress: this measure determined the process for the admission of new states into the union—an accomplishment often regarded as the most significant achievement by Congress under the Articles of Confederation. Once delegates had this task behind them, there was a collective sense that they should bide their time until receiving word from Philadelphia. Richard Henry confidently expected that they would receive a copy of the convention's report shortly, and he notified others as to his expectations. He informed his cousin to look for a "federal [government] of 3 branches, with independent powers, and supreme for external matters, Revenue & Commerce—with an Executive well toned and of reasonable duration."[15]

While he waited in New York City, he eagerly waited for these revisions as he began hearing disturbing reports from Virginia reminiscent of Shays's Rebellion of a year earlier. He wrote to another cousin in Virginia, Richard "Squire" Lee, thanking him for intelligence that "especially relates to the welfare of my family." Richard Henry had worried about rumblings among the struggling farmers in the Northern Neck who were burdened by heavy debts. He commented on how "the friends to American honor & happiness here all join in lamenting the riots and mobbish proceedings in Virginia." Lee recognized that the burden of debt triggered the violent behavior, and he tried to assure his cousin that "Congress is endeavoring to lighten the public burthens by selling federal lands beyond the Ohio to pay the domestic debt which forms so great a part of our whole debt." Nonetheless, such unfortunate activity injures the "American name & character thro the world—And the wonder is that all good men in the country don't unite and suppress such evil doings, and punish the offenders." As Lee expressed his concerns about the internal rebellion, he also noted his confidence that the "federal Convention will rise this week," implying that Congress could then get on with the business of addressing the nation's domestic woes.[16]

As Richard Henry anticipated news from Philadelphia, he reacquainted himself with the instructions issued by Congress to the convention delegates in February 1787. The orders called for revisions in the Articles of Confederation: after those changes are "agreed to in Congress," they would be transmitted to the states for their confirmation.[17] Lee acted accordingly and prepared to receive the proposed changes in the Articles. The document arrived in New York

City on September 20, 1787; Richard Henry spent a week reading through the revisions and stood before Congress to submit a short list of amendments.

One object of concern related to the absence of a bill of rights, so he offered one patterned after George Mason's 1776 Virginia Declaration of Rights. He read into the record the standard litany, calling for freedom of conscience, the press, and speech. He sought guarantees for jury trials, and he called for frequent elections; an independent judiciary; a ban on cruel and unusual punishments and excessive fines; and provisions allowing for citizens to hold peaceful, public assemblies.[18] In addition, Lee recommended some modifications that actually strengthened the executive branch. He called for the establishment of a Council of State, or Privy Council, to assist the president. It would consist of eleven members, all selected by the chief executive. Lee suggested that the Philadelphia plan and its provision for senate confirmation of executive appointments represented a "dangerous blending of Legislative and Executive powers." Lastly, Richard Henry thought that representation ought to be increased to bolster the "democratic interests" in the United States.[19]

Lee did not in any way regard his proposed amendments as any kind of restriction on the powers of the national government as proposed by the Philadelphia Convention. To the contrary, he simply sought to clarify and actually enlarge the powers of the national government—the executive branch, in particular. His advocacy of a bill of rights added nothing new to the prevailing currents of political thought in America at the time, and Richard Henry certainly thought he was merely addressing an oversight on the part of the public-spirited men who attended the convention—many of whom were his friends. Some members of Congress reacted to Lee's modest proposals with panic because they were uncertain of his motives.

One such congressman and fellow Virginian, Edward Carrington, clearly revealed he had not a clue concerning Lee's designs. As Lee prepared to address Congress, Carrington quickly dispatched a note to James Madison, commenting that "one of our colleagues Mr. R.H. Lee is forming proposals for essential alterations in the Constitution, which will be in effect to oppose it."[20] Carrington made his comments four days before Richard Henry presented his amendments to Congress. Word quickly spread that Lee was opposed to the new plan and was seeking to destroy the good work accomplished in Philadelphia. Lee found the reaction of his fellow congressmen somewhat perplexing; he simply did not understand the prevailing mentality suggesting that the mere hint of amendments was tantamount to a rejection of the plan—especially since he knew better. As his colleagues became more strident in their accusations, Lee became increasingly suspicious of *their* motives.

Congress had reached an impasse once again. Richard Henry bolstered his position in Congress by reaching out to fellow concerned skeptics, such as

Melancton Smith of New York. After Congress rejected Lee's proposed amendments in their entirety and without debate, Lee presented a motion, seconded by Smith, observing that the thirteenth article of the Articles of Confederation provided for amendments but "did not extend . . . to the creation of a new confederacy of nine states," referring to the number required to ratify the new system. These maneuverings in Congress reminded Lee of the ugliness he suffered ten years earlier, and mild objections flared into a full-blown rejection; he no longer trusted the advocates of the Philadelphia plan—not because of the structure, but because of the character of the men supporting the scheme. As a result, Richard Henry refused to sanction the proposed constitution without the inclusion of prior amendments. Lee fought for clarification, but his efforts were of no avail; subsequently, he became even more suspicious and resentful when Congress announced the following resolution:

> Resolved unanimously, That the said report with the resolutions and letter accompanying the same be transmitted to the several legislatures in order to be submitted to a convention of delegates chosen in each state by the people thereof in conformity to the resolves of the Convention made and provided in that case.[21]

Lee resented the language of the resolution for implying unanimous consent, when that simply was not the case. He argued that the authors of the resolution inserted the word "unanimously" as part of a deliberate tactic, "hoping to have it mistaken for an unanimous approbation of the thing . . . [when] it is certain that no such approbation was given."[22] Once again, as far as Lee was concerned, battle lines were drawn, and he began preparing to meet the challenge.

IV

Richard Henry left New York City hastily at the beginning of October 1787; before leaving, however, he took time to meet with Melancton Smith and John Lamb, also of New York, both of whom now led the effort to amend the proposed constitution in New York state. After a short initial meeting, Lee departed and returned to Chantilly, where he contacted George Mason and began discussing strategies for securing amendments. He informed Mason that he believed the Philadelphia plan had "a great many excellent regulations in it and if it could be reasonably amended would be a fine system."[23] Lee hoped he would be able to promote an interstate effort to secure amendments. He noted that it would be a "great point to get Maryland and Virginia to join in the plan for amendments"; he urged Mason to contact Edmund Pendleton, who had relations in South Carolina, and if Pendleton agreed, "his opinion will have great weight with our ratifying convention." If Lee could bring these three southern states together and join them with Smith and Lamb's efforts in New York, then amendments could be easily secured. Unfortunately for Richard Henry Lee, this was not to be the case.

Soon after his return to Virginia, Lee drafted his proposed amendments, which he intended to publish in pamphlet form in the guise of a letter to Governor Edmund Randolph. In this letter, Lee observed that "the establishment of the new plan of government, in its present form, is a question that involves such immense consequences, to the present times and posterity, that it calls for the deepest attention of the best and wisest friends of their country and mankind." He ridiculed the fear mongers who claimed that if the new system was not immediately ratified, that civil war would ensue. Lee countered this absurd claim, noting that "to say a bad government must be established for fear of anarchy, is really saying we should kill ourselves for fear of dying!"[24]

The unfortunate dismissal of Richard Henry's modest proposals presented to Congress in September 1787 now forced him to scrutinize every aspect of the proposed constitution and examine every potential abuse of power to further his quest for amendments. He noted the heavy concentration of power that existed between the executive branch and the Senate. Within these two segments of the national government, Lee noted, all of the treaty-making authority and all of the appointive power for civil and military officers resided. He acknowledged that the impeachment process represented a potential check on any significant abuse of power, only to tear it down by suggesting the unlikelihood that senators would impeach one of their own. He asked, is this "not a most formidable combination of power thus created in a few?" He added that "the only check to be found in this system, is the House of Representative," which he characterized as a "mere shred or rag of representation."[25]

He also raised his concerns regarding ambiguous phrases scattered throughout the proposed constitution like "general welfare" and "supreme law of the land," suggesting that such phraseology offered no restraint of the power of the national government. Additionally, in the absence of a bill of rights, he complained that "the rights of conscience, the freedom of the press, and trial by jury, are at the mercy" of the government under the proposed system. Richard Henry also reminded his audience that "a bare majority can enact commercial laws, so that the representatives of the seven northern states, as they will have a majority, can, by law, create the most oppressive monopolies upon the five southern states."[26] The South would be the helpless pawn to the more powerful, northern mercantile interests.

In November 1787, the *Virginia Gazette* printed Richard Henry Lee's letter to Governor Randolph under the title "Observations on the Plan of Government Proposed by the Convention. By R. H. Lee, Esquire." At that time, George Washington read the document and forwarded a copy to James Madison. Washington noted that the pamphlet had been "circulated with great industry . . . and is said to have a bad influence."[27] Madison, however, seemed less concerned about Lee's views, noting that they do "not appear to be a very formidable attack on the new Constitution; unless it should derive an influence from the name of the correspondents," but "its intrinsic merits do not entitle" the pamphlet to any serious consideration.[28] Yet, in spite of Madison's cursory dismissal, the pamphlet had the effect of clearly identifying Richard Henry Lee as the leader of the "antifederalist" party in Virginia, as the opponents of the Philadelphia plan were then called. Lee's letter to Randolph attracted a considerable amount of publicity to him, most of it negative. In the days and weeks that followed the publication and distribution of his letter to Randolph, Richard Henry once again became a target. The invective commentaries that flowed from the pens of his political enemies prompted Lee to announce to stunned listeners in January 1788 that he was withdrawing from the public debate over the proposed constitution. That said, Richard Henry Lee returned to Chantilly.

V

Not long after Richard Henry Lee initially proposed his original amendments to the new plan of government, he met fierce criticism from his opponents. Some of the commentary was so strong and bitter that it prompted Lee to observe that "the malady of human nature in these states now, seems to be as it was in the years 1778 & 1779 with respect to the effect produced by a certain Combination."[29] The melancholy tone of this remark reveals that even before he sent his letter to Governor Randolph, he knew to prepare for attacks of a bitter and personal nature, like the ones he suffered through during the Deane–Lee imbroglio. He knew the men responsible for the denunciations made against him, and he recognized them as the same individuals that cast aspersions on his character ten years before. Ironically, however, the attacks were not because of anything Lee said or did. Instead, the assaults on Lee's character and personality occurred as a result of confusing him with New Yorker Melancton Smith.

After Lee, Smith, and John Lamb parted company in early October 1787, Smith returned to his residence in New York City, where he penned a series of essays later published collectively under the title *Letters from the Federal Farmer to the Republican*. Smith eventually wrote enough letters to fill two pamphlets; the first contained letters dated from October 8 to 13, 1787. Smith sent them to his hometown newspaper, the Poughkeepsie *Country Journal*, and they were later reprinted in other papers and eventually in pamphlet form. The appearance of these letters immediately spread alarm among the advocates of the proposed constitution. Edward Carrington sent a copy to Thomas Jefferson in France, commenting that the letters were "the best of anything that has been written in opposition" to the Constitution—but, he noted, "the author is not known."[30] The logical exposition offered by Smith, writing under the pseudonym the "Federal Farmer," galvanized the supporters of the plan, as indicated by the appearance of the first of a series of essays written by "Publius," a pseudonym used with great effect by Alexander Hamilton, James Madison, and John Jay; these essays, which also circulated in the New York papers, first appeared in print on October 27, 1787.

One tactic adopted by the proponents of the new constitution was to identify the "Federal Farmer" as quickly as possible and, once revealed, make him the target. On December 10, 1787, an essay written by Oliver Ellsworth of Connecticut under the pseudonym "A Landholder" named Richard Henry Lee as the author of *The Letters from the Federal Farmer*. The identification appeared in the sixth of a series of essays by Ellsworth, written in defense of the proposed constitution. Ellsworth had figured prominently in the anti-Lee faction in Congress, dating back to the days of the Deane–Lee imbroglio, when he characterized Lee as a leader of an "ass-ridden junto" in Congress in 1778.[31]

Ellsworth, in his "Landholder" essays, launched a series of very personal attacks on Richard Henry Lee and revived many of the unfounded rumors of 1777–1778 that identified Lee as the ringleader of the infamous Conway Cabal, just ten years earlier. Ellsworth wrote of the "factious spirit of R.H.L.—his implacable hatred to General Washington—his well-known intrigues against him in the late war—his attempt to displace him and give command of the American army to his relation General [Charles] Lee—is so recent in your minds it is not necessary to repeat them."[32] But repeat them he did. Ellsworth then added, after this litany of charges, that Lee was supposed to be the author of the recent scurrility being published in the New York papers, an oblique referenced to the *Letters from the Federal Farmer*.

Ellsworth did not stop there. He continued to focus on the rumored enmity between Lee and Washington in an attempt to cast the leaders against the proposed constitution as enemies of the revered general and as individuals willing to sacrifice the national interest for their personal gain. He asserted that the resistance to the Philadelphia plan of government in Virginia stemmed from two sources: "the madness of George Mason and the enmity of the Lee faction to General Washington." Ellsworth went as far as to suggest that "had the General not attended the Convention nor given his sentiments respecting the Constitution, the Lee party would undoubtedly have supported it, and Colonel Mason would have vented his rage to his own Negroes and to the wind."[33]

As Ellsworth continued his tirade in the Connecticut papers, another editorialist joined the cause against Richard Henry Lee. The writer, using the pseudonym "New England," repeated many of same charges made by Ellsworth, but he went one step further by positively identifying Lee as the author of the *Letters from the Federal Farmer*. "New England's" commentary first appeared in the *Connecticut Courant* on December 24, 1787, but before long, newspapers throughout the country reprinted the editorial. Soon, other advocates for the proposed constitution leapt upon the mistaken reference, and from that moment forward, rather than address the strong arguments set forth by Smith in his pamphlets, they attacked Richard Henry Lee's character instead. In the end, this effort, and the identification of Lee as the "Federal Farmer," represented nothing more than a political smear campaign trying to discredit Smith's exposition by tagging the authorship of the letters on a person who had been vilified by his political enemies from the very start of his career in the public's service.[34]

In response to the public humiliation, Richard Henry Lee made the decision to withdraw from the public debate over the proposed constitution. Several factors contributed to this determination on Lee's part. Publicly, Richard Henry declined to participate because of his poor health, and while this might have indeed been the case, other important developments intervened as well. One item that had to be of significant concern to Richard Henry involved a growing rift within his own family. Lee's brother Francis and oldest son, Thomas, had taken public stands endorsing the proposed constitution.

Before long, newspapers caught wind of this and made great sport by ridiculing Richard Henry's relationship with his son. The *Pennsylvania Gazette*, for example, published a piece reporting that "the eldest son of R.H.L.—, Esq., is one of the most zealous and active friends of the federal government in Virginia. In a letter to his father, while in New York, before he knew his [father's] sentiments, he unfortunately told him, that the constitution had no enemies in Virginia, but 'fools and knaves.'" On January 16, 1788, this same article appeared in the *Virginian Independent Chronicle*, no doubt much to the embarrassment of Richard Henry and his family.[35] Most likely, Lee's decision to withdraw resulted from the combined effects of the revival of the rumors of his enmity toward Washington and the personal attacks that Richard Henry suffered by his enemies, which Lee characterized as "temporary insanity."[36]

Another important factor that cannot be discounted is the close friendship that he had with George Washington, something they had shared since childhood. As the public debate over the constitution became more intense, the general made occasional references to the "bad company" that Lee was now associated with, a reference to Patrick Henry—someone neither Washington nor Lee had much patience for.[37] Richard Henry's decision, of course, shocked many prominent Virginians—not least of all, his youngest brother, Arthur Lee. When he heard of Richard Henry's decision, a stunned Arthur asked if the stories were true: "have [you] given up all idea of opposing the Constitution?"[38] Also, a disheartened George Mason complained that, without Richard Henry, "there will be no one . . . whom he can confide" with during the ratifying convention, hinting that Mason had little tolerance for Patrick Henry as well. In an attempt to dissuade Lee from this course of action, Mason expressed his concern that Lee "will be regarded by many as having deserted a cause in which you have published your persuasion of its being of the last moment to your Country."[39] Mason simply could not understand why Richard Henry had experienced this change of heart. He hoped Lee would relent and stand for election to the upcoming Virginia ratifying convention. Mason urged Lee to run as a representative from Fauquier County, where he could easily win. Arthur echoed Mason's comments adding: "I confess, I wish to see you elected whether you serve or not."[40]

Richard Henry, however, did not change his mind. He followed through on his commitment not to participate in the debate, although some suspected that Lee's action merely reflected a "Change of Conduct . . . not of Opinion."[41] Be that as it may, Lee had to look out for the integrity of his family; his two oldest sons, Thomas and Ludwell, had just launched political careers of their own. Thomas took a seat in Virginia's state senate in 1785, and Ludwell had just won his first election to Virginia's House of Delegates. By all indications, his two sons shared the views of their Uncle Francis and those of Richard Henry Lee, expressed by their father during the summer of 1787.

Despite his attempts to avoid controversy, it seemed to follow Richard Henry no matter where he went. Advocates for the proposed constitution would not let him rest. One Virginia essayist, writing under the pseudonym "State Soldier," wrote that Lee's October 1787 letter to Governor Randolph had "relieved us from any fear we might have had of being deluded by his abilities." "State Soldier" then proceeded to repeat the rumors of Lee's connection to the Conway Cabal, made current by Ellsworth's "Landholder" series. The Virginia essayist noted that "it is not at all surprising that Mr. Lee should be opposed to a government," which would probably begin with George Washington as president. The writer further impugned Lee's integrity by asking what "do you suppose are the real motives" behind Mason's and Lee's opposition? He answered by speculating: "Is it that Mr. Mason, who is a man of immense fortune, and Mr. Lee, who possesses as much pride and ambition as he does fortune, are really anxious to see all men raised up to an equality with themselves?—Or is it not rather from a fear that they themselves shall be reduced below the level of some other?"[42]

Another editorialist, "Cassius," continued the assault. After admitting that he had never met Lee, the writer indicated that he had always maintained a favorable opinion of the man until he heard Lee's views on the proposed constitution. This information led "Cassius" to the conclusion that "fame, like fancy, sometimes delights in fiction, and often, confers qualities and virtues on objects which are, really, destitute of both."[43] These kinds of personal attacks struck a sensitive nerve in Richard Henry Lee and no doubt confirmed in his mind that he made the right decision to steer clear from the public debate over the constitution. He had learned as a result of his experience in 1778–1779, during the Deane–Lee imbroglio, that if he personally addressed these comments with a public response, it would simply add fuel to the fire. He continued to follow the debate, and he would answer questions when asked; but he was always careful to end his response with remarks such as: "I have been obliged to write in haste, so that you may be sure this letter is not intended for the press."[44]

VI

Throughout the spring of 1788, Richard Henry Lee remained at Chantilly and followed the progress of the ratification debate in Virginia. He lamented the prevailing view that allowed only two choices for his state, either complete acceptance or absolute rejection of the proposed constitution. "I know of no power on earth," Lee observed, "that has . . . a right to propose such a question of extremity to the people."[45] Lee clearly resented being cast as either an unwavering opponent or unquestioning supporter of the proposed system of government, and he fought against this sort of simplistic breakdown on a question so vital to the future of the American nation. As other states began the process of ratification, Richard Henry expressed his disappointment as Massachusetts and other states adopted the new system on the mere promise of future amendments. He questioned his old friend Samuel Adams, asking "why submit to a system" that required such fundamental amendments? Lee continued defending the Articles of Confederation as well, noting that "the objections to the present [government], if accurately considered, will . . . be found to grow out of temporary pressures, created by along expensive war, which time and prudence may remove."[46]

As Virginia began preparing for its own ratifying convention, Richard Henry began sending his recommendations to friends, like George Mason, who he knew would be attending the gathering. Lee outlined a strategy for the opposition to the proposed constitution, urging the leading critics of the new system to gather together in a group of six or eight and organize a concise list of amendments. He urged them to keep their list to amendments protecting the basic freedoms of a democratic society and to avoid local and sectional issues at all costs. Lee recommended that the Virginia convention should endorse amendments already proposed by other states as a show of support, and he wanted them to resist all attempts by advocates of the plan to assert the notion that all proposed amendments threatened the national interest under the "pretext of losing all by attempting *any* change."[47] In anticipation of failure in the bid to secure prior amendments, Richard Henry urged his compatriots to conditionally adopt without amendments, adding that "if these amendments are not secured and obtained by the mode pointed out by the fifth article of the convention plan, in two years after the meeting of the new congress, that Virginia shall be considered disengaged from this ratification."[48]

In the end, all of Richard Henry's efforts proved to be of no avail. On June 25, 1788, the convention called for a final tally on the question of ratification. Those in favor of the new system narrowly carried the day, by a margin of ten votes: eighty-nine voting in favor of the constitution without prior amendments, and seventy-nine opposed. On that day, Virginia became the tenth state to approve the Philadelphia plan, leaving only New York, North Carolina, and Rhode Island still struggling to render their final decision on the matter. Lee's goal of mustering an interstate effort to secure prior amendments never materialized in time to mount an effective challenge against the advocates of the new system. In May 1788, John Lamb of New York sent Lee a packet containing copies of the *Letters from the Federal Farmer* and the *Additional Letters from the Federal Farmer*. Lamb hoped Lee would distribute copies of Melancton Smith's pamphlets in the Old Dominion and use them to sway Virginians in favor of arguments calling for prior amendments.[49] Richard Henry thanked his friend for the packet but indicated that he had received it too late to make effective use of the pamphlets in Virginia. Lamb's packet did not arrive at Chantilly until June 27—two days after the Virginia ratifying convention had approved the plan. Nonetheless, Richard Henry asked Lamb to let him know if he could contribute anything toward his efforts to secure prior amendments in New York.[50] In the end, advocates for the proposed constitution thwarted Smith and Lamb's efforts as well, and on July 27, 1788, New York became the eleventh state to ratify without prior amendments.

In many respects, Richard Henry Lee had come full circle by the end of 1788. Virginia's ratification of the new Constitution of the United States did not prove to be too disappointing. Lee always anticipated that the Philadelphia Convention intended to make substantial changes in the Articles of Confederation, and he endorsed those changes from the outset. The strident demands for amendments that characterized Richard Henry's correspondence between September 1787 and January 1788 did not reflect opposition to a new plan of government so much as it did his desire to secure the basic rights characteristic of a democratic society. Lee did not oppose the Constitution in and of itself; what alarmed him was the "certain Combination" that supported the new plan and advanced their agenda through the politics of personal destruction—public attacks on Lee's character of a very private nature. He was alarmed by thoughts of what these men would do if they retained power under a new constitution that did not have a bill of rights. Much has been made of Richard Henry's antifederalism, but in the final analysis, his criticism of the new constitution was always circumspect and cautious. When he learned about the decision reached at the Virginia ratifying convention, he did not act as if the world had ended; he simply made preparations to continue the fight for modest amendments and a bill of rights, once the new government took effect.

NOTES

1. R. H. Lee to Theodoric Lee, January 27, 1786, *Lee Letters*, 2: 410–11; R. H. Lee to John Hopkins, April 22, 1786, *Lee Letters*, 2: 413–14.

2. Lee, *Lee of Virginia*, 206–8. The ages of Richard Henry's children are as follows as of 1786: from his first marriage to Anne Aylett Lee, Thomas, 28; Ludwell, 26; Nancy, 22; and Hannah, 20. From his second marriage to Anne Pinckard Gaskins Lee, Ann, 16; Henrietta, 13; Sarah, 11; Cassius, 7; and Francis, 3. None of Richard Henry's children married before 1788, and most likely still maintained Chantilly as their primary residence.

3. R. H. Lee to Martin Pickett, March 5, 1786, *Lee Letters*, 2: 411–12.

4. Marks, *Independence on Trial*, 38.

5. R. H. Lee to George Washington, July 15, 1787, *Lee Letters*, 2: 426–27.

6. Norman K. Risjord, *Chesapeake Politics, 1781–1800* (New York: Columbia University Press, 1978), 257–59.

7. Risjord, *Chesapeake Politics*, 259–66, Jensen, *The New Nation*, 420–21; Marks, *Independence on Trial*, 91–95.

8. Henry Knox to George Washington, quoted in Flexner, *George Washington and the New Nation, 1783–1793* (Boston: Little, Brown, 1970), 99.

9. George Washington to Henry Lee, October 31, 1786, *Washington Writings*, 29: 34–35.

10. R. H. Lee to Edmund Randolph, March 26, 1787, *Lee Letters*, 2: 415.

11. R. H. Lee to Edmund Randolph, March 26, 1787, *Lee Letters*, 2: 415.

12. R. H. Lee to George Mason, May 15, 1787, *Lee Letters*, 2: 419–22.

13. R. H. Lee to George Mason, May 15, 1787, *Lee Letters*, 2: 419–22.

14. R. H. Lee to Francis Lightfoot Lee, July 14, 1787, *Lee Letters*, 2: 424.

15. R. H. Lee to Henry Lee, August 22, 1787, *Lee Letters*, 2: 433.

16. R. H. Lee to Richard Lee, September 13, 1787, *Lee Letters*, 2: 436–37.

17. "Confederation Congress Calls the Constitutional Convention," February 21, 1787, *DHRC*, 1: 187.

18. "Richard Henry Lee's Proposed Amendments," September 27, 1787, *DHRC*, 1: 337–38.

19. "Richard Henry Lee's Proposed Amendments," September 27, 1787, *DHRC*, 1: 338–39.

20. Edward Carrington to James Madison, September 23, 1787, *DHRC*, 1: 326.

21. "Journals of Congress," September 28, 1787, *DHRC*, 1: 340.

22. R. H. Lee to William Shippen Jr., October 2, 1787, *Lee Letters*, 2: 444.

23. R. H. Lee to George Mason, October 1, 1787, *Lee Letters*, 2: 439.

24. R. H. Lee to the Governor of Virginia, Edmund Randolph, October 16, 1787, *Lee Letters*, 2: 450.

25. R. H. Lee to the Governor of Virginia, Edmund Randolph, October 16, 1787, 2: 451–52.

26. R. H. Lee to the Governor of Virginia, Edmund Randolph, October 16, 1787, 2: 454–55.

27. George Washington to James Madison, December 7, 1787, *DHRC*, 8: 226.

28. James Madison to George Washington, December 20, 1787, *DHRC*, 8: 253.

29. R. H. Lee to William Shippen Jr., October 2, 1787, *Lee Letters*, 2: 444.

30. Carrington's comment as quoted in *The Complete Anti-Federalist*, 7 vols., ed. Herbert J. Storing, with the assistance of Murray Dry (Chicago: The University of Chicago Press, 1981), 2: 216.

31. The authorship of the *Letters from the Federal Farmer* has been the focus on scholarly debate for some time now. In addition to my article, "The Authorship of the *Letters from the Federal Farmer*, Revisited," see Gordon Wood, "The Authorship of the *Letters from the Federal Farmer*," *The William and Mary Quarterly* 31 (April 1974): 299–307; and Robert H. Webking, "Melancton Smith and the *Letters from the Federal Farmer*," *William and Mary Quarterly* 44 (July 1987): 510–28.

32. Oliver Ellsworth, "Landholder VI," December 10, 1787, *DHRC*, 3: 488.

33. Oliver Ellsworth, "Landholder VIII," December 24, 1787, *DHRC*, 3: 506.

34. McGaughy, "The Authorship of the *Letters from the Federal Farmer* Revisited," 158 n. 12.

35. *DHRC*, 8: 284. The actual source of this account is unknown, and the alleged quote from Richard Henry's son represents secondhand testimony that cannot be verified. In spite of the reservations such observations raise, the story is plausible, especially when recalling the views expressed by Richard Henry about the proposed constitution in his July 14, 1787, letter to Francis Lightfoot Lee. It also remains within the realm of possibility that F. L. Lee shared these sentiments with his nephew Thomas Lee, who was then serving in Virginia's state senate.

36. R. H. Lee to William Shippen Jr., October 2, 1787, *Lee Letters*, 2: 444.

37. George Washington to James Madison, January 10, 1788, *DHRC*, 8: 292.

38. Arthur Lee to R. H. Lee, February 19, 1788, *DHRC*, 9: 620.

39. Arthur Lee to R. H. Lee, February 19, 1788, *DHRC*, 9: 620. Arthur Lee related Mason's comments in the letter he wrote to his older brother.

40. Arthur Lee to R. H. Lee, February 19, 1788, *DHRC*, 9: 620.

41. Tenche Coxe to James Madison, January 23, 1788, *DHRC*, 8: 313.

42. "The State Soldier III," March 12, 1788, *DHRC*, 8: 485–88.

43. "Cassius II: To Richard Henry Lee, Esquire," April 9, 1788, *DHRC*, 9: 713–14.

44. R. H. Lee to James Gordon Jr., February 26, 1788, *Lee Letters*, 2: 460–62.

45. R. H. Lee to James Gordon Jr., February 26, 1788, *Lee Letters*, 2: 460–62.

46. R. H. Lee to Samuel Adams, April 28, 1788, *Lee Letters*, 2: 465.

47. R. H. Lee to George Mason, May 7, 1788, *Lee Letters*, 2: 466–69.

48. R. H. Lee to Edmund Pendleton, May 22, 1788, *Lee Letters*, 2: 473.

49. John Lamb to R. H. Lee, May 18, 1788, *DHRC*, 9: 814–15. Smith's second pamphlet contained letters dated from December 25, 1787, through January 25, 1788.

50. R. H. Lee to John Lamb, June 27, 1788, *Lee Letters*, 2: 474–76; and *DHRC*, 9: 825–26.

The Honorable Senator from Virginia

I

$\mathcal{I}$n the months following the adoption of the Constitution of the United States, Richard Henry Lee bided his time at Chantilly and continued to avoid public comment on the situation. By October 1788, the situation seemed to have calmed down in Virginia; as he initiated a quiet campaign for the new United States Senate, Lee began contacting old friends and allies in the House of Delegates who also opposed the Constitution during the ratification debates. He reminded his correspondents of his efforts to secure prior amendments, and he indicated that he would welcome an opportunity to pursue these matters "in the senate of the new legislature."[1] As news spread of Lee's candidacy for the Senate, several staunch advocates of the Constitution expressed their dismay. Edward Carrington expressed his concern over rumors regarding the nominations of Patrick Henry and Richard Henry Lee; he feared they would dismantle the new government as quickly as possible. Carrington was confident that Lee would easily win a seat in the Senate, unless advocates of the new plan found alternative candidates "very well established in the confidence of the people" to run against him. Carrington urged James Madison to place his name in nomination for the Senate in order to lessen Lee's chances of winning.[2]

Carrington's efforts failed, as on November 8, 1788, the House of Delegates elected Richard Henry Lee and William Grayson as that state's first two senators. The final ballot reflected strong support for Lee, as delegates awarded him ninety-eight votes, with Grayson a close second with eighty-six votes. Madison placed third in the contest. These results disappointed Carrington and his friends; many of them expressed their fears that after their long struggle to win the ratification contest, they were handing over the new government to the most ardent critics of the new plan. While men like Carrington fretted about the future, Lee's friends and family celebrated the news. Richard Henry's brother-in-law, William Shippen Jr., in Philadelphia, announced to his son that "R.H. Lee and Col. Grayson are chosen Senators for Virginia both fond of amendments to the new Constitution." He then added a chiding reference to Robert Morris, who was also appointed to a seat in the new Senate, commenting that the news from Virginia was "very disagreeable to Bobby & our warm Federalists."[3] The tone of the meeting of the First Federal Congress of the United States was already being set, as both sides once again prepared to take their seats in the nation's capitol.

II

As Richard Henry Lee prepared to return to New York City and take his place in the United States Senate, he still remained an unknown quantity as far as many of his contemporaries were concerned. No one was exactly sure how far he would go in his pursuit of constitutional amendments. George Washington believed that his friend only "wished to see the Government fairly carried into execution & that such alterations only should be adopted, as might be found necessary from its errors and defects."[4] Washington was quick to defend his old friend by countering alarming rumors that Richard Henry would sponsor "premature amendments" that would "render the government abortive." The general indicated his confidence that such talk "will be found untrue."[5]

Washington more than likely received reassurances from Richard Henry Lee, as the general's old friend stopped by Mount Vernon for a visit while on his way to take his seat in the United States Senate. Characteristically, Lee did not arrive in New York City until early April, since he was always desirous of waiting until the coldest weather had passed before traveling northward. Once he had arrived and taken his seat, the Senate began conducting its first matters of business. The new Constitution stipulated that senators would serve six-year terms and that members to the first Senate would be divided into three classes—the first class held their seats for two years, the second class would remain for a four-year term, and senators of the third class would serve out their full six years. As senators drew their lots to determine their class ranking, Lee announced that he was a senator of the second class and would retain his seat until 1792.

Items on the first order of business for the new Senate included electing members to fill offices, such as president pro tempore, and counting the votes for president and vice president of the United States. Much to Richard Henry's delight, George Washington won the highest office, with a majority of sixty-nine votes; Lee's old friend from Massachusetts, John Adams, came in second with thirty-four votes, making him vice president.[6] Upon confirming this final tally, Congress dispatched Charles Thomson and Sylvanus Bourne to notify and deliver certificates of election to Washington and Adams.[7] Lee wrote a letter to Washington indicating that his worst fear was that the general would not accept the office, adding the personal observation that "I am sure that the public happiness which I know you have so much at heart will be very insecure without your acceptance."[8] Washington did not disappoint his friend, as both he and Adams notified Congress that they would accept their respective offices in the new government of the United States.

Once Congress had this order of business behind them, members could turn their attention to other pressing matters of state. During Richard Henry Lee's tenure in the Senate, he attended all four sessions, and the first proved to be the most active, as both houses of Congress completed unfinished portions of the Constitution by further defining the executive branch and by establishing the framework for the federal judiciary. Additionally, Richard Henry followed debates in the House of Representatives regarding a bill of rights and eagerly anticipated receiving a finished document from the lower house. All the while, Lee kept a watchful eye on his long-standing political rivals who also occupied seats in the Senate, most notably, Robert Morris and Oliver Ellsworth. Because of their past history, Lee simply did not trust these two men, and he informed numerous correspondents that he would work to make sure that the new national government did not eclipse the state legislatures.[9] Richard Henry recognized that the Constitution was an unfinished document and that both the executive and judicial branches remained largely undefined; the ratifying conventions left that task for the First Federal Congress to complete. These represented the pressing matters that shaped the agenda of the first Congress, and Lee made it clear that he would work diligently to procure the "happiness, prosperity, and security of . . . union"; but he would not tolerate "one government founded on the ruin of the State governments."[10]

Despite his reservations about the new system of government that Richard Henry Lee so frequently voiced after arriving in New York City, he surprised many of his colleagues. Some of Lee's friends expected him to either demand a second constitutional convention or at least sponsor a series of structural amendments that would clearly direct political power back toward the states. He rejected these paths, recognizing their futility. Instead, he and his fellow senator from Virginia William Grayson set about the task of limiting federal authority through efforts to further define the executive and judicial branches. Richard Henry, however, made it clear that he would keep a watchful eye on his colleagues, predicting that they would "pass Laws of a nature so gracious as to quiet alarms"; but he hastened to add that "the safety of liberty depends not so much upon the *gracious manner*, as upon the Limitation of Power."[11]

III

Richard Henry Lee and William Grayson were the only two senators elected who had disparaged the Constitution during the ratification debates, although ten antifederalists won seats in the House of Representatives. Because his views reflected a minority position in the Senate, Lee understood that he would have to compromise and work with others to achieve his desired goals—that is, he would have to reach out toward others if he hoped to succeed. Richard Henry believed that his best opportunity to accomplish his objectives would be to cultivate his old ties with John Adams, who regarded his role as president of the Senate as an active position designed to marshal support for particular measures that impinged on executive departments. Initially, Richard Henry did not object to Adams's definition of his role; he regarded it favorably and saw it as an effective means to reestablish the old Lee–Adams alliance that dominated the Continental Congress from 1774 to 1779.

The first indication of the revival of the old Lee–Adams coalition appeared as the Senate addressed the issue of official titles for the president and vice president of the United States. At Adams's request, the Senate appointed a committee to consider various titles that might be bestowed upon the two chief executive officers. Adams clearly favored adopting appellations reminiscent of European monarchies, displaying a particular affinity for addressing Washington as "His Highness the President of the United States of America and Protector of Their Liberties."[12] Richard Henry endorsed Adams's view and made the observation before the Senate that "all the World [both] civilized and Savage called for the use of titles"; he then proceeded to make allusions to classical antiquity, the manner in which the ancient Greeks and Romans maintained republican institutions while allowing the use of titles.[13]

These efforts by Adams and Lee annoyed many of their colleagues; the entire discussion disturbed several senators, and they responded in jest, largely at the expense of John Adams. Given the vice president's proclivity for titles, some suggested that Adams take the title "his superfluous majesty" or his "rotundity." William Maclay, a senator from Pennsylvania, was convinced that "had it not been for [Adams] and Lee," no one in the Senate would have broached the subject of titles, which led him to ascribe political motives as the reason for Richard Henry's active participation in the debate.[14] Maclay noted in his diary, "this whole silly business is the Work of Mr. Adams and Mr. Lee." Those that endorsed the use of titles did so to gain political advantage from these two prominent men: "Mr. [Ralph] Izard [of South Carolina] follows Lee, and the New England men . . . always herd together follow Mr. Adams." Maclay added that his colleague Charles Thomson noted that "this used to be the Case in the old Congress."[15]

Maclay's assessment of Lee depended largely upon the skewed views expressed by his Pennsylvania colleagues Robert Morris and Charles Thomson, neither of whom had much regard for Richard Henry Lee. When Maclay first anticipated working with Lee in the Senate, he incorrectly described Lee as a "notorious Antifederalist" and characterized him as a "Jehru like Spirit," whose real aim it was to flatter Adams so Lee could "govern all the Members from New England." Maclay saw nothing but nefarious motives on the Virginian's part, as he voiced his suspicion that with Adams's support and "with a little assistance from Carolina or Georgia," Lee's power would be "absolute in the Senate."[16] Later, Maclay referred to Lee as the "perfect Ishmael" as a further illustration of his disdain for the honorable senator from Virginia.[17] Maclay seemed convinced that Lee was intent on establishing strong ties between the Senate and the executive branch at the expense of the House of Representatives, and the debate over titles clinched the notion in the Pennsylvanian's mind that "the Game that [Adams] & Mr. Lee appear to have now in View is to separate the Senate as much as possible from the House of Representatives. . . . [the] doctrine is that all honors & Titles should flow from the President and Senate only."[18]

IV

Although Maclay's observations astutely recognized Lee's desire to reestablish strong political ties with his old friend from Massachusetts, he did not fully understand Lee's motives. In all likelihood, Richard Henry viewed the issue of titles as a harmless, innocuous issue that did not have any bearing the distribution of power between state and local authorities. The use of titles would be limited to public ceremonies, and Lee understandably thought the judicious use of such titles would enhance America's stature in the eyes of a world still dominated by emperors and kings. But, when it came to issues that did in fact define the relationship between the legislative and executive branches, for example, Richard Henry remained consistent with his expressed views toward limited government—a stance that soon made it impossible to revive the Lee–Adams coalition of the 1770s and, in the process, killed an old friendship.

While members of the Senate debated the issue of titles, James Madison took the lead in the House of Representatives and began further defining executive offices. Four departments were established: foreign affairs (later Department of State), treasury, war, and attorney general. The Constitution offered very little specific guidance on this subject, other than to stipulate that such offices would exist. Madison interpreted the Constitution to mean that the president could select whomever he wished to these posts with the advice and confirmation of the Senate. Madison also believed that the men who held these positions could be removed from office at his will—a prerogative Madison believed was an inherent part of the executive appointment power.[19]

Richard Henry Lee echoed the sentiments of several of his colleagues when he disputed Madison's suggestion that the president could dismiss an appointee without at least first consulting members of the Senate. As the controversy moved to open debate, Lee and Adams once again dominated affairs, but this time they argued for opposite sides of the question at hand. Lee refused to endorse what he regarded as a dramatic extension of presidential power, and he viewed this sort of sweeping removal power as the first steps toward a despotic government.[20] Richard Henry argued that if the president could remove men from an executive office at will, then their advice would reflect only what the president wished to hear, not a candid, objective opinion. Lee added that "the absurdity" of such a position seemed too strong to ignore.[21]

A few days after the debate on the removal power began, Richard Henry arrived in Senate chambers early one morning and observed John Adams scurrying from desk to desk, openly attacking Lee's position in such a manner as to question Lee's honor and integrity. Richard Henry confronted Adams on the floor, demanding an explanation for his behavior. William Maclay later recorded in his diary that the "altercation" was not violent, but Lee was clearly hurt by the actions taken by his old friend; he was stymied and felt betrayed by John Adams. What made Maclay certain of his interpretation of the event was Lee's manner afterward. The Pennsylvanian noted that, for the remainder of the day, Lee "was languid, and much shorter [in speech] than ever I had heard him on almost any Subject."[22] The next day, the Senate voted on the provision, giving the president authority to remove officers without the consent of the Senate. The vote ended in a tie—ten for and ten against. John Adams then stepped forward and in his capacity as presiding officer in the Senate, cast the tie-breaking vote, thereby allowing the measure to pass.[23] Now that this particular issue was resolved, members of the Senate confirmed President Washington's first executive cabinet: Alexander Hamilton, secretary of the treasury; Thomas Jefferson, secretary of state; Henry Knox, secretary of war; and Edmund Randolph, attorney general.

V

Richard Henry Lee could barely contain his disgust toward this turn of events. He now spoke more openly of what he regarded as fundamental structural weaknesses within the new constitutional system, and he thus redefined his role within the Senate. Richard Henry Lee now questioned whether or not the vice president should be allowed to cast a vote in the Senate at all. He regarded this situation as dicey, especially if the matter before the Senate related to executive authority, since the vice president had such a "probable prospect" of gaining that office.[24] Additionally, Lee now welcomed every opportunity to criticize John Adams's conduct as vice president. Richard Henry's renewed awareness for the possibly corrupting concentration of power in the hands of federal authority occurred at a crucial time—just as James Madison in the House of Representatives began considering proposed amendments that would comprise a bill of rights as promised during the ratification debates a year before. At the same time, both chambers began the task of further defining the federal judiciary, as provided for by article 3 of the Constitution of the United States. As Lee participated in the discussions and debates over these issues, his suspicions grew; he spoke openly of a dangerous concentration of power at the national level. He revived older references to the virtues of a confederated republic, and he urged his friends to keep a vigilant eye on the events in Congress to ensure that the federal government did not encroach on the authority of the state governments.[25]

Richard Henry now pinned his hopes of limiting federal authority on the amendment process. He had followed the progression of a bill of rights in the House since the effort began in the spring of 1789. Initially, Lee expressed his apprehension that Madison's ideas and those of the Virginia ratifying convention were not similar.[26] He indicated that Madison's efforts focused on what Lee regarded as procedural amendments geared toward protecting civil liberties such as freedom of conscience; guarantees protecting trial by jury; and other such matters. Richard Henry noted, however, that the talk of amendments steered clear of structural amendments concerning the distribution of power between state and national government as well as within the three branches of the federal government.

Lee recognized the critical importance of the procedural amendments as the discussion advanced through the House; but by the fall of 1789, these alone were insufficient. After the Senate's debate over the president's removal power and his altercation with Vice President Adams, Lee became more insistent in his quest for structural amendments as well. As he faced criticism from some of his colleagues in the House and the Senate, including some old friends from the heady days of the American Revolution, he became increasingly disheartened. In one particular instant, Lee was incredulous when he heard that Roger Sherman of Connecticut opposed an amendment subordinating military authority to civilian government on the grounds that such a provision "'*would make the people insolent!*'"[27] After Richard Henry received a final draft of the House's proposed bill of rights, he despondently observed that "it is very clear . . . that a government very different from a free one will take place err many years are passed."[28]

VI

Richard Henry Lee's renewed suspicion toward the enlargement of federal authority not only prompted his despondent tone toward the proposed bill of rights, but it also influenced his position on the Federal Judiciary Act of 1789. In April 1789, the Senate appointed a committee chaired by Oliver Ellsworth, whose purpose was to bring forward a bill "for organizing the judiciary of the United States."[29] By the following June, the panel presented a measure to the Senate calling for the appointment of six Supreme Court justices, and they outlined a system of federal district and circuit courts as well. Richard Henry immediately took issue with some provisions in the bill and advanced the idea that federal judicial authority should be limited to admiralty cases and maritime law. Lee suggested that the extensive court system proposed by Ellsworth's committee threatened the established jurisdictions of state courts. Additionally, Richard Henry argued that a circuit court system could not adequately serve an area as large as the United States, and he sought clarification regarding how the appeals process would work. In spite of the concerns raised by Lee, he took a moderate stance when he simply proposed that the Senate be given more time to study the matter before bringing it to a final vote.[30]

Nonetheless, Lee's grievances raised several eyebrows in the Senate. William Maclay noted that the "effect of [Lee's] motion was to exclude Federal Jurisdiction from the states."[31] Up until this moment, Maclay's assessment of Lee had always betrayed a harsh tone because he had based his comments on the characterizations of the Virginian made by his political enemies. The debate over the Federal Judiciary Act of 1789, however, marks a steady shift in Maclay's demeanor toward Lee. The turning point for Maclay occurred as he witnessed the fight between Lee and Adams on the Senate floor in July 1789. That one event shattered a whole host of assumptions Maclay had about Richard Henry Lee and his overall conduct in the Senate. More important, however, Maclay now found a valuable ally in Richard Henry Lee, as both men shared the same sentiments toward the judiciary bill. The Pennsylvanian regarded the measure as a "Vile law system, calculated for Expence, and with a design to draw by degrees all law business into the federal courts [and] . . . to Swallow by degrees all the State judiciaries."[32]

Richard Henry Lee's public row with John Adams had taken place before the Senate renewed its debate over the Federal Judiciary Act of 1789. Maclay immediately detected that whenever Lee addressed the issue in debate, his speech "was more pointed than any of them"; and the senator from Pennsylvania began to realize how much he had in common with his colleague from the Old Dominion.[33] Maclay no longer regarded Lee as a "Jehru," or an "Ishmael," and as the debate over the judiciary began, Maclay noted that Lee used many of Maclay's points, adding that Richard Henry was "always . . . polite enough to acknowledge" Maclay's original authorship of the arguments.[34]

It seemed that in the process of losing one old friend, Richard Henry Lee had gained a new one. Lee and Maclay began working more closely with each other, and Richard Henry found a comfortable place among moderates in the Senate. Although many of their efforts failed when it came to reeling in the expansion of federal authority, a new coalition steadily emerged. The busy first session for the Senate came to an end in September 1789, and Lee left his new-found friends and happily returned to his beloved Chantilly-on-the-Potomac, where he would spend the winter among his dearest friends and family.

VII

The second session for the United States Senate was scheduled to begin in January 1790, after a three-month hiatus. Unfortunately, Richard Henry Lee's health declined steadily as the cold season began to chill the air along the shores of the Potomac River. As a result, Lee was unable to attend the opening of the new session. Yet, in spite of his health-related problems, Lee still found reason to celebrate. Between the first and second sessions, Richard Henry announced the birth of two granddaughters, one by Nancy and the other by Ludwell. Soon afterward, Lee found another reason to celebrate, as he announced the engagements of two more daughters, Mary and Hannah, to relations of President Washington. Mary wed William Augustine Washington, and Hannah married Corbin Washington. So, in between bouts of illness, there is little reason to doubt that Lee drank several toasts to the good fortunes bestowed upon his family.

It was May 1790 before he had finally recuperated and had the strength to return to New York, but as Lee resumed his seat, he was much more subdued. His old friend and fellow senator William Grayson died in March 1790, and Lee reflected on the loss of his only true friend in the Senate. Nonetheless, he returned to New York with new colleague John Walker at his side. Almost immediately after his arrival, however, Lee had to excuse himself from the public's business, as he suffered a bout of influenza and was confined in his room for almost a month. An epidemic swept through New York City that June. Theodoric Bland, a member of the House of Representatives from Virginia, fell victim to the disease and died. President Washington also succumbed but, like Richard Henry, soon began a slow recovery. While incapacitated by the virus, Lee told his nephew how he suffered through "a most dangerous attack of the influenza" in his "Lungs & Head which nearly destroyed" him. As he slowly regained his strength, he commented on the severity of his illness, indicating that it had nearly dispatched him to "that Country from whose Bourne no Traveller returns." Before long, Lee felt well enough to move about and go visit his dear friend the president. Afterward, he expressed his pleasure as he witnessed Washington "sitting in his easy Chair . . . [for the] greatest part of the day."[35]

When Richard Henry Lee had gained sufficient strength to resume his duties as senator, he found his colleagues embroiled in controversy as they debated the first of several reports submitted to Congress by Treasury Secretary Hamilton regarding the funding of the national debt. The most controversial aspect of Hamilton's first report was his call for the assumption of state debts by the federal government.[36] Richard Henry immediately chimed into the debates and voiced his disapproval of the assumption plan primarily because Virginia had paid off its state debt, and he saw no reason for his state now to be burdened with the fiscal irresponsibility of other states. Naturally, proponents of the assumption plan in the Senate represented those states that were saddled with large debts carried since the war with Great Britain. As the Senate divided over the issue, Massachusetts and South Carolina came together supporting Hamilton's initiative while Pennsylvania and Virginia, oddly enough, now found common ground and resolved to take a determined stand against the assumption plan.

In July 1790, William Maclay eagerly approached Richard Henry Lee with a plan to give Hamilton's plan a "decided stroke" to guarantee its failure. Lee listened patiently and told his young friend that they would discuss the matter later and more fully. Afterward, Richard Henry met with James Madison, and the two men discussed Maclay's proposal. Lee returned from the meeting and informed Maclay that, provided he made a slight change in the wording of his proposal, Lee would stand and second the motion after Maclay introduced it on the Senate floor. The exchange perturbed the Pennsylvanian because the specific change Lee insisted on made his proposal "much more obscure." But, in the end, Maclay bowed to Richard Henry's recommendations because he knew that without Lee's support, his measure would fail. The next morning, Maclay addressed his colleagues in the Senate and introduced his motion regarding the assumption plan. He stood there waiting for Lee's motion to second, but the senator from Virginia remained in his seat and watched Maclay's amendment "perish with the indifference of a stranger."[37]

Although the record remains murky, Richard Henry Lee, in all likelihood, deliberately misled Maclay, making him think he had Lee's support, thereby preventing him from garnering the support of others. Once the ruse was in place, Richard Henry could ensure the demise of Maclay's proposal by remaining in his seat and failing to second the motion. Maclay's determined effort to kill Hamilton's assumption plan fell victim to a much larger political battle that loomed in the background, as members of Congress debated the merits of the treasurer's financial program—the determination of a permanent location of the nation's capital.

As Massachusetts and South Carolina became more determined to secure passage of Hamilton's proposal to relieve their burden of debt, the assumption plan became inextricably linked to the question of a permanent seat of government for the United States. Congressmen from Massachusetts and South Carolina began talking openly with leaders from New York, promising to support plans to declare New York City as the permanent capital of the United States. As word of such discussions spread, advocates of a Potomac site panicked, as they feared their efforts to push the capital southward would be lost. Representatives from Pennsylvania who had endorsed the assumption plan complicated matters even more by hinting that they cared little about the location of the nation's capital and would support whichever side could guarantee the passage of Hamilton's assumption plan.

The dispute exasperated Richard Henry Lee as he began listening to the internecine wrangling occurring all around him. He told one correspondent that it was "impossible" for him to describe the scene, adding that in comparison "every thing met in my former life is mere trifling, compared with this, and you know I have been in very stormy legislative sessions."[38] In the end, proponents for a Potomac site carried the day as the Senate passed the Residence Bill on June 30, 1790, proclaiming that the seat of government would move to Philadelphia for a period of ten years, and then on to a permanent location somewhere along the shores of the Potomac River. Afterward, the measure moved on to the House of Representatives, for their consideration.[39] Initially, Lee was confident that the House would act quickly and adopt the Residence Bill; but those hopes were soon dashed, as Lee indicated in a letter to his nephew that "all the arts of division practiced in the Senate would be repeated in the H. of R."[40] Apparently, members of the House who were opposed to the assumption plan were gaining an upper hand; and since many were from Virginia, Madison had to work with them and gain their support for the assumption plan in exchange for a Potomac site for the nation's capital. While Madison worked with recalcitrant members of the House, Lee had to deal with antiassumption senators like Maclay. As a result of this wrangling, and much to Lee's delight, a few days later the House passed the Residence Bill, which President Washington happily signed into law on July 16, 1790.

The passage of the Residence Bill pleased Lee and his Virginia colleagues immensely, but they had to pay a price. In order to secure a Potomac River site, they had to guarantee passage of Hamilton's assumption plan. The treasurer approached Thomas Jefferson as early as June 6, 1790, suggesting a compromise linking the assumption plan with the residence debate. After this meeting,

Jefferson urged Madison in the House to marshal support for the assumption plan, so Madison worked with Lee in the Senate. Hamilton struck a nerve in dealing with this Virginia trio, and in the end, both sides achieved their desired goals.[41] As the backroom deals materialized, Madison maintained a public stance against the assumption plan so he would not anger his constituents in Virginia who were unaware of the larger issue at stake; all the while, he worked to convince Richard Bland Lee (R. H. Lee's cousin) and Alexander White of Virginia, as well as two additional votes from Maryland, to support the assumption in exchange for a Potomac site. In all likelihood, Richard Henry Lee played a similar role in the Senate by outwardly appearing to endorse Maclay's efforts to kill the assumption plan but remaining silent in the end. When Lee abandoned Maclay on the Senate floor at the last minute, the Virginian all but guaranteed the passage of Hamilton's assumption plan in the Senate—yet anyone who was not privy to the private conversations between Lee and Maclay on July 4 and 5, 1790, would swear Lee opposed the assumption plan.

James Madison accomplished everything that was expected of him toward fulfilling his end of the "dinner table bargain" between Hamilton and Jefferson, and Richard Henry Lee proved to an active, if not silent, partner in the affair. However, Lee maintained to the end the façade that he opposed the assumption plan, as he and John Walker wrote to the governor of Virginia, indicating "we are sorry to inform your Excellency that the assumption of State debts into the funds of the U.S. is likely to succeed at last." The senators from Virginia tried to put the best spin forward by adding that the "sum assumed [by Virginia] is $3,500,000, which being more than we owe, will serve to cover a part of the large balance that we claim from the Union."[42] Despite the apparent setback, Lee accepted the sacrifice in order to secure a permanent seat of government on the Potomac River. The backroom dealings, however, had taken a toll on Lee. Compounded by his weakened state of health and disturbing news from Chantilly, it was a situation that led Richard Henry to long for the end of this "tedious session" so that he could hasten back home once again.

VIII

Richard Henry Lee was distracted throughout the second session of the Senate by a host of personal matters. In addition to his own bout with influenza in May 1790, and not long after his recovery, he received disturbing reports from home. Just as the Senate began debating the location of the new American capital, Lee learned that his "family at Chantilly, & that of Stratford have been severely visited with the Measles."[43] As he learned that several members of his family began to recover, he became increasingly alarmed about his daughter Nancy, "whose situation [was] . . . by no means favorable," and he begged his brother Arthur to visit Chantilly and "relieve me from my anxiety on her account as soon as you can."[44] As soon as Congress settled the question on the location of the capital, Richard Henry left New York City and hurried back to Chantilly so that he could tend to the needs of those who were still ill.

Unfortunately, he knew that his stay in Virginia would be short. Congress had scheduled its third session to begin in December 1790. During this brief hiatus, the two-year terms for Senators of the first class expired, and the state legislature convened for new elections. Virginia's House of Delegates named James Monroe to succeed William Grayson's midterm replacement, John Walker. Monroe's appointment to the United States Senate was his first office under the new Constitution, but he did serve three years in the Continental Congress and had assisted in the negotiations of treaties with Native American tribes during Richard Henry Lee's presidency in 1784 and 1785. Lee intended to meet with his new colleague in Virginia so they could travel to Philadelphia together for the third session. Illness, once again, delayed Lee's plans. He informed Monroe and other political associates that he would not be able to resume his official duties until February 1791. This unfortunate turn of events put Monroe in a disadvantageous situation because, as soon as the new senator from Virginia arrived, the Senate began considering other controversial aspects of Treasury Secretary Hamilton's financial program—notably, the proposed tax on distilled spirits and the establishment of a national bank.

Senator Monroe recognized his lack of preparation on these matters and successfully carried a vote postponing the debate; then, he turned to his senior partner, who was still incapacitated at Chantilly, for advice.[45] Richard Henry responded quickly to Monroe's queries while profusely apologizing for his state of health, which "tho improving" kept him away from Philadelphia. Regarding the proposed excise tax on liquor, Lee urged caution because "the temptation to smuggle [was] already great," and additional duties may only serve to "tempt Men into the practise of violating law." Richard Henry believed the Senate should pursue a moderate path, noting that he did not object to "a reasonable & unabusive excise." As for the national bank, Lee simply noted his belief that banking was not public business and that members of the government should not become bankers "because such abuses practiced by Government, leave injured Individuals too much without redress." He referred his young colleague to Adam Smith's *Inquiry into the Nature and Causes of the Wealth of Nations*, describing Smith as "a very great Author" who had written on this very subject and had given "[the] obvious reason" why "banking is [the] kind of Traffic that tempts by interest to abuse." Lee concluded his commentary, noting that "the reasons assigned by that sensible Author against the Government of England being so engaged, must be seen by every person experienced in American Affairs, to apply with very increased force."[46]

Richard Henry's deference to Adam Smith on the question of a national bank put him in good company with a number of congressmen and senators. James Madison, also citing Smith, voiced his concerns about the potential problems associated with a national bank, as did William Maclay, who described banks as "machines for promoting the profits of unproductive Men."[47] There is little reason to doubt that Lee would have echoed Maclay's sentiments based on the Virginian's personal experiences with Robert Morris and his friends in the 1770s and 1780s. Monroe, acting on Lee's advice, opposed the bank measure once the Senate resumed the debate over the issue. He offered several amendments, such as reducing the proposed bank's charter from twenty to ten years; when that motion failed, Monroe sought a ban on the incorporation of other banks while Hamilton's national bank was in operation.[48] Proponents of the bank expressed their displeasure toward Monroe, using an invective tone that grouped the two Virginians together (in spite of Lee's absence) as part of a "Potowmack [sic] interest" that opposed the bank simply because it resides in Philadelphia and its existence might delay the transfer of the nation's capital from Pennsylvania to the Potomac River.[49] Despite Monroe's efforts, the bank bill passed on January 19, 1791.

IX

Richard Henry Lee did not return to Philadelphia until mid-February, just in time for the Senate to begin concluding business of the third session. Consequently, Lee happily returned to Chantilly, where he would remain until the next session, slated for October 1791. Although Richard Henry delighted at the opportunity to spend more time at home, his health continued to languish. Soon after he returned home, he suffered a debilitating injury to his right hand. This new wound, combined with his old injury from 1768 (in which he lost all for four fingers on his left hand), cost him the use of both hands—a state of affairs that now forced him to rely on a personal secretary to handle his correspondence.[50] Yet, as the fall of 1791 approached, Richard Henry, in spite of these health-related setbacks, began making preparations to return to Philadelphia and take his place in the Senate once again. He arranged to bring his son-in-law Charles Lee, whom he employed as his personal assistant, and he also made inquiries about apartments in Philadelphia "as convenient to the State house as possible, [so] that my gouty feet may sustain no injury from the wintry weather."[51] Yet, despite these careful arrangements, disaster struck. While traveling to Philadelphia, Lee's carriage overturned, and the injuries Richard Henry sustained in the accident prevented him from resuming his seat until the end of December 1791.

After recovering from the accident, Lee rejoined his colleagues in the Senate while they were in the midst of a series of debates concerning the ratio of representation in the House of Representatives in relation to the general population. The Constitution established a ratio that provided one representative for every 30,000 citizens. Congressmen from the North wanted to increase that number by 3,000—an initiative opposed by Lee and many other southerners who argued that the proposed measure would "abridge the representation of the South, and add to that of the North."[52] Nonetheless, the bill managed to pass both houses of Congress and proceed to President Washington's desk. Washington listened to his closest advisors, after which he handed down his first presidential veto. Congressional advocates for the increase failed to secure the needed two-thirds majority to override the veto, and their effort thus failed—much to the delight of Richard Henry Lee.[53] After the debates over representation in the Senate, Vice President John Adams announced that he planned to take a month's leave of absence, and Richard Henry's colleagues accorded him the honor of electing him president pro tempore. Most of the Senate's business had been complete, and the honor proved more to be a reflection of the esteem many of Lee's associates had for the Virginian than anything else.

Congress adjourned on May 7, 1792, and Richard Henry hurried home to be with his family once again. The conclusion of the fourth session of the Senate also marked the end of the terms for senators, like Lee, who were of the second class. As Virginia's legislature gathered in the fall 1792, Richard Henry learned from friends that he remained at the top of the list of senatorial candidates under consideration. After learning this, he submitted a letter to the House of Delegates requesting that his name be withdrawn from consideration. He wrote: "I feel . . . compelled by the feeble state of my health to retire from the service of my Country." He mentioned how he had "grown gray in the service of my country," suggesting that he would have gladly accepted another term in the Senate had it not been for "infirmities that can only be relieved by a quiet retirement."[54] The House of Delegates and the Virginia Senate read Lee's request, and the state senate responded promptly by adopting the following resolution:

> Resolved unanimously, That the speaker be desired to convey to Richard Henry Lee, Esq. the respects of the Senate; that they sincerely sympathize with him in those infirmities which have deprived their country of his valuable services; and that they ardently wish he may, in retirement, with uninterrupted happiness, close the evening of a life, in which he hath so conspicuously shone forth as a statesman and patriot; that while mindful of the exertions to promote the public interests, *they are particularly thankful for his conduct, as a member of the Legislature of the United States.*"[55]

Lee cordially responded to the resolution, thanking them and wishing that it "may be the good fortune of those who follow me, to serve masters willing to crown their labours, by bestowing upon them a reward so respectable as I have been favored with."[56] Thus ended Richard Henry Lee's long career in the public's service.

When Lee first arrived in New York City as a Senator from Virginia in 1789, several members of Congress expressed concern over Lee's reputation as an opponent of the new Constitution. To a limited extent, their concerns were justifiable. Lee annoyed many senators by voicing his objections in debates without hesitation, but he always worked through the appropriate constitutional channels allowed by the new plan of government. In the end, Richard Henry Lee won the respect of many members of Congress. William Maclay, who began his career in the Senate as one of Lee's most vocal critics, soon referred to Richard Henry as "the Man who gave Independence (in One Sense) to America" and as "a Man of clear head, and great experience in public business."[57] This sort of honor accorded Richard Henry Lee by colleagues at the state and national level led them to finally award him with the "quiet retirement" he so desired.

NOTES

1. R. H. Lee to Theodoric Bland, October 15, 1788, *Lee Letters*, 2: 477–78; R. H. Lee to John Jones, October 15, 1788, *Lee Letters*, 2: 478–79; and R. H. Lee to William Cabell, October 15, 1788, *Lee Letters*, 2: 479–80. Additional secondary works consulted for this chapter include Charlene Bickford and Kenneth R. Bowling, *Birth of the Nation* (Madison, WI: Madison House Publishers, 1989); Chitwood, *Richard Henry Lee*, 183–95; Stanley Elkins and Eric McKitrick, *The Age of Federalism: The Early American Republic, 1788–1800* (New York: Oxford University Press, 1993), 31–76, 303–74, and 581–641; and Joseph C. Miller, *The Federalist Era, 1789–1801* (New York: Harper & Row, 1960), 1–98.

2. Edward Carrington to James Madison, October 19, 1788, *The Documentary History of the First Federal Elections, 1788–1790*, 3 vols., ed. Gordon DenBoer, Lucy Trumbell Brown, and Charles D. Hagerman (Madison: University of Wisconsin Press, 1984), 2: 260–61. Hereafter, cited as *DHFFE*.

3. William Shippen Jr. to Thomas Lee Shippen, November 18, 1788, *DHFFE*, 2: 377.

4. George Washington to Benjamin Lincoln, November 14, 1788, *DHFFE*, 2: 374.

5. George Washington to Henry Knox, January 1, 1789, *DHFFE*, 2: 386.

6. *Senate Legislative Journal*, April 6, 1789, *Documentary History of the First Federal Congress*, 14 vols., ed. Linda Grant DePauw, Charlene Bangs Bickford, and LaVonne Siegal, et al. (Baltimore, MD: Johns Hopkins University Press, 1972–1996), 1: 8. Hereafter cited as *DHFFC*.

7. Charlene Bangs Bickford, "'Public Attention is Very Much Fixed on the Proceedings of the New Congress': The First Federal Congress Organizes Itself." *Inventing Congress: Origins and Establishment of the First Federal Congress,* ed. Kenneth R. Bowling and Donald R. Kennon (Athens: Ohio University Press, 1999), 141–42.

8. R. H. Lee to George Washington, April 6, 1789, *Lee Letters,* 2: 483.

9. R. H. Lee to Samuel Adams, April 25, 1789, *Lee Letters,* 2: 483–85; R. H. Lee to the Governor of Virginia [Beverly Randolph], May 26, 1789, *Lee Letters,* 2: 485–86; and R. H. Lee to Patrick Henry, May 28, 1789, *Lee Letters,* 2: 486–89.

10. R. H. Lee to Samuel Adams, April 25, 1789, *Lee Letters,* 2: 484.

11. R. H. Lee to Samuel Adams, April 25, 1789, *Lee Letters,* 2: 484.

12. Elkins and McKitrick, *The Age of Federalism,* 48.

13. *The Diary of William Maclay and Other Notes on Senate Debates,* May 8, 1789, *DHFFC,* 9: 27. Hereafter, cited as *Maclay's Diary.*

14. *Maclay's Diary,* May 14, 1789, *DHFFC,* 9: 39.

15. *Maclay's Diary,* May 8, 1789, *DHFFC,* 9: 29.

16. *Maclay's Diary,* April 29, 1789, *DHFFC,* 9: 10. Jehru was an ancient Israeli king (c. 840 B.C.E.) who, at the instigation of the Prophet Elijah, took over the kingdom of Israel and weakened the state to such a degree that the Hebrew kingdom became a weak dependency of other powers in the region.

17. *Maclay's Diary,* May 28, 1789, *DHFFC,* 9: 57. In the book of Genesis, Ishmael, the son of Abraham, is described as "a wild donkey of a man / his hand will be against everyone / and everyone's hand against him / and he will live in hostility toward all his brothers."

18. *Maclay's Diary,* May 14, 1789, *DHFFC,* 9: 39.

19. Elkins and McKitrick, *Age of Federalism,* 50–55.

20. *Maclay's Diary,* July 14, 1789, *DHFFC,* 9: 112.

21. R. H. Lee to Samuel Adams, August 8, 1789, *Lee Letters,* 2: 497.

22. *Maclay's Diary,* July 15, 1789, *DHFFC,* 9: 113.

23. *Maclay's Diary,* July 16, 1789, *DHFFC,* 9: 115.

24. R. H. Lee to Patrick Henry, September 27, 1789, *Lee Letters,* 2: 505.

25. R. H. Lee to Patrick Henry, September 27, 1789, *Lee Letters,* 2: 506.

26. R. H. Lee to Patrick Henry, May 28, 1789, *Lee Letters,* 2: 487.

27. R. H. Lee to Samuel Adams, August 8, 1789, *Lee Letters,* 2: 496. (Lee's emphasis.)

28. R. H. Lee to Francis Lightfoot Lee, September 13, 1789, *Lee Letters,* 2: 500.

29. *Senate Legislative Journal,* April 6, 1789, *DHFFC,* 1: 11.

30. "Debate on the Judiciary Act [S-1] Motion by Lee to limit federal courts to Admiralty jurisdiction," June 22, 1789, *DHFFC,* 9: 475.

31. *Maclay's Diary,* June 22, 1789, *DHFFC,* 9: 85.

32. *Maclay's Diary,* July 17, 1789, *DHFFC,* 9: 116.

33. *Maclay's Diary,* July 17, 1789, *DHFFC,* 9: 116.

34. *Maclay's Diary,* July 14, 1789, *DHFFC,* 9: 112.

35. R. H. Lee to Thomas Lee Shippen, May 8, 1790; R. H. Lee to Thomas Lee Shippen, May 14, 1790; R. H. Lee to Thomas Lee Shippen, May 18, 1790; and R. H. Lee to Thomas Lee Shippen, May 23, 1790, *Lee Letters,* 2: 510, 513, 515, and 517.

36. Alexander Hamilton, "Report Relative to a Provision for the Support of Public Credit," January 9, 1790, *The Reports of Alexander Hamilton*, ed. Jacob E. Cooke (New York: Harper & Row, 1964), 43–44.

37. *Maclay's Diary*, July 4–6, 1790, *DHFFC*, 9: 312–14.

38. R. H. Lee to Patrick Henry, June 10, 1790, *Lee Letters*, 2: 523–24.

39. R. H. Lee to Thomas Lee Shippen, June 30, 1790, *Lee Letters*, 2: 530.

40. R. H. Lee to Thomas Lee Shippen, July 6, 1790, *Lee Letters*, 2: 532.

41. The events surrounding the so-called Compromise of 1790 are still shrouded in mystery, and many notable scholars have disputed the notion of the sort of wrangling described in this account. Those interested in the controversy should consult Kenneth R. Bowling, *The Creation of Washington D.C.: The Idea and Location of the American Capital* (Fairfax, VA: George Mason University Press, 1991); as well as the following exchange: Jacob E. Cooke, "The Compromise of 1790," *The William and Mary Quarterly* 27 (1970): 523–45; Kenneth R. Bowling, "Dinner at Jefferson's: A Note on Jacob E. Cooke's 'The Compromise of 1790,' with a Rebuttal by Cooke," *The William and Mary Quarterly* 28 (1971): 629–48; and Norman K. Risjord, "The Compromise of 1790: New Evidence on the Dinner Table Bargain," *William and Mary Quarterly* 33 (1976): 309–14.

42. United States Senators from Virginia to the Governor of Virginia, July 25, 1790, *Lee Letters*, 2: 534.

43. R. H. Lee to Thomas Lee Shippen, June 5, 1790, *Lee Letters*, 2: 522.

44. R. H. Lee to Arthur Lee, June 10, 1790, *Lee Letters*, 2: 525.

45. *Maclay's Diary*, January 12, 1791, *DHFFC*, 9: 359.

46. R. H. Lee to James Monroe, January 15, 1791, *Lee Letters*, 2: 541–42.

47. William P. Cowin, "The Invisible Smith: The Impact of Adam Smith on the Foundation of Early American Economic Policy during the First Federal Congress, 1789–1791," in *Inventing Congress*, 284–92; *Maclay's Diary*, January 17, 1791, *DHFFC*, 9: 362.

48. *Senate Legislative Journal*, January 19–20, 1791, *DHFFC*, 1: 534–36.

49. *Maclay's Diary*, January 19, 1791, *DHFFC*, 9: 364.

50. R. H. Lee to General John Armstrong, May 1, 1791, *Lee Letters*, 2: 543; R. H. Lee to Thomas Lee Shippen, September 21, 1791, *Lee Letters*, 2: 543–44.

51. R. H. Lee to Thomas Lee Shippen, September 21, 1791, *Lee Letters*, 2: 543–44.

52. [United State Senators from Virginia] to Governor Henry Lee, January 21, 1792, *Lee Letters*, 2: 545.

53. R. H. Lee to William Lee, April 7, 1792, *Lee Letters*, 2: 550.

54. R. H. Lee to the Speaker of the House of Delegates, October 8, 1792, *Lee Letters*, 2: 550–51.

55. Speaker of the Senate [of Virginia], November 5, 1792, *Lee Letters*, 2: 552 n. 1.

56. R. H. Lee to the Speaker of the Senate [of Virginia], November 5, 1792, *Lee Letters*, 2: 552–53.

57. *Maclay's Diary*, June 12, 1790, *DHFFC*, 9: 290.

• 11 •

Twilight

I

$\mathcal{O}$nce Richard Henry Lee had finalized his decision to retire from public service, he devoted his full attention to taking care of his wife and children; he took control of directing the education of his two youngest boys, Cassius and Francis; and he delighted in his newfound role—grandfather. Sadly, these joyous moments soon faded. Just barely a month after his retirement, Lee learned he would have to witness the burial of another sibling. In December 1792, Arthur Lee contracted a fever that kept him confined to his bed. A few days later, just before he celebrated his fifty-second birthday, Arthur became violently ill and died on December 12. In accordance with his brother's wishes, Richard Henry took on the responsibility as "sole executor" of his brother's estate. Ludwell Lee penned a short verse in remembrance of his uncle:

> Closed are those eyes that beamed celestial fire
> That mouth that virtue did inspire;
> Cold is that heart, which beat for public good
> Fled is that mind, which most things understood.[1]

There is little reason to doubt that Richard Henry shared the sentiments expressed by his son.

Now, Lee began the tedious process of reviewing his brother's account books and listing all of Arthur's outstanding debts, which would have to be paid before dividing up his estate as instructed in his will. Richard Henry immediately ran into complications as he encountered "2 or 3 small bills" submitted to Arthur's estate that he could not verify; thus, Richard Henry launched an investigation. The immediate question Lee felt compelled to address concerned that the bills were long overdue, which seemed unlikely because of his brother's renowned punctuality when it came to settling debts. Consequently, Lee notified the collectors that he would not remit payment "until legal, i.e. impartial proof is produced" that would clarify the exact nature of the disputed obligations.[2] At the same time Richard Henry tried to deal with these suspicious debt claims, he realized that Arthur had failed to include several close family members as recipients in the will. As word spread, many of them turned to Richard Henry for an explanation, but he did not have one. As he told his nephew, "it is impossible for me to tell, any more than I can account for the omission of my daughter . . . who was known to be a favorite Niece."[3]

These complications made the management of Arthur Lee's estate a daunting and depressing chore for Richard Henry Lee and, no doubt, contributed to his resolve to make sure his own affairs were in order so that similar problems would not plague his family after his death. As Lee suffered through frequent illnesses and attacks of gout, he reviewed his own will, and on July 18, 1793, he filed what would become the final draft of his will, at the Westmoreland County Courthouse. He left specific instructions for his executors not to "pay any demand against my estates but as such as are supported by evidence strictly legal, or such demands as they or any of them know to be just." He defended this provision by observing the "great injury being done to he estates of persons deceased, by fictitious, false demands and accounts trumped up and sworn upon a mistaken supposition that such oaths give legal validity" to such claims. Lee's tone clearly reflected the battles he had to fight with his brother's creditors.[4] After addressing the resolution of his debts, he turned to specific matters relating to his internment. He requested that he be buried in the Burnt House Field, and he indicated his desire that his first wife's body be placed next to his, expressing his desire to lie "as near to my late wife as possible." Richard Henry left additional instructions to leave room so that the present Mrs. Lee could placed next to him on his other side "so my body may be laid between those of my dear wives."[5]

Having addressed these preliminary issues, Richard Henry turned next to the distribution of his property. He left Ann Lee full title to the two plantations that he owned, Chantilly and another one, called Hallow's Marsh. Lee's three oldest sons, Thomas, Ludwell, and Cassius, each received equal shares of property in Fauquier and Prince William Counties, while the oldest received all of the Chantilly slaves with the exception of a few left to his other children. Cassius received a bricklayer named Phil; Francis was left with a slave named Anthony, a skilled blacksmith; and Richard Henry's daughter Mary Lee Washington received a young slave girl named Letty, since Letty had "usually waited on her."[6] Richard Henry certainly thought that Thomas Lee would need the bulk of the slaves to work the lands he managed in the area around Dumfries,

Virginia, in Prince William County. Ludwell Lee—like his father—spent most of his time practicing law and engaging in politics. Ludwell built a stately home just outside Alexandria, Virginia, which he called Shuter's Hill.

As for his other possessions, Richard Henry Lee divided most of his library between his two youngest sons. He gave Cassius his "Encyclopedia or dictionary of arts and sciences in ten volumes, [and] Millots elements of general history in five volumes." Francis received all of his father's books pertaining to law, no doubt to assist him in his future career as an attorney. Richard Henry divided the rest of his property among all of his sons and daughters and, for the younger ones, unspecified sums of money to be given them on their twenty-first birthdays.[7] After Lee had made these decisions and filed his will in the county courthouse, he could then turn his attention to other matters that concerned him, with relative confidence that he had addressed the potentially divisive issues pertaining to his estate in advent of his death.

II

After Richard Henry Lee retired, he devoted much of his time to improving the area immediately around Chantilly. He never traveled far from home, and he spoke of the pleasure he derived from the solitude of his quiet plantation. Lee did, however, mention what he regarded as slight drawbacks in living in such an isolated area. He informed one correspondent that living in this "retired part of the Northern Neck" made it difficult to "dispose of our grain and furnish our family with supplies." To address this problem, he proposed launching a modest business venture with friends and neighbors to "purchase a small vessel in partnership" for transporting products to market and returning with supplies.[8] This sort of project occupied much of his time, and his injured hands still forced him to rely on his personal secretary to handle his voluminous correspondence.

Although he no longer held public office, he still craved information relating to political matters confronting the new nation, and much to his delight, he found that on occasion his former colleagues still valued his opinion and sought his advice. During the first year of his retirement, Congress found itself more and more frequently having to address foreign policy matters in the wake of mounting tensions between France and the United States. Four years earlier, the French Revolution began, which soon led to dramatic changes in that old European kingdom. Richard Henry Lee followed the events in France closely since the beginning of the Revolution. In 1789 Lee, like most Americans, warmly supported the revolutionary leaders. He noted that "the eyes of Europe are now turned upon the meeting of the states general [Estates General] in France," and he observed, with a hint of admiration, that "if [the

French] people succeed in restoring their ancient liberty, France will be the most potent power in Europe."[9] A few weeks later, when Lee seemed to be depressed about the state of American politics in the aftermath of his public fight with Vice President John Adams, Lee sardonically observed that "the love of liberty has fled from hence to France."[10]

Richard Henry soon modified his view toward the French Revolution after the revolutionary regime removed King Louis XVI and Marie Antoinette from the throne and subsequently ushered in a violent phase, with the execution of the king in January 1793. "How the mighty have fallen" Lee observed as he tried to make sense of Louis XVI's death while pondering the future of the French nation. He noted that "it is not easy for a mind of sensibility not to feel for the King & Queen of France—for the latter especially." He acknowledged that from his point of view, it was "difficult to judge," but he could no longer restrain his anger. He regarded the execution of the Louis XVI as "cruel, unnecessary, and highly impolitic; he characterized those that performed the deed as "murderers." He summed up his sentiments by quoting Queen Elizabeth I: "'God may forgive his Murderers, but I never can.'"[11]

The violent turn of events in France led Richard Henry to scrutinize events in that country more closely, to the point where he could no longer conceal his contempt for the revolutionary regime. After hearing reports of French seizures of British and Dutch merchant ships, Lee remarked that these acts of "robbery & piracy" will be avenged, as the "British Lion will claw these fellows handsomely for their misdoing."[12] With this frame of mind, Lee began responding to the correspondents seeking his opinions on such matters, and he used this opportunity to secure information regarding the movements of the new French envoy to America, Edmond Charles Genet. The envoy's demeanor astounded Lee. "This person," he complained, "even before his credentials were presented & admitted, whilst yet no more than a private Man, began to assume powers & practices that nothing could justify." He characterized Genet as "rude and violent," while he praised President Washington's response to the envoy. As Genet sought to draw the United States into the war France launched against the great powers of Europe, Richard Henry characterized Washington's proclamation of American neutrality as "well-conceived" and "wise."[13]

The tremors generated by Genet's controversial visit to the United States led Richard Henry Lee to be more circumspect about American involvement in European affairs. He was delighted by the fact that the United States was staying out of the "ruinous war, where everything may be lost & and nothing can possibly be gained." He still warned his correspondents that they should not become so preoccupied with France that they ignore other potential problems— notably, Spain. Lee reminded his audience about the many problems that punctuated American–Spanish relations dating back to 1776, especially Spain's reluctance to grant Americans access to the Mississippi River. Lee remained critical of Spain's misplaced "National jealousy" because of the Spanish empire's approximation to the southern United States.[14] Great Britain was the only European nation that Lee spoke of favorably. His views toward Britain differed sharply from many of his colleagues in Virginia. Several of Richard Henry's contemporaries advocated efforts obstructing debt payments to British merchants. Virginia's state leaders delighted in blaming all of America's problems on Great Britain, from the continued attacks on American ships in the Mediterranean from Barbary corsairs to the attacks launched by Native Americans along the frontier. Lee characterized these as specious reports, and he vocalized his criticism of Thomas Jefferson and James Madison for advocating trade sanctions against Great Britain. Lee complained that "commerce is a subject of too delicate a nature to be coerced by the Theoretic ideas of bookish men." Additionally, he complained that Jefferson's and Madison's anti-British pronouncements were "partial, illtimed, and totally unnecessary."[15]

Lee thought the best course the United States could pursue was one toward improving relations with Great Britain. Southern dependence on British markets was a strong factor dictating this view, but the Virginian acknowledged that the continued presence of British troops on American soil could not be ignored. He remained confident that the two nations could resolve their differences and reach an equitable solution. Richard Henry again departed from many of his contemporaries when he placed the onus for the British occupation on Americans who steadfastly refused to the terms of the 1783 Treaty of Paris and still had not paid their debts to British merchants. While others expressed their alarm at reports that the British were constructing "forts in their own territory near ours," Lee viewed the situation favorably as an indication that the British were preparing to withdraw from American lands and move to Canada.

The political views expressed by Richard Henry Lee in the twilight of his life seemed a rather dramatic departure from his earlier role as a revolutionary leader, but there was a remarkable degree of consistency. Lee's views toward France in the early 1790s were shaped by French recklessness and the indiscretions of Genet during his visit to the United States. Genet's manipulations certainly reminded Richard Henry of similar tactics employed by another French diplomat fifteen years earlier, Conrad Gerard, and his collusion with Robert Morris and Silas Deane during the critical debates over the French alliance in 1778 and 1779. He believed that if America maintained close ties with France, it would be detrimental to the United States. Without hesitation, Richard Henry Lee welcomed every opportunity to publicly confirm his opinions regarding the French. At one point, Richard Henry joined with his cousin Henry Lee, who then served as governor of Virginia, and his son-in-law Charles Lee at a public rally in support of President Washington's call for American neutrality. In front of a hostile crowd, the two younger Lees delivered their speeches, wholeheart-edly supporting the president's opinion. Richard Henry, too ill to speak to the audience, sat on the stage next to the podium as a demonstration of his support for what his relations had said. As Lee continued expressing his sentiments, he increasingly revealed his sympathies for the nascent Federalist Party.[16]

III

As Richard Henry Lee participated in the anti-French rally staged by his cousin, his health steadily worsened. Several times during 1793, his weakened state alarmed members of his family. Lee's oldest son, Thomas, wrote to his father after one particularly severe illness and expressed his hope that Richard Henry would "find both strength and health" once the weather turned warm again.[17] Richard Henry spent the remainder of the year dividing his time between Chantilly and the homes of friends and family. While Lee visited his son Ludwell and his granddaughter Matilda at Shuter's Hill, much to everyone's surprise, President Washington stopped by to visit his old friend. Richard Henry remained at Shuter's Hill for an extended stay because Matilda, who was just three years old, had fallen from a tree and almost died from her injuries. Richard Henry refused to leave until he was sure Matilda would recover from the fall.[18]

After Richard Henry returned to Chantilly, he wrote the president, fondly recalling their visit together but sadly acknowledging that he had not "enjoyed one day's health" since and was now "closely confined to home." As Lee continued languishing at Chantilly, he repeated his endorsement of Washington's policies, telling him that the "success & happiness of the United States is our care, and if the nations of Europe approve War, we surely may be permitted to cultivate the arts of peace."[19] Washington appreciated Lee's warm endorsement and wished his friend a speedy recovery, but that was not to be. On June 19, 1794, with his body no longer able to withstand the constant pain, Richard Henry Lee died at his home on the Potomac River at the age of sixty-two. Five days later, Richard Henry's oldest surviving brother, Francis Lightfoot Lee, and two other associates arrived at Chantilly to serve as executors of Richard Henry's estate. They compiled an inventory of all of Lee's belongings and ascribed a monetary value to each item. In the end, the inventory listed all of the furniture found in each room in Chantilly; it cataglogued Lee's library, which consisted of more than 200 volumes of books, most of which pertained to history and literature; and it listed the fifty-seven slaves living at Chantilly.

After the executors of Richard Henry Lee's estate worked to complete their business, the family held a quiet funeral; and in compliance with his will, they buried him in Burnt House Field. At the time of Lee's death, the contested politics of the early 1790s once again generated an acrimonious atmosphere for his family, as indicated by the lack of public reaction at the time of his death. Almost a month after Richard Henry died, the *Virginia Herald* published a brief obituary, noting, incorrectly, that Lee had died in "the 61st year of his age."[20] The announcement did not contain a single reference to his family or his long, illustrious career in public service. Thus ended Richard Henry Lee's life in quiet ignominy, a reflection of the contentious times in which he lived.

NOTES

1. Potts, *Arthur Lee*, 280.
2. R. H. Lee to Thomas Lee Shippen, April 15, 1793, *Lee Letters*, 2: 555–56.
3. R. H. Lee to Thomas Lee Shippen, March 24, 1793, *Lee Letters*, 2: 555.
4. "Richard Henry Lee's Will," in *Lee of Virginia*, 202.
5. "Richard Henry Lee's Will," in *Lee of Virginia*, 202.
6. "Richard Henry Lee's Will," in *Lee of Virginia*, 202–3.
7. "Richard Henry Lee's Will," in *Lee of Virginia*, 203.
8. R. H. Lee to General Otho Williams, June 22, 1793, *Lee Letters*, 2: 559.
9. R. H. Lee to Patrick Henry, May 28, 1789, *Lee Letters*, 2: 488.
10. R. H. Lee to Francis Lightfoot Lee, September 13, 1789, *Lee Letters*, 2: 501.
11. R. H. Lee to Thomas Lee Shippen, April 15, 1793, *Lee Letters*, 2: 555–56.
12. R. H. Lee to Thomas Lee Shippen, April 15, 1793, *Lee Letters*, 2: 555–56.
13. R. H. Lee to Thomas Lee Shippen, December 11, 1793, *Lee Letters*, 2: 562.
14. R. H. Lee to Richard Bland Lee, February 5, 1794, *Lee Letters*, 2: 571.
15. R. H. Lee to Richard Bland Lee, February 5, 1794, *Lee Letters*, 2: 571; R. H. Lee to George Washington, March 8, 1794, *Lee Letters*, 2: 581.
16. John C. Miller, *The Federalist Era* (New York: Harper & Row, 1960), 7, 102. Lee's biographer Oliver Perry Chitwood sharply disagreed with Miller's identification with the Federalist camp, but the evidence falls squarely on the side of the assertion made by Miller. Chitwood, *Richard Henry Lee*, 276 n. 41. See also, Elkins and McKitrick, *The Federalist Era*, 632–33.
17. Thomas Lee to R. H. Lee, April 17, 1793, Jessie Ball Du Pont Memorial Library, Stratford Hall Plantation. This letter represents the only surviving correspondence between Richard Henry Lee and any of his children.
18. Matilda Lee Love did survive the fall, and in 1866, at age seventy-seven, she recalled the episode, writing that "when I was about three years old, I came very near losing my life from a fall; on that occasion I remember seeing my grandfather." Lee, *Lee Chronicle*, 284.
19. R. H. Lee to George Washington, March 8, 1794, *Lee Letters*, 2: 580.
20. "Richard Henry Lee's Obituary," July 17, 1794, *The Virginia Herald*, Virginia Historical Society, Richmond, VA.

Epilogue: Legacies

I

$\mathcal{A}$s I stood above Richard Henry Lee's grave marker in Burnt House Field and read the plaintive statement "we cannot do without you," I could sense how the comment reflected a deeply felt sense of loss expressed by Richard Henry's surviving family members and how it hinted at the reality that no one left was strong enough, or capable enough, to maintain the energetic role that Lee played throughout his adult life. As the realization set in that Richard Henry was truly gone, Anne Lee took Cassius and Francis, gathered their belongings, left Chantilly, and moved to Alexandria, where she and her young sons lived with Charles and Nancy Lee. She lived there for two years, until her death in 1796.[1] Information concerning Anne Lee's life after the death of her husband is scant; however, one thing that is certain is that she was not buried in Burnt House Field, in accordance with Richard Henry Lee's wishes expressed in his will. By this time, all of Richard Henry's children, with the exception of Cassius and Francis, who were still teenagers, had established homes of their own and were busily raising their families and managing their plantations. Ludwell Lee remained as Richard Henry's only son that expressed much interest in pursuing a political career; Lee's son-in-law Charles, however, was appointed as President Washington's attorney general in 1795.

Richard Henry Lee's oldest son, Thomas, seemed content to continue farming and practicing law in Dumfries, Virginia. He died in 1805 at the age of forty-seven, as a highly respected member of that small community. Ludwell Lee continued his career in Virginia politics, while managing his Shuter's Hill plantation near Alexandria. By 1795, Ludwell's family included three children—two daughters, Matilda and Cecilia, and one son, his grandfather's namesake, Richard

H. Lee II. In 1800, Ludwell Lee's political career culminated with his election as Speaker of the Virginia Senate, where he served as an active member of the Federalist Party. He resigned his seat, however, after Thomas Jefferson was inaugurated as the third president of the United States, in 1801. Ludwell Lee made it known that he could not stomach Jefferson as president, and he chose early retirement as the best way to register his disapproval. He never reentered politics, choosing instead to spend the rest of his days divided between spending time at Shuter's Hill and practicing law in Alexandria until his death at the age of seventy-six, in 1836.

Richard Henry Lee's son-in-law Charles Lee remained the only other member of the Lee family to maintain an active role in politics. After serving as Washington's attorney general from 1795 to 1797, President John Adams offered him the post as Chief Justice of the Supreme Court after Oliver Ellsworth announced his plans to retire. Charles Lee, however, declined the appointment and chose instead to practice law privately. The comparatively short political careers of Ludwell and Charles Lee illustrate the degree to which the Lees had become identified with the Federalist Party and their respective disdain for the men who soon dominated the political scene in the late 1790s and early 1800s—John Adams and Thomas Jefferson.

As for Richard Henry's surviving siblings—Francis Lightfoot, Alice Lee Shippen, and William—only Alice survived into the new century. William Lee returned to America in 1784 and, after returning to his home, Green Spring, served one term in the Virginia Senate. For years, William Lee suffered from an illness that was causing him to go blind. In June 1795, he died as a result of this illness and other health-related complications. Francis Lightfoot lived on for another two years, passing on in February 1797. After his death, Alice Lee Shippen remained as the last of the Stratford Lees, but she made her home in Philadelphia, where she spent the remainder of her days as a highly respected matriarch in that community. She died in 1817 at the age of seventy-seven. The deaths of William and Francis left no one that could really fill the void left behind after Richard Henry's death in 1794. Consequently, the family no longer represented the powerful force in the political debates and controversies that it once did in the past.

II

In the absence of a person with a strong personality like that of Richard Henry Lee, the family faded into quiet obscurity; and as the Lee family became less prominent, so did Lee's grand estate, Chantilly-on-the-Potomac. After Richard Henry's death, Anne Lee vacated the residence and moved to Alexandria. After her death in 1796, Charles Lee assumed control of the property and sold the home and the surrounding 500 acres to Thomas Swan of Alexandria sometime around 1800. Swan, however, never occupied the residence, and it began to slowly deteriorate. During the War of 1812, as British warships made their way up the Potomac River on their way to Washington, D.C., the invaders shelled Chantilly, causing extensive damage to the home. Consequently, the home was valued at less than $500 by the end of 1814.

Chantilly, once regarded as one of the most palatial homes on the Potomac River, now stood in ruins. Although the structure itself excited little attention during the early decades of the nineteenth century, the location proved to be of great importance during America's bloody civil war. Richard Henry Lee built the home and its dock system beyond Currioman Bay along the shores of Cold Harbor Creek, thus concealing Chantilly Landing from the traffic that moved along the Potomac to all except those who knew the area best. The seclusion of Chantilly's dilapidated pier provided a convenient base in Virginia for Maryland's Confederate sympathizers who would transport supplies across the Potomac. They would make their way into Currioman Bay and up Cold Harbor Creek, stockpiling food and other contraband while remaining hidden from other traffic that made its way up and down the Potomac River. Zack Sanders of Virginia's Fifteenth Cavalry would receive these items from Virginia's Maryland friends, then transport them inland by taking Chantilly Road from the dock and passing the ruins of the old manor house as he would deliver the supplies to those men fighting the Union.

Remnants of Richard Henry Lee's once grand estate remained standing but were a mere shadow of what they once were. In 1871, a traveler named George William Beale visited the site and reported that "not a vestige of the old edifice remains save a rude mound of stones, half concealed beneath briars and weeds." Beale noted that only the fireplace and chimney from the kitchen remained standing as he looked upon the ruins of Chantilly.[2] Sixty-four years later, in the midst of the Great Depression, witnesses recall seeing trucks loaded with bricks leaving the Chantilly property, removing the last pieces of the home. Today, nothing remains that indicates a home once occupied the location where Richard Henry Lee once lived, with the exception of an occasional brick found by a passerby.

III

In many respects, the fate of Chantilly-on-the-Potomac serves as sort of a metaphor for how Richard Henry Lee's name and reputation has faired in the hands of chroniclers and historians since his death in 1794. Soon after the

United States won its independence from Great Britain, numerous people wrote histories of what they were convinced were truly momentous times. John Marshall, while serving as Chief Justice of the Supreme Court, contributed to this effort by writing a five-volume history of George Washington and his times, first published between 1801 and 1807.

As Marshall's book discussed events approaching the eve of America's declaration of independence, the chief justice credited Richard Henry Lee as the author of "An Address to the Inhabitants of the Colonies," a copy of which was also sent to King George III. Later, upon reviewing this section of Marshall's study, Jefferson disputed the attribution, telling his correspondent John Adams that he was "certain" that the pamphlet "was not written by [Lee]." Jefferson based his argument on his observation that the pamphlet's author wrote with clarity, whereas Lee's writing style was "loose, vague, frothy, [and] rhetorical."[3] Two years later, Jefferson and Adams discussed another history of the American Revolution by an Italian scholar, Carlo Guiseppo Guglielmo Botta's *Storia della Guerra Americana*. Many reviewers of Botta's history regarded it as the "best history of the revolution" yet written. Adams noted that "this Italian Classick has followed the example of Greek and Roman historians, by composing speeches for his Generals and Orators." He went on to observe that Botta's translations of Richard Henry Lee's speeches favoring independence represented "A splendid [morsel] of oratory"; but, he told Jefferson, "how faithful, you can judge."[4] Jefferson agreed with his correspondent that Botta put "speeches into mouths which never made them."[5] The correspondence between Adams and Jefferson clearly indicates that neither of them held Richard Henry Lee in very high regard. Both men lived long lives and worked with Lee at critical junctures in America's early history; but it also must be remembered that both of them had bitter disputes with Lee, which no doubt influenced how they recalled events that occurred forty years before.

Several external factors also shaped how Jefferson in particular reacted to the histories of the American Revolution. At the time Marshall began his multivolume biography of Washington, Jefferson was convinced that this was a purely political effort to discredit him and the Democratic-Republican Party as the 1804 election approached. Consequently, Jefferson and his friends were prepared to challenge every aspect of Marshall's history. The president wrote that "John Marshall is writing the life of General Washington from his papers. It is intended to come out just in time to influence the next presidential election. It is written therefore principally with a view to election purposes"[6] These external concerns on the part of Thomas Jefferson encouraged a mindset that tended to discredit anything that spoke favorably of the president's political opponents.

Jefferson maintained an uneasy relationship with Richard Henry Lee, a situation that in many respects mirrored the contentious association that existed between Jefferson and Marshall. Richard Henry emerged as one of Jefferson's harshest critics for his conduct as Virginia's wartime governor; and still later, after Lee won election to the United States Senate, the two became even more distant as Richard Henry disparaged Jefferson's pro-French foreign policy as secretary of state. The relationship between Lee and Jefferson was a marked contrast to that which developed between Lee and Marshall. Throughout his life, John Marshall's connection to Richard Henry Lee remained close. When Marshall was but ten years old, his father was not yet financially secure enough to purchase property, so he leased 330 acres from Lee. The agreed-upon terms were generous, stipulating an annual rent of £5 "for and during the natural lives of . . . Thomas Marshall, Mary Marshall his wife, and John Marshall his son and . . . the longest liver of them."[7] The family resided on Lee's property for ten years before moving on to better lands. In 1782, when John Marshall took his seat in the Virginia House of Delegates, Richard Henry took him under his wings. As Lee and Marshall maintained a cordial bond, Lee and Jefferson grew further apart.

The Lees remained as thorns in Jefferson's side long after Richard Henry's death. As he resigned his seat in the Virginia state legislature, protesting the results of the election of 1800, Ludwell Lee's public display no doubt irritated Jefferson. A few years later, Richard Henry's son-in-law Charles Lee annoyed Jefferson as he took on a prominent role as part of Aaron Burr's defense team during the treason trial of 1807. Lastly, Lee's grandson and namesake, Richard H. Lee, struck a raw nerve with Jefferson while discussing the revered Declaration of Independence in the early 1820s. Lee indicated that only a "small part of that memorable instrument" should be attributed to Jefferson; the rest, "he stole from *Locke's Essays*."[8] Jefferson was so upset by Lee's remark that he wrote the young man to explain that his goal was

> not to find out new principles, or new arguments, never before thought of, not merely to say things which had never been said before; but to place before mankind the common sense of the subject, in terms so plain and firm as to command their assent. . . . Neither aiming at originality of principles or sentiments, nor yet copied from any particular or previous writing, it was intended to be an expression of the American mind. . . . All its authority rests then on the harmonizing sentiments of the day, whether expressed in conversation, in letters, printed essays, or the elementary books of public right, as Aristotle, Cicero, [and] Locke.[9]

Jefferson's response to Lee's characterization of his contributions during the debate over American independence simply reinforced an already established tendency to relegate his opponents to minor roles at best.

IV

Richard H. Lee II's commentary on the originality of the Declaration of Independence was the result of his efforts to publish a biography of his grandfather. He came to believe that the Lee family's role during the American Revolution had been slighted and, beginning in 1821, set on the task of rectifying this matter. Lee sought information from men who knew and worked with his grandfather. John Adams was one of the principal figures Lee contacted while doing his research. After Adams received his query from Lee's grandson, he responded cordially by simply noting that he had "served with your grandfather in Congress from 1774 to 1778 and afterward in the Senate in 1789." Adams added that Lee's grandfather was "a gentlemen of fine talents, of amiable manners, and great worth. As a public speaker, he had a fluency as easy and graceful as it was melodious, which his classical education enabled him to decorate with frequent allusion to the finest passages of antiquity."

Adams indicated that he could no longer remember specific details about events in the Continental Congress. As he related events to his questioner, he gave Richard Henry Lee only a minor role in the push for independence, noting that "Mr. R.H. Lee was preferred for the motion for independence because he was from the most ancient colony" and because he had "made a speech in favor of a declaration of independence, I have no doubt, and very probably more than one, though, I cannot take upon me to repeat from memory any part of his speeches, or any others that were made upon that occasion."[10] Additionally, perhaps as a result of memory lapse or malice, Adams had a tendency to give George Wythe, Jefferson's mentor, credit for Richard Henry Lee's accomplishments during those critical days in the Continental Congress.[11] Unfortunately, Adams did not take the time to consult his diary, which contained a detailed account of Richard Henry Lee's role in the dispute with Great Britain.

After Richard H. Lee finished his biography in 1825, he dedicated the work to the surviving signers of the Declaration of Independence—John Adams, Charles Carroll of Carrollton, and Thomas Jefferson—and sent them all a complimentary copy. After Jefferson read his, he wrote to Adams. "I presume that you have received a copy of the life of Richd. H. Lee, from his grandson." Jefferson went on to note that both of them knew that Lee "merited much during the revolution. Eloquent, bold, and ever watchful at his post." Jefferson also found much to criticize and concluded that he was not "certain whether the friends of George Mason, of Patrick Henry, yourself, and even of Genl. Washington may not reclaim some feathers of the plumage given him, notable as was proper the original coat."[12]

V

Thomas Jefferson's review of *The Memoir of the Life of Richard Henry Lee and his Correspondence* seems odd and a bit disingenuous, as the biography represents primarily a catalogue of committee posts—official actions occasioned by speeches and correspondence. In addition, the author repeatedly paid respects to the individuals mentioned by Jefferson. Unfortunately, the characterizations set forth by men such as John Adams and Thomas Jefferson set the stage for other commentators and historians to interpret Richard Henry Lee in the decades following the sage of Monticello's death in 1826.

In the middle of the nineteenth century, nationalistic historians such as Jared Sparks, George Bancroft, and James Parton began publishing their celebratory presentations of America's past, at a time as the reputations of revolutionary leaders like George Washington and Benjamin Franklin reached mythic proportions. In their attempts to convey the tense drama of the American Revolution, Sparks and Bancroft attached a tremendous amount of significance to events such as the Conway Cabal and its alleged ringleader, Richard Henry Lee. Additionally, as Parton published his biography of Franklin, he cast Arthur Lee as the villain in the drama and referred to the "peculiarly constituted brain of Arthur Lee."[13] All of these accounts affected other histories, as repeated references to Arthur Lee as a "malignancy" and a "monomaniacal"character that infected his brothers began to appear in numerous historical accounts. Eventually, such interpretations had a real impact. In 1842, Congress passed a resolution vindicating Silas Deane and awarded his descendants an award of $37,000 on the grounds that the charges made against Deane during the American Revolution were "*ex parte*, erroneous, and a gross injustice." The monetary award, by implication, officially impugned the Lee family since they were the ones who had leveled the most serious charges against Deane during the contentious disputes in Congress in 1778–1779.

In the aftermath of these events, historical scholarship reflected unkindly on the Lees of Virginia, specifically Richard Henry's supposed lead role in the Conway Cabal. In 1888, such characterizations reached new levels with the publication of Francis Wharton's *Revolutionary Diplomatic Correspondence of the United States*. Wharton, a descendant of Thomas and Samuel Wharton, devoted a large section of his introductory volume to the enmity between George Washington and the Lees, as well as their rumored hostility toward the French alliance during the War for American Independence. Wharton's conclusions regarding the Lees, perhaps more so than anyone else, has shaped the way Richard Henry Lee and his family has been viewed by historians during the twentieth century. Scholars such as Samuel Flagg Bemis, Richard B. Morris, and James Thomas Flexner incorporated Wharton's characterizations without question into their works.[14] Similarly, the conclusion that Lee was the author of the *Letters from the Federal Farmer to the Republican* and the *Additional Letters from the Federal Farmer to the Republican* persist in recent studies.[15] The perceptions of Richard Henry Lee's reputation and contributions during the American Revolution set forth by Jefferson and Adams had the effect of shaping how nineteenth- and twentieth-century historians have interpreted Lee ever since. Consequently, contemporary historians tend to identify Lee as a paradox or an enigma because they have found the different mantles he wore over the course of his political career difficult to reconcile.[16]

VI

Richard Henry Lee is best understood as the epitome of the conservative revolutionary. Throughout his adult life, he fought to preserve and promote the society that his family helped create. In this capacity, Lee's role often shifted between being a person who resisted new policies and someone who emerged as an active agent of change. In actuality, Lee was one of the few consistent political figures of his time. The animosity that arose between Richard Henry and his contemporaries led to the many controversies that then shaped his political life, affected his personal life, and largely determined his legacy. Richard Henry Lee devoted his life to protecting his family and preserving the only world that he knew. The ambiguity of his legacy resulted from the rapid changes that followed his death in 1794; and as the society he sought to protect changed dramatically, so did the historical perception of the man.

Today, standing at his graveside, the visitor does not see monuments or statues, only a small cemetery in an otherwise empty field. After studying the life of Richard Henry Lee, I get the sense that he would not have wanted it any other way. He devoted his life to his family and public service, so there is little doubt that he would be content with the sincere, heartfelt, sentiments expressed by his family with the epitaph: "We cannot do without you."

NOTES

1. A court document in the Virginia Historical Society, dated February 23, 1796, named George Lee Turberville as the executor of Anne Pinckard Lee's estate.

2. George William Beale, "Chantilly: The Home of Richard Henry Lee," *Old Dominion Magazine* (July 1871): 423.

3. Thomas Jefferson to John Adams, August 22, 1813, *The Adams-Jefferson Letters*, 2 vols., ed. Lester J. Cappon (Chapel Hill: University of North Carolina Press, 1959), 2: 369–70.

4. John Adams to Thomas Jefferson and Thomas McKean, July 30, 1815, *Adams-Jefferson Letters*, 2: 451.

5. Thomas Jefferson to John Adams, May 5, 1817, *Adams-Jefferson Letters*, 2: 513.

6. Jean Edward Smith, *John Marshall: Definer of a Nation* (New York: Henry Holt and Company, 1996), 333.

7. Smith, *John Marshall*, 30, 537 n. 58.

8. Pauline Maier, *American Scripture: Making the Declaration of Independence* (New York: Alfred A. Knopf, 1997), 171.

9. Carl L. Becker, *The Declaration of Independence: A Study in the History of Political Ideas* (New York: Vintage Books, 1958), 25–26.

10. John Adams to Richard H. Lee, February 24, 1821, *The Works of John Adams, Second President of the United States*, 10 vols., ed. Charles Francis Adams (Boston: 1850–1856; reprint, Freeport, NY: Books for Libraries Press, 1969), 10: 395–96.

11. Selby, "Richard Henry Lee, John Adams, and the Virginia Constitution of 1776," 395.

12. Thomas Jefferson to John Adams, December 18, 1825, *Adams-Jefferson Letters*, 2: 612.

13. *The Revolutionary Diplomatic Correspondence of the United States*, 1: 529.

14. Samuel Flagg Bemis, *The Diplomacy of the American Revolution* (Bloomington: Indiana University Press, 1935), 176–77; Richard B. Morris, *The Peacemakers: The Great Powers and American Independence* (New York: Harper & Row, 1965), 10, 151; and James Thomas Flexner, *George Washington in the American Revolution, 1775–1783* (Boston: Little, Brown 1968), 255–59.

15. Despite the best efforts on the part of Gordon S. Wood, Robert Webking, and myself, the attribution of Lee as the Federal Farmer persists. See Jean Smith, *John Marshall*, 117, 569 n. 7.

16. Maier, *The Old Revolutionaries*, 164.

Index

About the Author

J. Kent McGaughy is a professor of History at Houston Community College (HCC), Northwest and currently serves as the director of the HCC, Northwest Honors Program. He received his B.A. in history from the University of Texas at Austin and his M.A. and Ph.D. in history from the University of Houston. He has published articles in *New York History, History in Dispute: The American Revolution*, and *The Encyclopedia of Conspiracy Theories* and has appeared on C-Span's *Washington Journal* discussing Richard Henry Lee as one of America's Founding Fathers. He resides in Katy, Texas.

Made in the USA
Lexington, KY
10 February 2015